# The Bridegroom's Song

### Sarah Ramsey

Copyright © 2020 Sarah Ramsey

All rights reserved.

ISBN: 9798639052927

## *Acknowledgments*

…He has given each one of us a special gift through the generosity of Christ. Ephesians 4:7

God draws us and calls us , and He sends us the Helper who equips helpers. I have had so much help in writing and publishing The Bridegroom's Song. It has been a long journey.

God gave me teachers—Ephesians 4:11-13 says their responsibility is to equip God's people to do His work and build up the church, the body of Christ…..until we will be mature in the Lord. Jesus gave me wonderful teachers who knew the journey of Song of Solomon…Mike Bickle, Watchman Nee, Wade Taylor ( and Madame Guyon, even though I don't use her quotes in The Bridegroom's Song). I treasure the teachers God has so richly blessed me with. Their insight into God's Word builds a great foundation.

Also, God brought and surrounded me with members of His Body that had gifts that I needed and I am dependent on each one of these who helped get this beautiful message in print.

Eileen was so faithful for so many years and was with me in the beginning.

Tibet's generosity and encouragement was untiring when the journey took twists and turns.

Tibet brought Julianne who edited and taught the Song with me.

And Carol came and helped me to finish.

Every part contributed.

As we began to publish, Tibet also enlisted Michael and he did the final edit and is helping get The Bridegroom's Song.

And then there all of you family and friends, so patient with me as I kept over flowing on you as the Song became so alive in me!!!

The fun surprise was when I was having dinner with my grandson AJ Carter and his friend. We were talking about things we were doing and I said I was trying to get a book cover designed for The Bridegroom's Song. AJ said, "I can do that". He saw my vision and made the beautiful cover.

Selah.

Every part contributed.

It's been a joint venture. My name just happens to be on the cover.

Each person was vital to the completion of The Bridegroom's Song.

Selah

## *Table of contents*

**Introduction**

**Chapter 1; The Song of Solomon – Pg. 1**

**Chapter 2; Draw Me – Pg. 9**

**Chapter 3; Self-Evaluation: Seeing Myself – Pg. 18**

**Chapter 4; The Plan – Pg. 30**

**Chapter 5; The Fragrance of Worship – Pg. 38**

**Chapter 6; Dove's Eyes – Pg. 48**

**Chapter 7; Stolen Identity – Pg. 56**

**Chapter 8; The Seasons Change – Pg. 71**

**Chapter 9; The Painful Compromise – Pg. 85**

**Chapter 10; Finding the One I Love – Pg. 100**

**Chapter 11; Coming Out of the Wilderness – Pg. 110**

**Chapter 12; A Place for Us Beside The King – Pg. 125**

**Chapter 13; I Will Go – Pg. 140**

**Chapter 14; A Call to the Mountains – Pg. 148**

**Chapter 15; The Ravished Heart of Jesus – Pg. 166**

**Chapter 16; The Garden Enclosed – Pg. 177**

**Chapter 17; The Garden Party – Pg. 189**

**Chapter 18; Another Challenge – Pg. 198**

**Chapter 19; When God is Silent – Pg. 216**

**Chapter 20; My Beloved Is – Pg. 231**

**Chapter 21; Awakening an Earnest Desire – Pg. 244**

**Chapter 22; The Bridal Attributes – Pg. 254**

**Chapter 23; The New Day Dawns – Pg. 267**

**Chapter 24; The Garden – Pg. 276**

**Chapter 25; The Daughters Bless the Bride – Pg. 286**

**Chapter 26; Take Hold of Me, My Beloved…I Am Yours – Pg. 297**

**Chapter 27; Come, My Beloved – Pg. 311**

**Chapter 28; The Lovesick Bride – Pg. 321**

**Chapter 29; The Hot, Fiery Seal – Pg. 336**

**Chapter 30; Little Sister – Pg. 346**

**Chapter 31; The King's Vineyard – Pg. 357**

## *Preface*

For it is God who works in you both to will and to do for His good pleasure.

Philippians 2:13 NLV

The journey into and through the Song of Songs is like no other. When I began this journey several years ago, I could not have imagined the satisfaction it would bring.

The Bridegroom's Song was and is God's idea. It is the second in the Are We There Yet? trilogy. Book I, Are We There Yet? Journey into the Presence of God teaches us 'how to come into the Holy of Holies', the Secret Place of the Most High God. It is a beautiful, scriptural pattern… I don't have to go to church or a Bible Study to come into God's Presence, but it teaches us that His Presence is the place I can dwell day to day. In Book II, The Bridegroom's Song, an unlikely little shepherdess will show us the way into an intimate relationship with the King of Glory, the Beloved.

The Bridegroom's Song begins as The Beloved King is revealed at the beginning of SOS. There is revelation in this mysterious little book in the middle of the Bible that only the Holy Spirit can unveil. The song called The Song of Solomon or The Songs of Songs unravels and reveals the struggle of the human heart that longs for intimacy with God. David spoke of God as the King of Kings and the Lord of Lords. Moses called God, the God of gods and the Song of Solomon is also called the Song of all Songs. Zephaniah tells us that… "the Lord our God will…joy over thee with singing." The Song of all Songs is "The Bridegroom's Song" to you and to me and to the Church as the Bride of Christ.

The Bridegroom's Song isn't just a book to read, it is an unfolding journey, not a love story about a one night stand. It is the journey into intimacy with the Beloved. It is the journey into an intimate relationship with the Lover of our souls that Song of Songs will teach us, if we accept this assignment. The Song will teach us how to receive God's love and how to love God with all our hearts, soul, mind, and strength. We are incapable, but God is able and the Holy Spirit will pour the love of God in our hearts and equip us to love with all our hearts.

The Song uses the most intimate language of love in an allegorical form that unveils The Bridegroom's love and sets His fire on the bride's heart. It's intimate language, that causes cheeks to blush, is full of figurative speech and symbolic language that requires the reader to depend on the Holy Spirit and the Scriptures for understanding and revelation. This progressive journey is a process…a pattern to follow and will take us along step by step. As we lean into the Holy Spirit and let Him lead us and guide us He will reveal intimacy with God fulfills the longing in the heart of man to love and be loved.

The truths in this Old Covenant love story are confirmed and fulfilled in the New Testament by Jesus Himself and in the Epistles.

Each of the 31 chapters of The Bridegroom's Song could be read individually as devotions—but The Song is progressive. It's journey is prompted by an overworked young maiden who sees the King of Glory and begins to see how she can draw near to Him. The young maiden is the Bride of Christ and is neuter in gender—ie., the Church (individually and corporately).

I'm excited you are considering this journey. It is powerful and never gets old. As I read the final edit, I said out loud, "O Song of all Songs, I have missed you!". My heart is full of passion and fire for my Beloved Bridegroom King. It is the hot fiery seal of God's love on my heart.

# Introduction

*To you it has been given to know the mysteries of the kingdom of God*

*--Jesus Christ* (Luke 8:10).

## A Love Story

The Song of Solomon, also called the Song of Songs or simply as The Song, has been a mysterious little book to believers throughout the centuries. It is a love story that parallels the believer's love story. Unwrapping its message is a marvelous experience and a gift I want to share with you. It is the story of a gallant, handsome, victorious king who chooses an unlikely shepherdess to be his bride. But this is not just a classic love story or fairy tale--this is the Word of God—the same as Romans or James or Revelation.

The Song is a true depiction, woven in allegorical form, of our relationship with God. Understanding it requires insight into a specific type of literature categorized within the Bible called the Books of Wisdom and Songs. Within this collection are found three books in the Old Testament written by Solomon: Proverbs, Ecclesiastes, and The Song of Solomon. These books were written to give us insight and understanding, and they continue to reveal timeless truths which can be applied in our relationships with God and others. Proverbs acts as a guiding hand for our instruction on daily living. Ecclesiastes presents the problem of finding the meaning of life. However, The Song unravels the heart and reveals the struggle to find intimacy with God. The Song of Solomon is written in poetic form, unlike Romans or Revelation, and must be approached as such. This format does not make it less applicable to our lives today, but in some ways the language can be more challenging.

The Holy Spirit wrote these words through King Solomon. The same Holy Spirit is ready to teach us their secrets. Referring to the Holy Spirit, Jesus told us that He would teach us all things (John 14). The Holy Spirit will give us the keys to unlock the secret doorway of "how to" do the first and greatest commandment; "to love the Lord your God with all your heart, with all your soul, and with all your mind" (Matthew 22:37). Simply put, the Song of Songs teaches us how to love God and how to be loved.

**Learning the Language of Love**

As we begin, let's talk about the language of The Song of Solomon. The Song is an intimate love story with its own love language, often thought almost too embarrassing to read or discuss. These are prophetic love words identifying the favorite of the Beloved King, the bride of Christ. The Song uses symbolic language, and we must depend on the Holy Spirit to reveal its message to us. Our culture has fed us so many perversions of love. We need the Teacher to take off our blinders and show us God's language of love in this Song. He is able to take away the blushes and embarrassment to create a hunger within us so we know the Bridegroom and accept our place as His bride.

Song of Solomon is an allegory[1] full of figurative speech and symbols. The symbolic language is uncovered and revealed in the Word of God. Scripture is the source for unlocking the secrets: The Word of God serves as its own commentary. In other words, we allow Scripture to interpret Scripture as we study the Song of Solomon. As we shall see, the truths revealed in this Old-Covenant love story are confirmed and fulfilled in the New Testament by Jesus Himself. This connection is especially evident in Paul's letters to the church.

**A Word About Parables**

Jesus often used the symbolic language of parables to teach. When we see why Jesus taught this way, we begin to value the language of love. Matthew 13:3 says, "Then He [Jesus] spoke many things to them in parables." He explains why in verses 10-17:

> And the disciples came and said to Him, 'Why do you speak to them in parables?'
>
> He (Jesus) answered and said to them, 'Because it has been given to you to know the mysteries of the kingdom

of heaven, but to them it has not been given. For whoever has, to him more will be given, and he will have abundance; but whoever does not have, even what he has will be taken away from him. Therefore I speak to them in parables, because seeing they do not see, and hearing they do not hear, nor do they understand. And in them the prophecy of Isaiah is fulfilled, which says:

> Hearing you will hear and shall not understand,
>
> And seeing you will see and not perceive;
>
> For the hearts of this people have grown dull.
>
> Their ears are hard of hearing,
>
> And their eyes they have closed
>
> Lest they should see with their eyes and hear with their ears,
>
> Lest they should understand with their hearts and turn,
>
> So that I should heal them.'

Jesus continues:

> 'But blessed are your eyes for they see, and your ears for they hear; for assuredly, I say to you that many prophets and righteous men desired to see what you see, and did not see it, and to hear what you hear, and did not hear it.'

Notice again what Jesus says: His disciples have ears to hear and eyes to see. He is talking about us! He spoke to them in parables because He wanted them to know the mysteries. Do you *see* this? A parable is a mystery, and you have been given a gift, a key, to unlock the door of these great and unfathomable mysteries. Mike Bickle says, "Parables make things simple and parables make things difficult so that only the hungry heart of love can experience them."[2] Rather than simply telling us, he gives us a puzzle, and when we unravel it there is so much more meaning to us than if it were just presented as it is.

Jesus taught in parables for these two reasons: To make the truth simple and to make the truth difficult. The Song of Solomon is a true love song. Jesus speaks in this poetic love language to reach down further inside of us than the normal mode of teaching can reach. It goes far deeper than intellectual understanding, which appeals to our minds. The deeper meaning in the Song speaks to our souls and spirits. It is the manifold wisdom of God. This poetic language, like parables, contains much more than can be gleaned from the surface. It is a mystery, awaiting revelation by the Holy Spirit. Paul speaks of this in 1 Corinthians 2:7, "hidden wisdom which God ordained before the ages for our glory." Paul goes on further to explain to the Corinthian church how only the spiritual man is able to discern these mysteries. "But the natural man does not receive the things of the Spirit of God, for they are foolishness to him; nor can he know them because they are spiritually discerned" (v.14).

**The Intimate Journey**

The Song of Songs is not a story about being born again, being baptized in water, or even being baptized in the Holy Spirit. When the book begins with the little Shulamite, the representation of the individual and personal Christian, is already in relationship with the King. As believers we come into relationship with Christ after being cleansed by the blood of Jesus, but this is just the starting place.[3] If you have trusted Jesus as your Savior, you are already in relationship with Him and have access to the Father. We are invited, *commanded* (Hebrews 4:16), to come boldly into the King's chambers! We are born into the Kingdom of God through faith in Him, but intimacy is not automatic. Her journey into an intimate relationship is progressive with many twists and setbacks. It is a process. You don't just wake up one morning and find yourself in an intimate love affair. Intimacy is built upon relationship. Our relationship with the Lord develops in the same way. The Song of Songs gives us a pattern to follow and will take us along the step-by-step journey into intimate love with Him.

**The Characters and Three Main Statements**

This little love story has three main characters:

- The king, who is the Beloved—Solomon, a symbolic picture of Jesus

- The love-smitten maiden (identified as the young Shulamite in 6:13), who is the bride—both in the natural and the spiritual. She represents the individual believer on a personal level and the church at large on a larger scale.
- The daughters of Jerusalem—friends of the bride; immature believers who lack discernment and who do not yet understand the various operations of the Spirit or the different seasons of God

Three main statements are made by the bride throughout the story. These declarations reveal the movement of her heart as the journey toward intimacy progresses.

- The first statement: "My beloved is mine, and I am his" (2:16). This statement is made in the early chapters. In the beginning, love is "all about me" to the little Shulamite maiden. The emphasis is on herself.
- The second statement: "I am my beloved's, and my beloved is mine" (6:3). As the journey progresses, her confession changes. Not only is He hers, but she is now His. Her focus is shifting from just her own needs and desires.
- Third statement: "I am my beloved's and his desire is towards me" (7:10). By the end of the journey, all of her emphasis is on the Beloved, her Bridegroom King, and the order of her declaration has reversed--she has given herself fully to her Beloved.

Can you see these three progressions? Our goal is to advance through these progressions ourselves towards spiritual maturity and intimacy with God. The Song of Songs is the story of the bride of Christ developing into maturity. This growth is an individual process, but it also happens corporately as the Church is made ready for her Bridegroom King.

**Awakening Love**

We are currently in this maturation process as the Body of Christ. As we draw near to Him (James 4:8) and listen for His heartbeat, the Holy Spirit is awakening this love and illuminating the Word of God. He chooses us and identifies us as His "fair one." Throughout the Song, the Beloved prophesies the bride's true identity and destiny into her heart. These spoken words take root, allowing us to realize who we are in Christ. The Song of Solomon is about awakening to see Jesus as He is and seeing ourselves as we truly are in Him.

**God's Ways**

God's ways are not our ways, and His thoughts are not like ours. Isaiah 55:8-9 tell us they are high above our ways and thoughts. Who would ever think the Song of Solomon would empower and equip the believer to do the first commandment?

This question was asked of Jesus by a lawyer:

> 'Teacher, which is the greatest commandment in the law?'

Jesus said to him, 'You shall love the LORD your God with all your heart, with all your soul, and with all your mind.

This is the first and greatest commandment'

(Matthew 22:36-38).

Again, God's ways are not our ways; but that does not mean we cannot change our ways! *Lord, my desire is that I may know Your way.* God loves us perfectly. Experientially here on earth, we have been shown imperfect representations of true love. We may have become confused and hurt by the actions of those who say they love us. We need God's way to be revealed. This may seem foreign to us at first, but He can open our eyes to see and receive His message from the Song.

Teach me Your way, O LORD;

I will walk in Your truth;

Unite my heart to fear Your name

(Psalm 86:11).

**My Story**

When I visited Paris with some friends, we visited Versailles, the massively opulent residence built in the 1700's by the king of France when Marie Antoinette was his queen. As we walked through Versailles, we came to a room with the marking "The King's Chambers" on the door. I was immediately interested because of this study on the Song of Solomon. As we stepped into the room, it became apparent it was the king's bedroom. We saw the beautiful, large four-poster bed with curtains to be used as privacy drapes. Elaborate, gold-crested moldings and walls adorned the room, painted by the best artists the world knew. In the New Living Translation, Song of Solomon 1:4 says, "Take me with you; come let's run! The king has brought me into his bedroom."

This experience was the highlight of my trip. As I stood in the king's chambers, I made the connection and was reminded of my King. My Beloved is the King of Kings. He is the King of the king who built Versailles, and He wants to bring me into His chambers. We have been invited into the King's chambers! If you dare to join me on this journey, you will not be disappointed. Dear believer, "That is what the Scriptures mean when they say, 'No eye has seen, no ear has heard, and no mind has imagined what God has prepared for those who love him'" (1 Corinthians 2:9, NLT).

Throughout the pages that follow, I will insert short prayers based on the information presented and the Scripture contained within each chapter. Boldly enter into the throne room and pray the Word of God with me.[4]

*King of Kings and Lord of Lords, thank you for inviting*

*us into your chambers.*

*Holy Spirit, open our eyes to see and our ears to hear*

*you.*

*Teach us your ways so that we may accept love and may*

*love you more perfectly.*

*Thank you, Jesus, our Beloved, for showing us the way*

*into perfect love.*

*Your blood cleanses us and your Word sanctifies us*

*completely.*

*Thank You for Your Spirit and for the mysteries*

*revealed within the Song of Solomon.*

*You teach us all things and lead and guide us into all*

*truth.*

*We don't have to be afraid of this journey with You.*

*May your kingdom come and your will be done in our*

*hearts as we surrender to You.*

Sarah Ramsey – The Bridegroom's Song

*Amen*

## 1

## The Song of Songs

*The song of songs, which is Solomon's*

(Song of Solomon 1:1)

**Weddings**

The Bible begins Genesis and ends Revelation with the same event; a wedding. In Genesis 2:18 God says, "It is not good that man should be alone." In the beginning He made Eve for Adam. Jesus began His ministry at the wedding in Cana of Galilee, not on the steps of the temple or through news networks or radio broadcasts. He performed His first recorded miracle at a celebratory banquet commemorating this sacred union when He turned the water into wine. "This beginning of signs Jesus did in Cana of Galilee, and manifested His glory; and His disciples believed in Him" (John 2:11). Weddings were important to Jesus.

His miracle at the wedding in Cana holds special significance even for those of us who were not in attendance. This snapshot foreshadows an even greater wedding celebration to come. We have all been invited to a magnificent event, but not simply as onlookers in the crowd. The King of Glory requests the honor of your presence as His bride at the most significant wedding banquet in history, one He has been planning since the beginning of time.

In His final discourse in Matthew 24-25, Jesus tells us to go out to meet the Bridegroom with our lamps full of oil. Jesus is the Bridegroom of the church, and we are His bride. We are instructed to be ready at midnight: "Behold, the bridegroom is coming; go out to meet him!" (25:6) Revelation 19:6-9 refers to the "marriage of the Lamb" (v.7), which is the culminating union of Christ and the church at the second coming of Christ. The last book of the Bible ends with the great invitation, "The Spirit and the bride say, 'Come!' And let him who hears say, 'Come!'" (Revelation 22:17a) The Song of Solomon ends with the same cry, "'Come away, my beloved.'" (NIV) Jesus is coming back for His church, His bride. You are that beloved his heart yearns for.

Let's get prepared together!

**The Divine Kiss**

> The song of songs, which is Solomon's.
>
> 'Let him kiss me with the kisses of his mouth....'
>
> (Song of Solomon 1:1-2a).

Just as Jesus is the King of Kings and the Lord of Lords (Revelation 19:16), this song is the Song of Songs. The Shulamite maiden reveals the beginning of a pattern as she asks for the King's kisses. This is her first request. The kisses of the King's mouth—the longing for intimacy—are not to be confused with an earthly kiss. The kisses are the Words that proceed from the mouth of God. Jesus said His words give life. "Man shall not live by bread alone, but by every word that proceeds from the mouth of God" (Matthew 4:4). Here, Jesus refers to the *rhema word* or "now word." This *word* is the Bread of Heaven, which feeds the believer's spirit. It is more than black ink on white paper. It is deeply personal—a kiss dropped from heaven—igniting the receiving heart. According to Hebrews 4:12, the word of God is alive and powerful. The Holy Spirit reveals God's love through His words as He deposits these "kisses" and satisfies our deepest longings.

Mike Bickle defines the Divine kiss as "a metaphor of intimacy with Jesus," as "God's hand touching my heart and pouring in love![1]" This image is not to be imagined as literally kissing Jesus on the mouth. Rather, Jesus embraces your spirit and awakens you to love by His Word! What a beautiful metaphor, indeed! My desire is for us to become deeply acquainted with our Beloved Bridegroom as we travel through the Song of Solomon. The first step is simply to begin in prayer and ask the Father, "Let me have the kisses of His mouth."

**Your Love Is Better Than…**

…for your love is better than wine

(Song of Solomon 1:2b).

Knowing Jesus is every heart's desire, whether fully realized or not. There is nothing more exhilarating than His love. The NIV says His love "is more delightful than wine" (Song 1:7-8). Wine is used as a metaphor for the best the world has to offer. Intimacy with Jesus is superior to success, worldly security, man's approval, or any fleeting pleasure of this age. His rivals all other loves. The love of Jesus transcends the temporary satisfaction which accompanies the lure of sin. The maiden expresses that His love is better than anything else she has experienced in her life. When Jesus miraculously turned the water into wine, the master of the wedding banquet proclaimed that the best had been saved until last (John 2:10)! The Bridegroom offers us His best, and His love is to be desired above all other blessings.

**Your Name**

Because of the fragrance of your good ointments,

Your name is ointment poured forth;

Therefore the virgins love you.

(Song of Solomon 1:3).

The Shulamite maiden's senses are overwhelmed with His love. First, she tastes His love, which is better than wine. Then, His name is fragrant ointment poured forth, filling her nostrils. Imagine the soothing effect of warm oil poured out on your skin and the tantalizing allure of its sweet fragrance. *Fragrance* is a recurring theme throughout the Song. Remember that *this* oil is the Holy Spirit! Oil repeatedly represents the Holy Spirit in Scripture. This aroma is thick with the presence of the Lord and creates a tangible aroma that draws her to Him.

Many years ago, as my journey with the Lord progressed, I memorized some of the names of God in Scripture. They became a wonderful tool to praise God. I encourage you to memorize God's names and declare them out loud. Speaking the names of the Lord aloud changes the atmosphere and releases a beautiful fragrance, enticing the virgins to love Him. The fragrance of love ignites a pure heart. Let's pour out his name:

- Jehovah-Tsidkenu—*Jehovah, our righteousness*
- Jehovah-m'Keddech—*Jehovah who sanctifies*
- Jehovah Shalom—*Jehovah is peace*
- Jehovah Shammah—*Jehovah is there*
- Jehovah Rophe—*Jehovah who heals*
- Jehovah Jireh—*Jehovah, my Provider*
- Jehovah Nissi—*Jehovah, my banner*
- Jehovah Rohi—*Jehovah, my shepherd*
- Jehovah Ishi—*Jehovah, my husband* [2]

Make it a goal to memorize these names so that you can use them as endearment whenever you desire. Explore Scripture on your own to find other ways His name is expressed. Now, spend some time hallowing His name, declaring His holiness. (Again, do this out loud. If you can't do this right now, make time later to pour out the Lord's name like purified oil and release His fragrance with your mouth.)

This is one way to become a doer of the Word of God--hear the Word, and speak it out loud. I overcome by the Blood of the Lamb, by the *word* of my testimony, and by not loving my life so much that I shrink from death or that I'm afraid to die (Revelation 12:11). We believe in our hearts and confess with our mouths (Romans 10:9-10). We are beginning to see the passionate imagery God is creating as He kisses us with His words and we cry out His name with our mouths. The Song of Solomon is not for the faint of heart! We are performing the Word of God and building with the Lord a foundation of intimacy.

**A Handbook**

Interestingly, this mysterious little book is found in the center of the Bible. While often misunderstood and overlooked, it reveals a pattern for the church to get ready for the big event. Large weddings require much preparation! Solomon was the wisest man to walk the face of the earth, apart from Jesus Christ. In his Song, Solomon tells of a young maiden's heart awakened to love. She has seen the King, but not just any king. He is the King of Kings and the Lord of Glory! Just one glimpse of Him sets her heart ablaze, and she longs for deeper intimacy. The Shulamite maiden sets out on a quest to find her true heart's desire. The Song of Solomon not only prepares us for the wedding night in the King's chambers but also ushers us into greater intimacy with Christ during these perilous days. Allow the Song of Solomon to be your inspiration in your pursuit of love as we embark on this journey!

The Song of Solomon will teach us who we are in Christ and will be a handbook of prayer and confessions. It will be only as effective as we are faithful. I encourage you to hold fast to these confessions and believe the kisses—the words of the Beloved's mouth. Repeat and meditate on them. Let faith be released as you begin to accept God's truth and use it as your mirror, as He sees you. Allow Him to embrace you with His words and declare who you truly are in His Kingdom. As the Bridegroom lifts the veil and we behold Him, we *will* be changed. Make your request and desires known to God. Let us cry out!

*Beloved King, kiss me with the kisses of Your mouth!*

*Let Your words journey into my heart and ignite fiery passion within me.*

*Open my soul to receive your love.*

*Your name, sweet King of Kings, is like ointment poured out.*

*The fragrance of your name fills the room as I confess it out loud!*

*Your wonderful scent envelopes me!*

*Thank you that, as I call, you are going to show me great and mighty things. Mysterious ways I do not know.*

*Show me the way into deeper love with You.*

*Amen.*

Don't you just want to drop back in your chair and take a deep breath? Selah! (*Selah* is a term used in the Psalms meaning "to pause and think about) We will have many "Selah" moments throughout the Song.)

# 2

**Draw Me**

*Draw me after you…*

(Song of Solomon 1:4)

**My Story**

A few years ago as I was writing *Are We There Yet? Journey Into the Presence of God* [1], the Lord showed me this simple prayer: "Draw me." That unconscious cry from my heart was the beginning of the process of discovering Jesus, the Bridegroom King. Sometimes we call this massive shift a "paradigm shift." A paradigm shift occurs when significant change happens, one fundamental view blossoming into another. It is a new perspective upon the same information. I already knew Jesus was my Savior and Deliverer. I knew Him as my Shepherd, Friend, Provider, Baptizer in the Holy Spirit, and more; yet, even though I intellectually knew the church as the bride of Christ corporately, I had not begun to "see" Jesus as my Bridegroom King. This perspective implies a deeper level of intimacy altogether. As I was learning how to dwell in His presence, I began to pray "Draw me after You." My spiritual eyes started to flutter open, and Jesus began revealing Himself to me as my Beloved, my Bridegroom King.

The spark which ignited this passion in me began after I heard Mike Bickle's personal testimony about receiving the hot, fiery seal spoken of in Song of Solomon 8:6. The speaker was on fire for Jesus and full of a passionate love that created desire and made me hungry for more. Although I was at the beginning of this journey, I had read the end of Solomon's book; and I began to ask for the hot, fiery seal as described in these Scriptures:

> Set me as a seal upon your heart,
>
> As a seal upon your arm;
>
> For love is as strong as death,
>
> Jealousy as cruel as the grave,
>
> Its flames are flames of fire,
>
> A most vehement flame.
>
> Song of Solomon 8:6

(We will get to this place in the Song. Many times our hearts run ahead of our minds as we walk in the Spirit.) My heart was responding to a desire my Creator had planted in me. He gave me this desire for Him--it was a divine yearning. Intellectually, I could not completely comprehend it, but I recognized a different kind of passion stirring up in me.

> "In my head I may not know,

what I feel down in my soul…."

(as my grandson Judah's song says) [2]

In hindsight, I can see how the Holy Spirit was drawing me. I wanted to be hot and fiery for God. I began to include in my prayer not only "Draw me," but "Set your hot, fiery seal on my heart." When I asked Jesus to come into my heart and confessed Him as my Lord, I didn't completely understand being born again. (I still don't get it all even now.) Likewise, when I was baptized in water, I didn't comprehend the magnitude of what was happening. Again, when I was baptized in the Holy Spirit, it was by faith that I received the power of God in my life, a choice which did not require a complete understanding. Actually, when I asked for this seal, I was pretty ignorant; but God knew the source of my desire and hunger. He had placed the hunger there, and only He could fulfill it! So I asked in faith, and He did it. The seed He planted began to grow.

Is there a longing inside you for more of Jesus? Love is not complacent; it is a fierce devotion. Even though you are satisfied with Him, faith always reaches for more. Do not mistake this hunger as a dissatisfaction with Jesus. It is a growing, divine yearning He wants to quench.

As we will learn when we come to chapter 8 in the Song of Solomon, Jesus Himself is the Bridal Seal; and He extends an invitation for us to take Him as a seal upon our hearts. This seal of fire ignites passion for Jesus. The journey starts with a longing for his kisses (Song 1:2), as we saw in the first chapter. It will end with a seal of true love upon our hearts (in the final chapter).

It begins with a longing; it will climax with an impartation of divine love upon our hearts. Yum!

**Draw Near**

God gives a precious and magnificent promise, "Draw near to God and He will draw near to you" (James 4:8). However, sometimes we need help even knowing how to "draw near" to Him. Jesus is no longer confined to flesh, instead living within the believers of His church here on earth. Jesus is sitting at the right hand of the Father. So how do I, a physical being on earth, draw near to Him in heaven? I believe the first step is simply to acknowledge Him. Talk to Him. Ask Him. The prayer, "Draw me," is the second request and implies three things: need, humility, and dependence. "Draw me" speaks of individual intimacy with Jesus. I need help drawing Him near. I exercise humility when I ask. I demonstrate dependence when I do what He says (obedience).

Psalm 42:7 says, "Deep calls unto deep...." You may—and should--physically cry out to Him with your mouth, but recognize that it is your spirit calling upon His Spirit. You may not see manifestation immediately in the natural world. As we ask to be drawn to Jesus, let's believe He is responding, drawing near, and setting a fire within. A fire will always leave evidence of where it has been. The same will hold true when He sets a fiery seal on your heart.

**Let Us Run Together**

This cry to be drawn is immediately followed by a decision; the decision is to run—not alone–but together.

> *Let us run together.*
>
> Song of Solomon 1:4a

This choice is a commitment; to the journey, to God, to myself, and to each other--*to run together*. Running with Jesus and joining with other seekers provides accountability and helps secure our ability to finish the journey. We must *do* what we learn and be diligent to finish what we begin. Hebrews 12:1-2 tell us, "...let us run with endurance the race that is set before us." Finishing takes endurance; but we must look "unto Jesus, the author and finisher of our faith."

As the young bride realized her inadequacies and prayed, "Draw me," the Bridegroom (Jesus) answered by bringing her into his chambers.

**The King's Chambers**

> The king has brought me into his chambers.
>
> We will be glad and rejoice in you.
>
> We will remember your love more than wine.
>
> Rightly do they love you.
>
> Song of Solomon 1:4b and c

The King's chambers will be the place for preparation. The little Shulamite maiden knows where she is. The King has brought her into His presence, His chambers, His throne room; the Holiest of All, the secret place of the Most High God. It is here that she will undergo the process of change--to become a mature bride ready for her Bridegroom. Then she commits: "We will be glad and rejoice....We will remember your love more than wine." She sees this as a time of rejoicing and being glad and remembering His love--having a *knowing* that loving Him is the right thing to do. Her expectations are great. That is right. Selah!

**In the Right Place**

This is the right place to hear from the Lord and find the tools needed to complete the journey. "The king has brought me into his chambers" (The Song 1:4b). If you don't know "how to" come into the King's chambers, my first book, *Are We There Yet? Journey Into the Presence of God,* can show you the way. All believers are invited--commanded--to come with boldness to the throne of grace, the mercy seat, to receive mercy and find grace to help in our time of need (Hebrews 4:16). In Revelation 4:1 Jesus referred to the throne room in heaven when he said to the apostle John, "Come up here." He is also telling us as believers, "Come up here." Allow the Holy Spirit to show you the throne room, the King's chambers, and bring you in. In the King's chambers is where we belong.

As we established earlier, I need help, and so do you. The King's chamber is the right place to seek help and ask some questions. In this paradigm shift, the chamber is the King's bedroom, the place of ultimate comfort, intimacy, and rest. There, I behold my Beloved, but I also see myself. In the King's presence, I inquire of the Lord.

David said it like this:

>One thing I have desired of the LORD,
>
>That I will seek:
>
>That I may dwell in the house of the LORD
>
>All the days of my life,

To behold the beauty of the LORD,

And to inquire in His temple.

Psalm 27:4

**The Manual**

We have what we need to finish the journey. It is awesome and wonderful, but it is not an easy journey. It will require diligence and patience. This little book; The Song, will guide us only *if we act upon it*, if we are willing to sow the seeds and cultivate them, we will see the bountiful harvest. Let us run together.

Pray with me:

*Draw me, Jesus,*

*Draw me after you.*

*Seal my heart with your hot, fiery love.*

*Thank You for bringing me into Your chambers.*

*I long to be in this place above any other place on earth.*

*We know what we want!*

*We make our commitment to run with you and each other.*

*We know where we live! (In the secret place of the Most High God, in the King's chambers.)*

*We will rejoice and be glad in You, our King.*

*We will extol Your love more than wine.*

*Only You are deserving; it is the right thing to love you!*

*Amen!*

## 3

**Self-Evaluation: Seeing Myself**

*But my own vineyard I have not kept*

(Song of Solomon 1:6).


The journey begins in the King's Chambers, in the light of God's presence. "In the light of the king's face is life, and his favor is like a cloud of the latter rain" (Proverbs 16:15). In His light I begin to see myself; and as I feel His acceptance and love, I am ready to look at myself. As the Shulamite maiden beholds herself, she says to the ones with her:

> I am dark, but lovely,
>
> O daughters of Jerusalem,
>
> Like the tents of Kedar,
>
> Like the curtains of Solomon
>
> Do not look upon me because I am dark
>
> Because the sun has tanned me
>
> My mother's sons were angry with me
>
> They made me keeper of the vineyards,
>
> But my own vineyard I have not kept.

Song of Solomon 1:5-6

In light of the King's acceptance, she has the courage to begin self-evaluation. She sees areas of darkness: "I am black," or "I am dark," another translation says. This is not referring to a certain skin tone. These areas of darkness represent the areas in our hearts that need to be confronted, the parts of our lives where we don't yet have complete victory. This is the struggle between the old nature and the new creation in Christ. She feels shame and condemnation because dark areas of her heart are being exposed. Paul deals with the contrast between the old and new nature in Romans 7. Then in Romans 8:2 he declares, "There is no condemnation in Christ." Although the maiden has imperfections, she is not shunned by the Bridegroom. She is able to acknowledge the darkness of her heart but still have confidence that she is lovely in the eyes of her King.

She contrasts the black tents of Kedar with the white linen curtains of Solomon. The contrast she describes was easily understood by the daughters of Jerusalem. They could relate to the phrase, "dark, but lovely." The tents of Kedar were made from the dark skins of wild goats. This imagery speaks of the darkness of the old nature, which hasn't been completely purged. However, Solomon's curtains, made of brilliant, white linen with fine embroidery, were located in the Holy Place within the temple and represent the inner sanctuary where sin is blotted out by the blood of Jesus and we find grace.

The bride, in essence, is saying, "I have been distracted and gotten dirty working in the vineyard--please don't stare at me! I am vulnerable and exposed in the light of His presence. I have tried to do too much in my own strength. I have tried to please too many, and my own vineyard has been untended." When she refers to her mother's sons, who became angry and made her tend the vineyards, she is dealing with shame and rejection. There is a subtle hint of placing blame, which often leads to unforgiveness and hinders relationships. When we are trying to please others, as the maiden is doing here with her brothers, we neglect our number- one priority, our relationship with the Lord. If we want intimacy, we need to be cleaned up (Ephesians 5:26) and to take responsibility for our condition.

**Inquiring of the Lord--the First Question**

Be alert! *Pay attention to the questions asked throughout the Song.* They are keys which help unlock revelations within the Song. The bride is a seeker. As the Song begins, she recognizes her need, seeks help, and begins to ask questions instead of hiding in fear and condemnation.

> Tell me, O you whom I love,
>
> Where you feed your flock,
>
> Where you make it rest at noon?
>
> For why should I be as one who veils herself

> By the flocks of your companions?
>
> Song of Solomon 1:7

She has three questions:

1. Where do you feed?
2. Where do you make your flock lie down at noon?
3. Why should I be veiled?

Her questions are legitimate: Where can I find food (spiritual nourishment and physical provision)? Where can I find rest? And why should I be so filled with shame and rejection?

**The Fairest of All**

The bride asks the right questions of the right person—the Beloved. His answers comes swiftly; he immediately responds:

> If you do not know, O fairest of women….
>
> Song of Solomon 1:8a

The Good Shepherd sees her actual need. Her identity has been stolen, and she doesn't know who she is. She identifies with her own darkness, but He addresses her as the "fairest among women." She identifies with her sin and is keenly aware of her imperfections, but He sees her as beautiful.

> Word Study: The word translated as "fair" is translated in most other versions of the Bible as "beautiful."

This term of endearment is meant to lavish the bride with favor and honor. Her tainted perceptions do not hinder the Beloved's ability to see her inner beauty. He is able to see her (both literally and figuratively) unveiled.

> He calls her beautiful even in the midst of her disorientation and failure. The Lord gives her an answer that shocks many of us. We would expect to be rebuked or to be accused or shamed by the Lord. He says, "I know your garden isn't being kept; I know you are like a veiled woman; I know you are serving at a distance; however, you are most beautiful to Me.

"Mirror, mirror on the wall, who is the fairest of them all?" [1]

"You are the fairest of all," Jesus tells His bride.

**Kate's Story**

As I was praying with a beautiful young friend of mine one morning before she was to compete in the local Fairest of the Fair pageant, the Lord reminded me of this verse. I told her, "Kate you are already the fairest! Just throw your shoulders back and walk out there knowing that you belong to Jesus. You are the King's fairest." The favor of God was on her, and she received the crown! *You*, Dear One, are the King's fairest, too!

**The Beloved's First Words**

The first words the little Shulamite hears from her Beloved affirm that she is accepted and not thrown aside by Him. Believing I am accepted is one of the first steps in a more intimate walk with Jesus. His work completed on the day He went on the cross made this divine exchange possible. He was rejected among men (Isaiah 53:3) that we might be accepted. Jesus identifies with our need for acceptance. We have all experienced rejection, although none to the degree Jesus did on the cross. The enemy uses rejection and shame to keep us separated from God and to hinder our relationships with others. Maybe rejection has been spoken over you by harsh words. Some rejection is overtly humiliating and cruel, but rejection also comes in the form of neglect or exclusion. Rejection may be unintentional and, in some instances, perceived only in our minds as a result of past rejection we may have experienced. Rejection breeds rejection. We can come to view ourselves as unacceptable and, therefore, rejected. It is easy to believe the *lie* of rejection. The truth is that we are accepted in the Beloved.

Word study:

> A *lie* is a false statement made with deliberate intent to deceive, a falsehood; something intended or serving to convey a false impression. [2]

Begin to ask the Lord to help you receive His love and acceptance. Receiving His acceptance is vital to this journey. Make a choice to believe what God's Word says, and no longer believe the *lie* that you are rejected. You may have been rejected horribly in the past in earthly relationships. You may still be experiencing rejection by those whom you love. Rejection causes pain, but *it does not define you*. God's Word defines who you are. Learn to recognize rejection when it comes to your door, and don't open it!

We can believe what He is saying to us. "Let God be true, but every man a liar" (Romans 3:4). The devil is a liar and accuser, but God's Word tells us we are "the fairest among women."

People who are struggling with a spirit of unbelief are constantly dealing with negative self-talk and convincing themselves that they are unworthy to be loved or to receive from God. That lie takes up residence in the heart and becomes a stronghold of unbelief. Please open your eyes and make the following declaration with me: "I renounce you, spirit of unbelief and spirit of lies and I command you to leave my life right now." [3]

## My Story

I experienced a real battle with rejection as a child and young adult. It was not until I received the Holy Spirit that I identified rejection as the enemy and learned how to be free. When I learned that Jesus was rejected so that I might be accepted, I went to war with the enemy of rejection. "He was despised and rejected by men, a Man of sorrows and acquainted with grief" (Isaiah 53:3). I had to take my thoughts captive and resist the lie of the enemy. The truth of God's Word set me free from rejection. Even though rejection still knocks on my door on a regular basis, I have learned how to recognize this enemy. I now guard my heart by not granting access to rejection, and I resist the fear of being unaccepted. Jesus accepted me for His pleasure, "to the praise of the glory of His grace, by which *He made us accepted in the Beloved*" (Ephesians 1:6, italics mine).

**Questions Receive Answers**

After the bridegroom assures her of acceptance, he begins to tell her in the very next verse how to find answers to her questions:

> If you do not know,
>
> O fairest among women,
>
> Follow in the footsteps of the flock,
>
> And feed your little goats
>
> Beside the shepherds' tents.
>
> Song of Solomon 1:8

The Beloved answers her questions and more. He tells her who she is, the fairest among women! Then he gives her three things to do.

- Stay with the flock. (Stay with the body, the church; if you are hungry, don't run; surround yourself with fellow believers; don't isolate and separate yourself. You will find spiritual nourishment within the body of believers. The flock needs the younger and the older, so don't be exclusive.)
- Feed your little goats. (Do the things that are your responsibility, and be faithful over the little things such as homes, finances, husbands and wives, children, jobs.)

- Luke 16:10 makes clear that whoever can be trusted with very little can also be trusted with much, but whoever is dishonest with little will be dishonest with much. Be faithful also, then, to finish what you start and follow through with the responsibilities set before you. Tend faithfully to your family and those in your sphere of influence.
- Remain beside the shepherds' tents. (Stay under authority; don't be a "Lone Ranger"; don't hide; don't get rebellious.) We all have "tents" of authority to stay under or preside over. In other words, you must remain not only under the Lord's spiritual authority, but also under authority in other relationships with, for example, your husband, father, pastor, teachers, bosses, etc. Likewise, do not abuse the authority given to you over others. Stay in line with godly authority. The importance of this submission cannot be overstated.

If you find yourself at a place in life when you don't know what to do, or if you are going through a particular struggle or identity crisis, just follow these instructions. These three directives will keep you out of trouble, and you will find what you are seeking: food, rest, and protection. In summary, stay with the flock, uphold your obligations, and stay under your appropriate authority.

**Keep the Gate Closed**

Getting free from rejection is an exhilarating way to begin this journey. The truth that I am accepted frees me from shame, guilt, and accusation. I can keep the gate closed when the enemy comes knocking, but he will try to get through the back door. God told Abraham in Genesis 22:17, "...your descendants shall possess the gates of their enemies." Learn to recognize the enemy; and when rejection comes, keep the gate locked! [4]

Say this out loud as we pray and confess:

*I am in Christ, and I am accepted in the Beloved.*

*Thank you, Jesus, for calling me the fairest one.*

*I am the Beloved's favorite!*

*I am not rejected.*

*I am redeemed.*

*I am the righteousness of God in Christ.*

*I no longer have to remain veiled.*

*Thank you, Jesus, for putting the enemy of rejection under*

*my feet.*

*Thank you, Jesus, for revealing the lie of the enemy and*

*for giving me the courage to speak the truth!*

*Show me now where to feed. Help me fulfill my*

*obligations and remain faithful.*

*Help me stay under proper authority when I find myself struggling or in areas of transition.*

*Thank you for revealing the truth of Your word.*

*Amen.*

## 4

## The Plan

*We will make you...*

(Song of Solomon 1:11)

**The King's Vision**

God's desire is for us to live in freedom from rejection. He offered the ultimate provision so that we can walk in the light of acceptance. When we walk in this light, He reveals Himself; and His plan becomes clearer. Using highly poetic language, the Beloved begins to share with the Shulamite maiden His vantage point. In the previous verses of Chapter 1, He has addressed her questions: "Where do you feed and rest? Why should I hide, be ashamed, or feel guilty?" He has answered lovingly, but now the Beloved has more to reveal to her. Previously He referred to her as "the fairest" or His favorite. Now He begins to share His vision of her through a series of comparisons. More importantly, His perspective is not flawed. Although she is not completely cleaned up yet, He affectionately affirms her once more by saying, "You are My love." His language is tender as He uses imagery to prophesy over her, declaring who she will become.

The Beloved speaking:

> I have compared you, my love,
>
> To my filly among Pharaoh's chariots.
>
> Your cheeks are lovely with ornaments,
>
> Your neck with chains of gold.
>
> We will make you ornaments of gold
>
> With studs of silver (Song of Solomon 1:9-11).

Let's look more closely at these comparisons; there is much to unpack in these few verses. He compares her strength to the costly war horses used in Pharaoh's cavalry. Egypt was known to have the strongest and best-trained horses in the world, and much was invested in these beautiful creatures. Solomon acquired thousands of these war horses for himself, but only the elite and most powerful of these horses were allowed to pull his personal chariot. The King is, in essence, saying, "You are my choice, my filly among horses. You, of all those trained for war, are the one I want to accompany me into battle." His righteousness is her strength. His words create, and she is being conformed to God's righteousness.

When we are trained in His righteousness and are in Christ, we have more strength than we can comprehend. The "yes" in your spirit is seen by God as strength.[1] Saying "yes" to Jesus supremely equips you to do battle and gives you the distinct honor of wearing His breastplate of righteousness into battle. Despite previous failures, such as the unkempt vineyard of the maiden, you are the best one suited for the task He has set before *you.*

The Beloved speaks about the strength of the maiden's spirit. He declares the reality of her true strength even when she sees herself as fragile and weak. Jesus does the same for us. "And He (the Lord) said to me, 'My grace is sufficient for you, for My power is made perfect in weakness'" (2 Corinthians 12:9a).

As He continues to describe the maiden, He draws attention to her cheeks, which speak of emotions. Upon our faces are painted the pictures of emotion and desire. Our cheeks reveal joy, sadness, embarrassment, anger, etc. We were created in God's image with emotions, a beautiful palette which enhances our experiences and decorates our lives with color. Our emotions are attractive to Him, and later in the Song we will see His Words come to pass. She learns submission to His Spirit with bridled emotion and sincere devotion to Jesus. Her cheeks reflect the glow of His presence within her.

From there, He goes on to describe her neck, which represents her will. He sees beauty in the nape of her submissive neck, which is supple and bowing, not stiff towards correction. A stiff neck is a sign of a rebellious will and faulty thinking. In contrast, a teachable spirit is a will that is yielded and humble- and is beautiful to the King.

The Beloved continues to reveal His plans for her as He brings her to the King's table. When He says, "*We* [plural] will make you ornaments of gold with studs of silver," He is speaking of the triune Godhead. The same type of reference is seen in Genesis during the creation account of man. "Then God said, 'Let *us* make human beings in *our* image, in *our* likeness'" (1:26, emphasis mine). Here, I believe the plural form "*We*" refers to the Trinity (Father, Son, and Holy Spirit) and is the Beloved speaking. These divine qualities, purity and deity, are distributed only by the ministry of the Godhead. Gold symbolizes royalty, purity and deity; and silver symbolizes redemption. He adorns her yielded and humble neck with jewels that are beautiful and valuable.

Her soul--mind, will, and emotions--are obedient and willing for the King. He affirms her desire to be drawn and to follow after Him. He has the plan and does the work of developing our divine character through His sanctifying grace. "For it is God who works in you, both to will and to do of His good pleasure" (Philippians 2:13). We must decide to believe His Word. This choice we make is not based upon how we feel or see ourselves. It is based upon how God sees us and what the Word of God says about us. We discover and rightly establish our identity in Christ when we agree with what God says about us.

**The King's Table - the Provision of the King**

As the King continues to answer her question, "Where do you feed?" He reveals the King's table.

> While the king is at his table,
>
> My spikenard sends forth its fragrance.
>
> Song of Solomon 1:12

This verse is so significant that we will take it in two parts. For now, let's focus on the King and His table. The King's table, where the bride will receive nourishment, is the place of fellowship and communion with the King and is where His great provision is revealed. The table holds the bread: Jesus is the Bread of Life. At the table we begin to learn who we are in Christ. Jesus says in John 6:52, ff., "Eat my flesh, drink my blood." Unless we partake in His flesh and blood, we have no life. Jesus knew some of his disciples would not receive this teaching, and many have turned away in disbelief upon hearing it.[2] Do not turn away in disbelief about what the Lord has done and is doing for you or stop short of allowing Him to complete the process. God has provided the divine exchange. That is, His flesh and blood have been sacrificed at the altar for your forgiveness and complete restoration.

**The Divine Exchange:**

1. Jesus was punished that we might be forgiven.
2. Jesus was made sin by our sinfulness that we might be made righteous with his righteousness.
3. Jesus died our death that we might share His life.
4. Jesus was made a curse that we might receive His eternal blessing.
5. Jesus endured our poverty that we might share His abundance.
6. Jesus bore our shame that we might share His glory.
7. Jesus endured our rejection that we might enjoy His acceptance.[3]

This exchange is the finished work of Jesus on the cross, God's provision. When we receive Him, our old self dies (on the cross) so that the new self will rise and live (through Him).[4] You can never deserve to be included in the divine exchange. You cannot earn a place at the King's table. It is the outworking of God's sovereign grace. It is the expression of His measureless love. The exchange is provided at the cross. He bought our seat next to Him at the King's table! We have a VIP pass. This is the golden table of showbread where we eat in His presence.[5] "For all the promises of God in Him (Jesus Christ) are yes and amen to the glory of God through us" (2 Corinthians 1:20). The Beloved Bridegroom King is giving this seat as a gift to His bride. He has provided the dowry and asked for the maiden's hand of acceptance.

Now it's your turn to do something: Receive His Word personally. Come to the table and eat! Sit down in your place. Be with the King. Eat His provision. "Taste and see that the Lord is good" (Psalm 34:8). Do the Word He speaks over you, serving Him whole-heartedly.[6] Partake in the goodness of the Lord! He has already made it available to you. Enjoy!

In the next chapter we will finish this verse and learn how the bride expresses her thankfulness for the bounty of the King's table. Before we move on, take time to confess and pray the Word of God over yourself. His Word is written personally, specifically for you. If no one gives you a word of encouragement, speak His word and prophesy to yourself! His words are true and can be trusted.

> *I am loved and highly prized by You, Jesus.*
>
> *Your plans for me are like ornaments of gold on my neck,*
>
> *pure and divine.*
>
> *I bend my neck in submission so that You may adorn me*
>
> *with chains of gold.*
>
> *To You all praise, glory, and honor are due.*
>
> *You have finished Your work on the cross, offering me an*
>
> *abundant life in exchange.*
>
> *You overcame and are helping me overcome.*

## Sarah Ramsey – The Bridegroom's Song

*You are working out Your good and perfect will in me.*

*I am becoming more like You every day.*

*Thank You for putting Your robes of righteousness on me*

*and clothing me with Your salvation.*

*Thank You for inviting me to Your table.*

*I come to you to sit, eat, and worship in Your presence.*

*Amen.*

# 5

## The Fragrance of Worship

*My spikenard sends forth its fragrance*

(Song of Solomon 1:12).

### The Journey Progresses--Joy Overflows

The King has brought me into His Chambers, to His Table! He answers my questions and blesses me with His own Kingly presence. He reveals His table of provision; my heart is full! He is here, sitting with me in intimate communion, waiting to nourish and strengthen me. This is where I converse with my Bridegroom. My cup overflows!

### Spikenard

> While the king is at his table,
>
> My spikenard sends forth its fragrance.
>
> Song of Solomon 1:12

"My spikenard sends forth its fragrance"--the fragrance of sacrificial worship. This kind of worship will cost me something. Spikenard is a valuable and fragrant ointment derived from the dried roots of the herbal plant called *nard*. By the first century, it was already being imported from its native India in alabaster boxes. Because of its costliness, spikenard was used only for very special occasions.[1]

Mary, the sister of Lazarus, whom Jesus resurrected from the dead, made dinner for Jesus and invited Him into her home:

> Then Mary took a pound of very costly oil of spikenard, anointed the feet of Jesus, and wiped His feet with her hair. And the house was filled with the fragrance of the oil.
>
> John 12:3

Spikenard illustrates spontaneous and affectionate worship.[2] Mary's costly offering of spikenard symbolized her worship of the King at His table. Mary's sacrificial offering filled the whole house with its sweet fragrance, much as the preparation of a savory meal fills the home with an alluring aroma. As I partake in His lavish provision and remember the abundant suffering He endured for me, I am moved to offer a sacrifice of thanksgiving; and a fragrance of worship envelops the space where I abide.[3]

Let's practice right now:

*Thank you, Jesus, for Your abundant provision.*

An old hymn rises up in my spirit, spontaneous worship!

> I am a child of the King.
>
> My Father is rich in houses and land.
>
> He holdeth the wealth of the world in His hands!!
>
> Of rubies and diamonds, of silver and gold--
>
> His coffers are full, He has riches untold!
>
> I am a child of the King, a child of the King,
>
> With Jesus my Savior I'm a child of the King![4]
>
> Selah!

*Jesus, I remember Your lavish provision through Your suffering.*

**Myrrh**

Spikenard is the first of a tri-fold expression of worship revealed by the symbolism of three fragrances: spikenard, myrrh, and henna. Myrrh is the next beautiful expression of the bride's worship.

> A bundle of myrrh is my beloved to me,
>
> That lies all night between my breasts.
>
> My beloved is to me a cluster of henna blooms
>
> In the vineyards of En Gedi.
>
> Song of Solomon 1:13-14

Myrrh is a sweet perfume which is symbolic of suffering and is referenced eight times in the Song of Solomon. Myrrh was also used as an embalming fluid and is thus symbolic of death. Its beautiful aroma covered the stench of death. It was very expensive and was used only by the wealthy in burial rituals. Myrrh was significant both in the beginning and at the end of the life of Jesus.

- Jesus' birth was honored with myrrh (Matthew 2:11). The wise kings brought this embalming spice to Jesus as a prophetic symbol of His death. (They actually brought three prophetic gifts: gold, frankincense, and myrrh-- symbolizing His deity, His ministry, and His death.)

> Throughout the Song of Solomon we will see repeated references to these three prophetic symbols.
> - Jesus was buried with myrrh. He was given a King's burial. When Mary went to the tomb, she brought more myrrh and spices to put upon His body.[5]

It was uncommon to have a bundle of expensive myrrh as a sachet between the breasts. Myrrh would have been an extravagant gift from the King to His bride. When she says, "You are a bundle of myrrh," she is saying, "I understand the abundance of Your suffering. I understand a little bit of what you went through for me in order to make available this table of eloquent provision." As the Shulamite maiden sits at the King's table, she remembers the price the Beloved (Jesus) paid for her, and is prompted to worship to honor that sacrifice and dedication to her.

She places between her breasts the bundle of myrrh which represents "The Beloved." You will see throughout the Song of Solomon that the breasts symbolize passion. The myrrh is placed there, close to her heart, where it lies during her night seasons. During times of suffering, like a sweet fragrance, it permeates her spirit in the quiet darkness and brings her Beloved like a sachet near to her heart. This representation is most precious.

The fragrance released from the myrrh keeps me ever mindful of the price which has been paid for me and how He suffered to bring me to His table. As I sacrifice parts of myself to Him, I die an extravagant death and release the same sweet fragrance to

Him. And in the night seasons, the sweet fragrance of myrrh serves as a reminder that He never leaves me nor forsakes me. I am not alone. Jesus said, "I am with you always, even to the end of the age" (Matthew 28:20). Do you find yourself in a night season? We will find myrrh sprinkled throughout the Song. Jesus will never leave you or forsake you either. Let the myrrh remind us our Beloved is near and familiar with our suffering and knows the very details of what we are experiencing.

**My Story**

As I began to learn about the sachet of myrrh, my sweet friend gave me a locket full of myrrh to wear around my neck. It is precious to me and reminds me of Jesus' suffering. I am encouraged to depend on Him in the night seasons that are abundant, seasons of darkness in my life. I have learned to meditate upon the price paid for me, an act which brings the comfort and hope that morning will come, and the Son will shine and bring warmth into the dark.

**Provision Is Expensive**

Maturity comes with suffering. Jesus learned obedience through the things He suffered. It is not the suffering itself which grows us, but it is allowing suffering to teach us to obey. Not everyone who suffers grows in maturity. Some fall under its weight. Jesus, however, learned obedience through His trials. He is the Author of the book on obedience and offers us salvation as a reward. We should run to Jesus and not away from Him when adversity comes.

> "He learned obedience." Why was this necessary for Christ? What is the blessing He brings us? *"Though He were a Son, yet He learned obedience by the things which He suffered. And... became the author of eternal salvation unto all who obey Him" (Hebrews 5:8-9).* Suffering is unnatural to us and therefore calls for the surrender of our wills and submitting to His guidance."[6]

> "We continue to obey God in the midst of trials. We grow stronger as we submit to God's wisdom whenever people slander us, gossip about us, mistreat us or try to hurt us, or when we've just lost our job, received a bad report from a lawyer or doctor, or don't know where needed funds are going to come from. We choose, [in the midst of] the hardship, to believe God, even if it appears to be to our disadvantage. We choose to resist the evil that attacks us, first and foremost by obeying God's Word. This is when true spiritual growth occurs."[7]

The apostle Peter says in 1 Peter 4:1, "Since Christ suffered for us in the flesh, arm yourself also with the same mind, for he who has suffered in the flesh has ceased from sin."

**The Henna--A Bouquet in the Desert**

These expressions of worship are producing an overwhelming sense of awe within the maiden (and within me as I do them)! Her worship releases the love in her and removes fear. Perfect love casts out fear. Her next statement is:

> My beloved is to me a cluster of henna blooms
>
> In the vineyard of En Gedi.
>
> Song of Solomon 1:14

The Song of Solomon is full of references to fragrances. The sense of smell is a powerful trigger of memories throughout our lifetimes. The maiden compares her Beloved to a desert bouquet of henna blooms. Henna, a lovely flower filled with sweet fragrance, is found in the vineyards of En Gedi. (En Gedi was famous for the intense fragrance of its henna blooms.) My Beloved is a sweet fragrance, a cluster of fragrant flowers, not burdensome, but a sweet, delightful, intense, and intoxicating fragrance. The Bride worships with abandon. Jesus, you fill up my senses! Do you recall "Annie's Song" by John Denver?

> You fill up my senses like a night in the forest
>
> like the mountains in springtime, like a walk in the rain,
>
> like a storm in the desert, like a sleepy blue ocean.
>
> You fill up my senses, come fill me again….[8]

I love singing songs to Jesus! Isn't it wonderful how secular songs can so often be sung as worship to our Beloved? Why not take a moment right here and sing a song to your Beloved? Spikenard, myrrh, and the sweet fragrance of henna make a sweet sacrifice of praise as we give thanks, praise, and worship. It has been said that the fragrances of childhood provoke the most powerful memories. I have some young friends who are wonderful, powerful worshippers. I love to see the beautiful abandon with which they worship Jesus. The fragrance of the worshippers fills the room with a sweet aroma.

Selah! Worship breeds worship. I desire to worship, too. Why don't you join me?

Confession and Prayer:

> *Your fragrance is wonderful to me, Jesus my Beloved.*

# Sarah Ramsey – The Bridegroom's Song

*O Jesus, You are a bundle of myrrh, a sachet of myrrh between my breasts.*

*I want the fragrance of Your abundant suffering close to my heart all the night.*

*As I remember that you suffered for me, I am able and equipped to endure the night seasons--the times when darkness surrounds me.*

*I know your relationship with me cost you dearly!*

*You finished the work and made provision available for me at Your table.*

*You are to me a cluster of henna blossoms, and You smell*

*wonderful!*

*Help me meditate upon the cross and remember how You*

*suffered to give me this great salvation.*

*Thank you, precious Lord. Come and fill my senses with your love and enable me to love you more completely.*

*Amen.*

# 6

## Dove's Eyes

*Behold my love...you have dove's eyes.*

Song of Solomon 1:15

**The Voice of the Beloved**

When we sit across a table and share a meal, it is more enjoyable if conversation occurs. For the most part, this is the natural flow of breaking bread together. The King's table is a place where communication happens frequently. The Bridegroom gives words of affirmation to the Shulamite maiden when she is seated at His table.

> Behold, you are fair, my love!
>
> Behold, you are fair!
>
> You have dove's eyes.
>
> Song of Solomon 1:15

The NASB translation says, "How beautiful are you my darling, How beautiful you are!" God created us with the desire to feel beautiful, and He is ready to fill us with the assurance of how beautiful we really are to Him. Unfortunately, we are bombarded by counterfeit claims that try to satisfy this longing. However, true satisfaction comes only from knowing I am beautiful to my Beloved.

We see emphasis through the repeated phrase, "Behold, you are fair, my love. Behold you are fair." The repetition gives power to His words and signals to us an important concept. In the New Testament when Jesus says, "Verily, verily," or "truly, truly I say unto you," we know to listen up! The same is true here when He states the phrase twice. It is not easy for our damaged souls to receive these words of great love and affirmation from the Bridegroom. But remember, the Bridegroom is also our Creator. If anyone knows our value and beauty, it is the One who crafted us. Allow God to give Himself a compliment for how well we have been designed by affirming you. Have you ever met anyone who could not receive a compliment? When it isn't received at face value, it is frustrating and discredits the one who is offering it. Let's believe our Creator and Bridegroom when He tells us we are fair (beautiful) to Him!

He does not stop, but continues to compliment her, "You have dove's eyes." He sees her eyes focused on Him alone. She has a singular vision for Him. Her eyes are set on an audience of One, which is attractive to Him.

**The Eyes of a Dove**

Throughout the Song the eyes are a strong emphasis. Jesus views His bride as one with singleness of vision. Mike Bickle teaches in "Song of Songs--The Ravished Heart of God," about the dove and singleness of vision.

1. The dove has been a picture of the Holy Spirit through Scripture, beginning with Noah in Genesis.
2. The dove speaks of singleness of purpose. The dove does not have peripheral vision; rather, its focus is clearly set on the object in front of it. It also reveals singleness of devotion. The dove only has one mate.
    a. Doves are totally faithful in mating, one dove mating with only one other dove throughout their life spans. If one of them dies, they will never mate again.
    b. Without peripheral vision, a dove can see only straight ahead. A dove's eyes cannot focus on two things at the same time.
3. The Holy Spirit has the single purpose of bringing glory to Jesus by spreading his presence. It is impossible for the Holy Spirit to be anything but perfectly faithful to Jesus. Jesus said about the Spirit, "He shall glorify me" (John 16:14).

4. Her "dove's eyes" reveal her ability to see redemptive truths. They speak of her eyes of faith and vision. He gave her the ability to see!

5. She is single minded in grace. She does not waver between security and calm one moment and condemnation the next. The Lord is saying, "Your eyes see truth. Single vision resists and conquers compromise

and double-mindedness. Having a double mind is a sign of a divided heart.[1] In the Psalms, David prays for an undivided heart:

Teach me your way, Lord, that I may rely on your faithfulness; give me an undivided heart that I may fear your name.

Psalm 86:11, NIV [2]

The Lord is always faithful and has His eyes set on us. Likewise, He yearns for us to have a faithful heart with a mind which does not stray from His truth.

**Another Answer**

Then He answers the second part of her question—such a beautiful sequence! She asks, He reveals who she is, and she sees provision—the King's table. Recall that back in Song of Solomon 1:7, one of her questions was, "Where do you make your flock rest at noon?" He reveals the provision for this rest in the next two verses:

Behold, you are handsome, my beloved!

Yes, pleasant!

Also our bed is green.

The beams of our houses are cedar,

And our rafters of fir (Song of Solomon 1:16-17).

Finding His rest is a process: Receive His words, believe His words, confess His words. *Then*, find rest. The rest comes only as a consequence of trusting in the words He speaks. Once the young maiden believes His words, she responds to her Beloved with praise and worship from a place of genuine rest and assurance.

**A Responsive, Voluntary Lover**

It is in this pleasant company that the maiden sees the place of rest (the bed or couch) which she calls "our bed" in verse 16. She responds to the Beloved's affectionate words and proclaims, "You are handsome, my Beloved." The spontaneous communion reveals enjoyment in being together. Someone once said that communion is the vehicle of fellowship. He tells her who she is, how magnificently special she is to him, and she responds accordingly. She is a responsive, voluntary lover. Love cannot be forced, or else it ceases to be love. She is able to express and give love without coercion--it is simply a response. Our love for God should be a response to who He is and to His affection for us. I am beautiful to my Beloved, and He is handsome to me. The relationship is alive and green with life. She also sees their houses (not house, but houses), a place of security, enduring forever. The houses are built of cedar beams and rafters of fir, which do not decay. She can rest assured in this strong fortress.

She releases worship to her handsome and pleasant Beloved in this place of peace and seclusion. Jesus talks about rest in Matthew 11, and Hebrews 4 also teaches us about it. He invites us, saying, "Come to me." When we come to the Lord, He gives us rest; but we must first go to Him. She is secure in His love for her. Again, coming to Him is a response to an invitation of a lifetime, and the security of their bed and home provides an environment for intimate worship and praise for both of them to be satisfied.

**My Story**

I was lost in a sense of newness and unfamiliarity when I first came into the King's chambers. I did not know what to *do*. Despite my uncertainty, I practiced coming into the Lord's presence by faith. Faith operates in an unseen realm; faith is a risk, an uncertain step into the unknown. I took my seat beside Him and learned to inquire of the Lord. I became more comfortable with the Beloved as I continued to commune in His presence. My awkwardness began to melt away and I began to enjoy being with my God. This has been a work of the Holy

Spirit in my life, and He helps me worship and learn how to live out this heavenly life here on earth. This is not only how we commune; it is also how we live--by faith. The just live by faith (Habakkuk 2:4).

Several years ago our grandchildren were part of the cast in a local production of *The King and I*.[3] I listened intently as the musical's English teacher, Anna, sang the following words: "Getting to know you, getting to know all about you, getting to like you, getting to hope you like me." Anna's song reminded me of the Song of Solomon--my own story of *The King and I*. As the melody and words resounded in my mind, I said. "Yes! I am getting to know You, my King. I like You, and I hope you like me, too!" These feelings can be likened to infatuation, the early stages of intimacy. We want to express our feelings and hope they are reciprocated. We are getting to know the King of Glory and learning to dwell in His chambers and eat at His table.

**More Answers**

Earlier in verse seven she had also asked, "Where do you feed? Where do you give rest? And why should I hide?" One of the promises of God's word is, "When you seek, you will find" (Luke 11:9). He is quick to give answers to the maiden's seeking heart. We are hearing the truth and finding God's abundant provision. His house will stand forever, and His love is alive for me! We find nourishment and life here! The journey into intimacy has begun, but we are not all the way there yet. This journey is so good, but it will get even better!

Confession and prayer:

*O, thank you, Jesus, that I am beautiful to you even before*

*I'm completely cleaned up!*

*You have made me Your love and say my eyes are like doves, for You alone.*

*Thank you for first fixing Your eyes upon me.*

*I will say, "I have found favor (grace) in your eye; I am Your fair one."*

*Now, give me an undivided heart--that I may fix my eyes upon You.*

*Teach me your ways, O Lord, as you did for David, and I*

*will rely on Your faithfulness.*

*I will praise You with all of my heart and glorify Your name forever.*

*Amen.*

## 7

## **Stolen Identity**

*The thief does not come except to steal…*

(John 10:10).

**Identity**

Song of Solomon Chapter 2 begins on a high note with revelation of the identity of the bride; but as we will discover, it does not end on that same note. Begin now to absorb some important concepts by asking the Holy Spirit to help you recover your stolen identity. The thief comes for one sole purpose: to steal. But there is good news! "When the thief is found, he must restore sevenfold" (Proverbs 6:31). Amen! Do you remember reading the Dr. Seuss book *Are You My Mother?* [1] The little character asks everyone he encounters the same question, "Are you my mother?" He is searching for his identity, he needs to know to whom he belongs. We, too, need to know who we really are. Our answer comes not by asking the world and meeting its standards, but by looking into the mirror of God's Word. Only there will we find our true identity-because God's opinion is the only one that really matters.

At this point in the Song of Solomon, the bride does not know who she is. The King wants this little Shulamite shepherdess, His bride, to know how He sees her. However, she only can begin to establish her identity as the bride as she comes to know Him. Isn't the same true in our relationship with God? We can only truly understand who we really are and where we belong as we come to know Him more fully.

**Believing the Truth**

A major theme in Chapter 2 is obedience. Believing the truth is not enough. We must make deliberate choices to obey what is revealed to us in the Word of God. Otherwise, we become deceived, even in our knowledge of the Word. "If you accustom yourself to studying the Bible without an earnest and very definite purpose to obey, you will harden yourself in disobedience." [2]

Remember the maiden's first confession, "I am dark but lovely" (1:5). As she sits at the King's table and begins to see herself in the light of His presence, she makes her second great "I am" confession:

> I am the rose of Sharon,
>
> And the lily of the valleys.
>
> Song of Solomon 2:1a

Some interpreters see the lily and rose as Jesus. For this study, however, we will consider this metaphor coming from the maiden herself. The interpretation we are using takes the symbolism of the lily to mean the believer in Jesus, not Jesus Himself. The rose and the lily have the same identity--the believer--throughout the Song. Jesus refers to the believer as the "lily" in Matthew 6:28. The lily is a symbol of purity. The maiden is beginning to see herself as pure in Him, a lily in the dark valleys of life.

This response to the Beloved, "I am the rose...and the lily," redefines her whole life, as it will redefine yours. I am not just dark and lovely. I am the rose and the lily. I am the bride of Christ. Just as it is foundational in the relationship of the maiden with her Beloved, comprehension and understanding of who Christ says I am in His word securely establishes my true identity.

**The Truth that Overcomes the Lie**

God is in earnest pursuit of our souls. Deep down, everyone desires to be pursued by their lover. I am the one God is looking for! I am a lover of God and am loved by God, my Creator. That realization is amazing! When I believe this truth in my heart, my self-worth overwhelms me, and I am able to better follow what

He wishes for our relationship. I am a voluntary lover; and as I confess it with my mouth, I feel valued by God.

Just pause a minute, and say it a few times:

> I am the rose of Sharon,
>
> And the lily of the valleys.
>
> Song of Solomon 2:1

This confession awakens a powerful truth in me and helps me overcome the lies of the enemy--lies of fear, shame, and rejection. God loves and accepts me; I am not condemned or cast aside. God's acceptance is more powerful than any condemnation or rejection I may have experienced from others who wish to bring me down and raise themselves higher.

> "...in God I have put my trust;
>
> I will not be afraid.
>
> What can man do to me?"
>
> Psalm 56:11

In the next verse, the Beloved agrees with the maiden's

confession when He says,

> Like a lily among thorns, so is my love among the daughters.
>
> Song of Solomon 2:2

He is telling her she is separated, set apart, from the ones (other daughters) who still have other beloveds, those whose eyes are not yet singly focused on Him. She is the one in His chambers spending time with Him alone. We can set ourselves apart as being genuine, whole-hearted God-seekers. Many believe, but not all seek with the same earnest devotion.

The King desires that all of us come to His chambers, a place of intimacy and rest; but it is ultimately an individual choice we must make. The bride makes the choice to surrender and enters into this place of intimacy. Jesus the Bridegroom reaffirms her confession by singling her out and praising her efforts in the midst of a life among thorns.[3] Not only is she setting herself apart from the world, but He also sets her apart as His love, a pure lily, a lover of God. Jesus desires a committed bride. Let's be His rose of Sharon, beautiful and fragrant despite our weaknesses and sharp thorns. His declaration of adoration over us is our true identity--who we were created to be--wholly His.

**Confess With Your Mouth**

What does it mean to *confess*? Confession means acknowledgement--avowal, admission--to own, to admit as true--especially to a priest. Jesus is the high priest of our confession.[4] We can confess sin, but we also confess salvation. We are saved when our mouths speak what we believe in our hearts. Romans 10:9 says, "With the mouth we confess, and with the heart we believe unto salvation." Here, the Scripture is referring to confession of salvation, not of sin. We can also confess--or admit as true--what He says about us, our identity.

Let's make a confession of what we are learning:

*I am the one the King seeks;*

*I am His fair one.*

*I am the lily--pure in His eyes;*

*I eat at the King's table. His Words feed me.*

*Jesus loves me! Jesus, the King, loves **me**!*

*Jesus loves me. This I know... I am His fair one, indeed!*

My soul sings; and as I believe these words, my mouth overflows with praise.

Did you make the confession out loud? When you confess and speak out loud several things happen:

1. You hear yourself.
2. You remember better.
3. Your words create what you say. (Remember that your words have real power.)

## A Responsive Lover

The maiden is enjoying being in His presence. As the love dialogue continues, she responds with praise for the Beloved:

> Like an apple tree among the trees of the woods,
>
> So is my Beloved among the sons.
>
> I sat down in his shade with great delight,
>
> And his fruit was sweet to my taste.
>
> Song of Solomon 2:3

Worship proceeds from within her as her King says that she, indeed, is the fairest of all! The overflow begins, and thankfulness and praise flow from her mouth. She is a lily, and He is the apple tree. He awakens her beneath this apple tree. Can't you imagine a big apple tree filled with fruit and the little bride's amazement as she sits beneath its relaxing shade and eats the juicy food. Selah. In Chapter 8 He will remind her of this time under His shade tree when she sat, rested, and ate His fruit. She will remember this comparison with great delight. O, Yum! She is making memories. Her history with the King is being written. Don't you just love it when He reminds you of precious times you have spent together? Pause now and try to remember a sweet time you spent with the Lord.

> I have considered the days of old,
>
> The years of ancient times.
>
> I call to remembrance my song in the night;
>
> I meditate within my heart,
>
> And my spirit makes diligent search.
>
> Psalm 77:5-6

**Sitting Down and Finding Rest**

This refreshing encounter reveals that He is a tree full of fruit to be enjoyed, with shade and a time to rest. Sitting down underneath His shade is the beginning place. Mary sat at the feet of Jesus to glean from His fruit. He told Martha, who was distracted and troubled about many things, that Mary had chosen the "one thing." Our undivided attention, or devotion, is the "one thing" Jesus desires from us. Jesus has seated us beside Him in heavenly places (Ephesians 2:6). This "knowing" brings great spiritual pleasure. Ruth was instructed to "sit still" until she knew how the matter would turn out (Ruth 3:18). Let's sit down at His feet and eat His fruit in the shade and find rest. *Sit* and *rest* are action verbs. They represent something we actively do; and it takes effort and discipline, sometimes even greater effort than to *go* and *do*.

Here the maiden receives answers to the questions she posed in the last chapter. Remember that she had asked Him, "Where do you feed and rest?" He is bringing her to a new place. She experiences pleasure sitting under the shade of the refreshing apple tree.

> Come unto me, all you who are weary and heavy laden and I will give you rest. Take my yoke upon you and learn of me, for I am meek and lowly in heart, and you shall find rest in your soul. My yoke is easy and my burden is light.
>
> Matthew 11:25

Sitting down, delighting in Him, and eating His fruit bring a fresh revelation.

**Fresh Revelation**

The rest and joy give way to a fresh revelation and celebration:

> He brought me to the banqueting house,
>
> And his banner over me was love.
>
> Song of Solomon 2:4

The King brings her to His banqueting house. Some versions say *banqueting table*, or *the house of wine*. Wine is a symbol of the Holy Spirit.[5] This celebration is a time of filling her with His Spirit, pouring the love of God into her heart. It is truly a celebration of abundant joy. The banner displayed over her is love. One of the names of God we declared is Jehovah Nissi, which means "Jehovah My Banner." At the banqueting house, she receives the declaration of His love. A banner is hung publicly. It is a demonstration bearing a slogan or theme for all to see. At the banqueting house, a banner also displays the victorious outcome of a battle. When I believe His banner over me is love, it conquers a multitude of things: tribulation, distress, fear, peril. "Yet in all these things we are more than conquerors through Him who loved us (Romans 8:37). I am waving this banner. "Love is the flag flown high from the castle of my heart when the King is in residence there!"[6]

**Lovesick--The Cry for More**

This visitation of the Holy Spirit awakens a deeper desire. She has learned to ask, "I want more of you my Beloved," so she prays and cries out in the next verse:

> Sustain me with cakes of raisins,
>
> Refresh me with apples.
>
> For I am lovesick.
>
> Song of Solomon 2:5

She has tasted and seen that Lord is good (Psalm 34:8), and she wants more! She knows she cannot sustain herself, but she has the confidence to humbly ask for more of the

refreshing, nourishing fruit of the apple tree. "Sustain me with cakes of raisins, refresh me with apples," she requests. She has no inhibition and acknowledges her desperate state. With a humble and contrite heart she declares, "I am lovesick!" When we taste something so delightful, don't we always want more than just a small bite? Faith always reaches and yearns for more--even in the midst of the blessing. The Lord delights in such abandon from the one who is lovesick for Him.

> These are the ones I look on with favor:
>
> those who are humble and contrite in spirit,
>
> and who tremble at my word.
>
> Isaiah 66:2 (NIV)

She experiences the thrill of loving and being loved. The King responds to her request and draws her near, into His embrace, protected by love. I imagine her trembling at His touch, not out of fear, but in excitement and contentment.

## A "Selah" Moment

> His left hand is under my head,
>
> And his right hand embraces me.
>
> Song of Solomon 2:6

Are you seeing how this works? She asks and receives. She seeks and she finds. She knocks and the door is opened. Don't forget to make your request known out loud. Use His words in the Song, but don't be afraid to use your own words, too. Let Him hear your voice, cry out with a lovesick heart. He is no respecter of persons. What He has done for one, He will do for all. He doesn't withhold his love from anyone who asks for it.

> It is no secret what God can do
>
> What He's done for others,
>
> He'll do for you
>
> With arms wide open,
>
> He'll pardon you;
>
> It is no secret what God can do.[7]

When we ask, He will respond. (We will see this posture again in Chapter 8 and learn more about the two-armed embrace; but for now—just envision yourself in this embrace.) Allow yourself to imagine His right arm wrapped around you with His left hand under your head. This is not awkward--it is divine. This is not a one-time, side-armed hug. It is a full-fledged embrace in which they meld together. He holds my head, my understanding, in His hand and gentle touch. The head represents the intellect or understanding. I just love this image. I don't have to understand everything to rest in His embrace! My ability to understand is in His keeping. I may not be able to comprehend everything, but I can trust my understanding into His capable hands. This *trust* is *faith*! I can just enjoy the pleasure of His company and "give up" my analytical tendency to try to figure things out. In this embrace, I learn to trust in the Lord with all my heart and not lean on my own understanding.[8] Can you feel His left hand under your head keeping your eyes focused on His? Can you feel His right hand drawing you close in His embrace? Oh! "I just faint dead away," Madame Guyon[9] said. I agree! Selah!

**Do Not Disturb!**

Now, the Beloved leaves orders for the daughters of Jerusalem as He hangs out the "Do Not Disturb" sign:

> I charge you, daughters of Jerusalem,
>
> by the gazelles or by the does of the field.
>
> Do not stir up nor awaken love.
>
> Song of Solomon 2:7

He is guarding her during this season. Her Bridegroom Jesus sees the necessity of her experiencing this season of personal rest and satisfaction before she enters the next season. She has found rest in His presence, in His arms. Now that's protection! She rejoices in her growing intimacy with the King and embraces her newfound identity as she rests in His arms. How beautiful! Enjoy this season, fair one. Selah!

I want to end this chapter with a personal challenge to you, dear reader. Let these lessons the little Shulamite is discovering become a reality in your life as well. Incorporate the principles we are learning, and put them into practice. Don't just read this as someone else's story--let it become your story, too. Her journey can be your reality. Take the time to apply these truths and live out your own love story with the King of Kings. He desires your own personal history to be written on His heart. You will be forever changed! That's a promise!

# 8

## The Seasons Change

*To everything, there is a season…*

(Ecclesiastes 3:1.)

**The Awakening Call**

Seasons change. Daniel 2:21 reminds us God changes them, and the seasons in our spiritual lives change, too--winter, springtime, summer, and times of harvest. In this secret place of the King's chambers, the little Shulamite has found food (provision) and rest. There is no reference to how much time elapses in this season of rest. Perhaps it is different for each individual, depending upon the depth of healing and nurturing needed. But the journey is progressing for the maiden. She has found love and acceptance as the fairest. She has savored the taste of His succulent gifts. She longs for more from her Beloved and has asked for more, a welcomed request. As we shall see, a deeper relationship beyond His provision is going to require heeding a different call. It has been said that the only thing constant is change itself. The identity she has found in Him, however, will never change.

As the season of rest nears an end, she hears the Beloved and sees Him coming!

# Sarah Ramsey – The Bridegroom's Song

> The voice of my beloved!
> 
> Behold, he comes
> 
> Leaping upon the mountains,
> 
> Skipping upon the hills.
> 
> My beloved is like a gazelle or a young stag.
> 
> Behold, he stands behind our wall;
> 
> He is looking through the windows,
> 
> Gazing through the lattice.
> 
> Song of Solomon 2:8-9

She hears and recognizes the voice of the Beloved. There is a familiarity now which is unmistakable. Jesus said, "I am the Good Shepherd; I know My sheep and am known by My own....my sheep know my voice and they follow me."[1] Not only does she hear the voice of the Beloved, but she also sees Him in action. In the passage above, there are seven expressions of His actions: He

- Comes
- Leaps
- Skips
- Looks
- Stands

- Gazes
- Speaks

Earlier, she had been sitting and lying in His embrace; He was holding her. But the scene is changing. Here He is standing and ready for action--gazing at His bride. The Beloved has come to call her into the next season, to come away with Him. However, the bride is behind a wall that separates them. He is peering through the windows, watching her through the lattice, and bidding her to come. This invitation requires her willingness to move beyond her walls of comfort so that she may enter into a new season, a time of transition, a time of discomfort, even a new level of faith—something she has never before experienced. She has been (as we are) called to abide in the King's chamber and under the shade of His apple tree, but the Beloved is also calling her to a new place. The new-found provision and rest she has discovered in her identity with Him are permanent. This is a sweet time with her King, a time of building trust and enjoying communion. However, she will soon find there is much beyond this prosperous "honeymoon" season in the King's chambers. The Beloved has come to conquer, and He desires that she join Him in this quest.

She sees the ease of His movement over the mountains--quickly moving over the obstacles and difficulties in life. This view should give her confidence in His ability to carry her over the mountainous trek. Mountains and hills are symbolic of the challenges we face in life--the enemies, obstacles, and demonic opposition (dominions). Jesus taught us to speak to the mountains:

> So Jesus answered and said to them "Have faith in God. For assuredly, I say to you, whoever says to this mountain, 'Be removed and cast into the sea,' and does not doubt in his heart but believes that those things he says will be done, he will have whatever he says."

Mark 11:22-23

Jesus says we are equipped for mountain moving, not just mountain climbing. He leaps over the mountains and hills like a gazelle or young stag who fearlessly conquers all opposition. What a happy thought! Previously He had invited her to rest, but now He is calling her into action with Him.

**Rise Up, My Love**

She sees the Beloved and hears His voice calling to her, asking her to respond:

> My beloved spoke, and said to me:
>
> 'Rise up, my love, my fair one,
>
> And come away.
>
> For lo, the winter is past,

## Sarah Ramsey – The Bridegroom's Song

The rain is over *and* gone.

The flowers appear on the earth;

The time of singing has come,

And the voice of the turtledove

Is heard in our land.

The fig tree puts forth her green figs,

And the vines *with* the tender grapes

Give a *good* smell.

Rise up, my love, my fair one,

And come away!

Oh my dove, in the clefts of the rock,

In the secret *places* of the cliff,

Let me see your face,

Let me hear your voice;

For your voice *is* sweet,

And your face *is* lovely.'

Song of Solomon 2:10-14


What a majestic appeal, "Rise up, my fair one and come away"! Can you imagine turning down that call? The Beloved prophetically commands and encourages her to rise up and see what is happening around her. He beckons her to remember how successful the past season has been: "Winter is past; the rain is over and gone; flowers appear; the time of singing has come." Fruit is appearing on the fig trees, and the vines are in bloom promising a harvest. It is springtime! Then He calls her a second time (in verse 13), "Rise up, my love, my fair one and come away." He gently coaxes: Come on--come with Me, beautiful one that I love. You can do this. He gives her reasons to have faith, not fear, and to obey as He calls again.

He desires her companionship and longs for her to join Him. He calls her "My fair one" or "My beautiful one", at each stage in her spiritual growth, even while she is not yet mature in the process. In the same way, Jesus never condemns or accuses. He beckons us to come into His presence. If we can see that the enemy is the accuser[2], we have gained some understanding. Then when we are accused or begin to accuse others, we can remember the source of the accusation.

**The Call to Come Out of the Comfort Zone**

The time has come for the maiden to take action--to rise and come away. The Bridegroom arrives, displaying His great power and authority by leaping upon the mountains and skipping effortlessly over the hills like a gazelle or young stag. He placed her in a place of rest, but now He asks her to respond to a different call. (This realization is important.) He is omniscient—He knows she is about to exhibit her shortcomings at this stage in her immaturity, but He continues to call her "My fair one" all the same. He even says the declaration twice!

He challenges her comfort zone. He is calling her to scale the mountains alongside Him--to go mountain climbing, so to speak. This journey is sure to be a n exciting and fulfilling adventure! He wants her with Him in the heavenly kingdoms. But, for whatever reason, she wants to remain behind, where her surroundings are familiar. She is enjoying the thrill of the celebration in the new wine of the Holy Spirit. The mountains may seem unsurpassable or too rocky, with uncertainty about what lies on the other side. From a natural perspective, fears loom large. Whatever her hindrance, He still encourages her to remain in intimacy and approach the obstacles and places of opposition with Him. She continues to call Him "my Beloved" throughout the Song, even though she is about send Him away.

This request is a call to warfare, and she does not want to fight. She likes the place of rest and security inside the walls, eating raisin cakes and apples, the green bed of vibrant rest, and the house of cedar that will not decay (1:16-17). He is asking her to be both a lover and a warrior alongside Him, warring to overcome the darkness. The darkness cannot comprehend the light! This move takes faith. It is risky to leave this comfort zone and go to the mountains—a truly frightening place. The young bride did not yet want to be a warrior! But faith is part of the mystery of kingdom life, as she will soon learn.

The first appeal uses reason to beckon her to Him. The second appeal reveals the King's heart of love. We can also see His appeal to us when we look closely.

- He defines where she will be--in safety and protection. It is a secret place in the cleft rock. Surely, she will be surrounded by the strong walls of the mountains.

- He sees her in the cleft Rock. Jesus is the Rock, and He created a fortress "in the secret places of the cliff," a place for us in Him, when He died on the cross. This haven of safety is His completed work. He wants to see *your* face and hear *your* voice in the cleft of the Rock. To Him, "*your* voice is sweet and *your* face is lovely!"

- He tells her why he wants her to go. He wants to see her lovely face and hear her sweet voice while he wages war for her. He simply desires her company. Again, I swoon at the thought of His abundant love!

The Beloved is going upward and onward, and he appeals to the maiden to step out in faith and go with Him--out of "comfort zone Christianity." He passionately woos her with bridal love and promises faithfulness even though He knows she will deny Him. He says, "The voice of the turtledove is singing...." He sees her with dove's eyes. Remember the characteristics of the dove, unique in loyalty and devotion. His invitation of love says, "Rise up, My love, My fair one and come away."[3] He persistently asks her, but He does eventually go on without her when she does not respond. What an appeal the Beloved makes! How could I ever refuse You, my Beloved? Yet in our Christian walk, haven't we all been afraid and refused to follow at some time, many times, perhaps?

**The Lure of the Comfort Zone**

The comfort zone feels good. We all like to stay comfortable. But genuine Christianity is not a place of perpetual comfort. Just ask Jesus. We are called to follow Him, and He went to some very uncomfortable places. He warned us, "In the world you will have tribulation, but be of good cheer, I have overcome the world" (John 16:33). He leads us out of the comfort zone in order that we may be overcomers with Him.

The Shulamite maiden likes the comfort zone. She has a plan of her own. She wants everything laid out on the table before she obeys. Notice the stipulation she offers in place of direct obedience:

> Catch us the foxes,
>
> The little foxes that spoil the vines,
>
> For our vines have tender grapes.
>
> Song of Solomon 2:15

Instead of abandoning herself and surrendering and trusting, she is still looking at the obstacles that hinder "the little foxes." Maybe these are prayers not yet answered, expectations not yet met. Maybe she still sees areas in herself that are not yet perfected. Somehow, she finds excuses, as we all so easily do. She has her own agenda, timetable, and expectation of the way things are supposed to look. She wants to wait until the little foxes are caught before obeying His call to come away. She is afraid something is going to spoil the success of His plan, for the "tender grapes" are yet not ready in her eyes. The harvest is not complete. The truth is that He is ready for me *just as I am*. He wants to see my face and hear my voice. How many times have we wanted to clean ourselves up before we go away with Jesus? He wants to clean me up as I go! Of course, He is aware of my immaturity and imperfections, but I don't have to "have it all together." He just wants me to come and rest in his arms!

**My Story**

I remember several times early in my married life that I did not go with God. I really didn't know at the time that I just wanted my own way. I did not know the Holy Spirit well. It was a surprise from God that helped me find the way. Me, my husband Paul and our two little girls had been in Cookeville two years when we built our first house there. We moved in when Jenny Lynne was beginning first grade and Susannah was two years old. We had a three-bedroom house--a bedroom for each of our little girls, and my plans did not involve getting pregnant again.

(Some sweet readers are laughing already.) But in the summer of 1970, I got pregnant. That wasn't my plan for the future! I got mad at both my husband and at God! But I kept on doing all the right things I was supposed to--I went to church and went visiting on Thursday to invite others to come to church. I worked with the children on Wednesday night, read my Bible and prayed every day, even though the Bible was just "black ink on white paper" to me. I loved the Lord, and I wasn't going to turn away from Him; but I did not like this place, and I lay on the couch with my bulging stomach and pouted! But as I see it now, God's plan was so wonderful! As I recounted in my first book, it was through the birth of our third child, Paul, that God truly revealed the Holy Spirit to me. Now that baby is my pastor at Church on the Hill in Algood, Tennessee. He has a wonderful wife, and they are the parents of four of my eight grandchildren! *O, God! I love your plan! Lord, lead me and guide me in Your ways!* God didn't leave me or forsake me, but gently led me to find His way, the one he knew would be the best for me. *God, help me find the way! Always draw me back to you! Thank you Jesus for leading and guiding me!*

**The Words that Reveal the Heart**

The Shulamite maiden wants help with the little foxes and won't turn loose just yet. But, as her words reveal, she is making progress. Her words in the next verses reveal her heart:

> My beloved is mine and I am His.
>
> He feeds His flock among the lilies.
>
> Song of Solomon 2:16

You are mine. I am Yours. And I know where You feed. At this beginning point, it is all about her and about getting her needs met. She states, "My beloved is mine!" The progression of the bride into maturity is a process. This declaration is the first of three possessive statements the bride makes throughout the Song of Solomon that reveal this process. We will revisit these declarations several times farther on because they are of utmost importance.

- "My Beloved is mine and I am His" (2:16): He belongs to her, first. She belongs to Him, second.
- "I am my Beloved's and He is mine" (6:3): His agenda is first; hers is second.
- "I am my Beloved's and His desire is towards me" (7:10): The order changes. Finally, His desire for her makes her want to be His alone; she delights in pleasing Him, which becomes her motivation.

These three statements, placed strategically throughout the Song of Solomon, help us follow her process of maturity. Her first statement says much about where she is spiritually. First she says, "My Beloved is mine." She places the Beloved *after* herself. This order will change as she matures.

Just like newborn babies, we Christ-followers all begin at the same place, desiring our needs to be met. That's okay. We grow through nurturing and finding safety in His provision. We must *learn* to let Jesus meet our needs. It is a starting point. Our desire is to progress and to mature and not to get stuck as the journey progresses. Do you see yourself as the bride making the journey?

**Confession and prayer:**

*Thank You, Beloved, for calling me away from my comfort*

*to deeper places with You.*

*You call me Your fair one, even in my imperfections and immaturity.*

*I am safe with you, even when my heart is not completely surrendered to You.*

*You leap effortlessly over the mountains and hills in my life.*

*No obstacle is too great for You.*

*You hide me in the clefts of the Rock.*

## Sarah Ramsey – The Bridegroom's Song

*Jesus is my hiding place.*

*My voice is sweet to You.*

*You love to gaze upon my face, just as I am.*

*Give me the courage to rise and face a new season with You.*

*Your provision is great, and in You I find safety.*

*The little foxes are no match for You.*

*Give me confidence to rise when I hear Your tender voice,*

*Calling me away with You.*

*Amen.*

## 9

## The Painful Compromise

*A double-minded man, unstable in all his ways*

(James 1:8)

### The Refusal

The bride has just made the beautiful proclamation that the Beloved is hers and she belongs to Him. However, immediately thereafter, she makes the terrible decision to refuse His call and invitation to go away with Him. She sends Him on His way alone and stays behind, nestled in the past season of comfort and ease.

> Until the day breaks
>
> And the shadows flee away,
>
> Turn, my beloved,
>
> And be like a gazelle
>
> Or a young stag
>
> Upon the mountains of Bether.
>
> Song of Solomon 2:17

We have seen her overcome fear and rejection. Now she is challenged with compromise (or double-mindedness), and she gives in. She refuses to go even though she knows He feeds His flock among the lilies outside the wall. The lilies represent other believers desiring purity. We run together with Him and beyond the walls with others seeking the Lord in a deeper way. This relationship of reckless abandon is essential in the maturity process. He places the lilies strategically in our lives. He wants us to run together, to rejoice and be glad. But the voice of compromise lures her to procrastinate--to wait until things get "fixed." He already knows all the dark shadows of her heart, but she prefers instead to wait until the night season has ended. She is content to wait until things get better in her own heart. In this hesitation she announces her decision, "Turn, my Beloved!" Is she commanding Him onward? She not only refuses to go, but she also tells Him to go to the mountains of Bether without her. The word *bether* means "separation."[1] She knows exactly what she is saying: "Go on without me! Hurry and go and come back later, after I get my life in order."

Learn from her painful mistake, dear one. Accept that Jesus loves you and wants you just as you are. Don't hesitate when He calls. He knows how to deal with the shadows in your heart. Can you hear the Beloved calling you out of your comfort zone? What will your response be? You don't have to wait for your spouse, children, or friends to respond. In fact, you must put the Beloved in first place. The decision is yours to make.

**Separation**

The maiden seems to hesitate with the statement, "Turn, my Beloved!" Yet she still allows him to leave without her. We must keep the gates closed on the enemies of compromise and double-mindedness. Compromise begins with small choices. Often, it is repetitive "minor" violations of His will which, in effect, lead to strongholds and habitual struggles with sin. The path of separation is walked in tandem with compromise over multiple small steps far more often than it occurs in one, sudden, giant leap off a cliff. Double-mindedness is often the herald of compromise and helps rationalize ungodly actions. James 1:6-8 makes clear that the double-minded man is unstable in all his ways. The maiden thinks she can disobey His voice and still have it all.

She sends Him away, as the Song says, "Until the day breaks and the shadows flee." He beckons her to come immediately, in the night. There is still darkness, and she prefers to stay behind in it. She is enjoying the provision, or "presents" from her Beloved, more than she desires being in His "presence." She has failed to remember what it was like without His presence. She has forgotten that even the "presents" are empty without Him. Both the darkness of sin and the failure to obey in His callings can hinder our intimacy with Christ.

**The Greatest Test of All**

The season of prosperity is often the greatest test of all. One of the challenges when experiencing great blessing is to avoid becoming passive and negligent in responding to God's voice. When living in the midst of blessing and outpouring, it is easy to become distracted by the provision instead of keeping our eyes on the Provider. Heeding the Beloved's voice to arise and come away can be carelessly pushed aside.

Jesus warns us in the parable of the sower in Mark 4:

> "Now these are the ones sown among thorns; they are the ones who hear the word, and the cares of this world, the deceitfulness of riches, and the desires for other things entering in choke the word, and it becomes unfruitful."
>
> Mark 4:18-19

Decisions have consequences, but the pattern in the Scripture of the Song reveals hope despite our failures. The Lord has promised never to leave us or forsake us[2], and He will not. Still we must accept the discipline brought about by our wrong choices, such as the young maiden's decision to push away her Beloved.

Scripture teaches, sadly, that we can miss the day of His visitation. Jesus wept over Jerusalem in Luke 19:41-44 because He knew they were missing their day of visitation. He said, "If you had known, even you, especially in this your day the things that make for your peace! But now they are hidden from your eyes...because you did not know the time of your visitation." Upon His triumphal entry into the city, Jesus knew He was getting ready to face rejection and ridicule. He came to bear witness to the truth as a light to the world but ultimately faced one of the cruelest punishments by Roman crucifixion. In the same way, let Jesus find no reason to say about us, "If only you had known….". We do have knowledge of the abundant life Jesus has in store; let us not be afraid, then, to embrace His invitation and go deeper still in a dark season or even in the midst of a season of prosperity.

**The Night Season**

As the Beloved goes on without the maiden, the painful reality of her failure to obey sets in; and she realizes His absence. Nighttime comes again, and she is in bed alone. A new chapter begins:

> By night on my bed I sought the one I love;
>
> I sought him, but I did not find him.
>
> Song of Solomon 3:1

The season has changed, and the absence of her Bridegroom's presence causes her to re-evaluate the situation. Realize this: It is not *whether* night will come, but *when* night will come. Night always follows the day! In this night season she sits in their house and eats her raisin cakes alone, trying to enjoy the provision without Him. She continues to compromise and attempts to seek from her bed, to no avail. "By night on my bed I sought the one I love; I sought him, but I did not find him." Notice that it is no longer "our" bed, but "my" bed from which she seeks.

The maiden's refusal of her Bridegroom's invitation begins to affect her ability to feel His presence (manifest presence). Refusal to "come away" or obey His call quenches God's Spirit. The Spirit of God is *omnipresent*. An attribute of God's character, *omnipresence* means He is present everywhere, throughout both time and space. We cannot flee from the presence of God or make Him disappear, according to Psalm 139:

> Where can I go from your Spirit?
>
> Where can I flee from your presence?
>
> If I go up to the heavens,
>
> you are there;
>
> if I make my bed in the depths, you are there.

> If I rise on the wings of the dawn,
>
> if I settle on the far side of the sea,
>
> even there your hand will guide me,
>
> your right hand will hold me fast.
>
> Psalm 139:7-10, NIV

The maiden is experiencing a loss of the tangible expression of their fellowship together, and He seems distant from her. When I refuse to obey or do not respond to the nudging of the Spirit of God, His voice becomes quieter and harder to recognize. This break in communication gives me the feeling that He has departed, and I must learn to lean on the Word. The maiden, though, finds that all the comforts and provision are empty without the Beloved; so she becomes willing to seek again.

**The Seeking Bride**

The bride is a seeker. Sometimes it takes awhile to realize we have taken the wrong turn or made a bad choice. We make mistakes! Free yourself from the false ideology that you have to be perfect. For some time she stayed behind the wall enjoying the provision and became isolated. How many times are we tempted to do the same? Isolation is one of the enemy's favorite strategies, and he deceives us into it. When we become isolated, we are vulnerable to attack. We do not know how long this dark and empty season lasted in the life of the maiden, but it marked a significant turning point. Thankfully, the bride is a persistent seeker even after she makes bad decisions. That, in fact, is the most important time to seek! She teaches us a very valuable lesson. She does not quit when she can't find Him right away. She sets her will in motion and announces it is time to get up, fully submit and obey, and *go seek*.

> "I will arise now," I said,
>
> "And go about the city;
>
> In the streets and in the squares
>
> I will seek the one I love."
>
> Song of Solomon 3:2

Word study: Seek--baqush (Strong's #1245)--To seek, to diligently look for, to search earnestly until the object of the search is located. We are instructed to seek the Lord with all of our hearts. *Baqush* occurs more than 210 times in the Bible.[3] The Lord's face (presence) must especially be sought, as stated in Psalm 27:8.

> When you said, "Seek My face,"
>
> My heart said to You,

"Your face, Lord, I will seek."

**I Will**

I will arise and seek now! What a great decision. Setting my will, getting my soul in line, is a decision to obey. The maiden gets aggressive and decides to obey without a second of hesitation. Instead of giving in to another compromising attitude, the bride sets her heart, face, and will not to be complacent. She becomes more desperate to find her lover. From the words of a classic American folk hymn, "I will arise and go to Jesus, He will embrace me in His arms; In the arms of my dear Savior, O There are ten thousand charms!"[4]

There is a great lesson here when she seeks but does not immediately find: Rise, don't give up. The bride is teaching us to seek with diligence. Notice that "sought" is repeated twice in verse one and again the third time in the second verse:

> I sought him, but I did not find him.
>
> Song of Solomon 3:2b

The fact that this passage emphasizes "sought" three times tells me I need to pay attention and hear truth. Yet she *still* does not find him. For the second time she has sought without finding him--the first being the search from the comfort of her bed.

The point is that I need to do it His way and not stay in bed. The call is to arise now and go! "I **will** go about the city, in the streets and in the squares!" (emphasis added). She is bringing her mind, will, and emotions in line with the Spirit of God. Look how determined she is with the use of "I wills!" She did not let failure stop her. She is persistent in her pursuit and is looking everywhere, leaving no stone unturned.

Sometimes thoughts of regret flood my mind: "Why didn't I obey? Where did I go wrong? Why didn't I do this? Why did I do that?" But I can't get lost in these thoughts. I must pursue like the bride and keep seeking. I will not give up! Jesus said, "Seek and you shall find (Luke 11:9). I must believe I will find Him again, which will take faith.

The discipline of seeking nurtures a persevering heart, one that is not easily distracted or dismayed. We may want to give up in the nighttime. Romans 5:3 tells us we also glory in tribulation, knowing that tribulation produces perseverance. Understanding God's affection for me when I am weak draws me to Him. This acceptance helps me run to Him and not away from Him when difficulty comes. He is drawing me into a deeper pursuit of Himself, but I must make the decision to seek.

**Night Time Does Not Last Forever**

Seeking without finding is challenging. Everyone experiences night seasons--it is part of the journey. You are not alone in this struggle. Learning how to come through the darkness is so valuable and is a sign of maturity. Remember, the night does not last forever. Psalm 30:5 reminds us, "Weeping may endure for a night, but joy comes in the morning." If we get up and do not give up, we will find what we seek--God promises it. Notice what happens next. When she obeys, the watchmen (spiritual authorities) find her:

> The watchmen who go about the city found me,
>
> I said, "Have you seen the one I love?"
>
> Song of Solomon 3:3

After her decision to arise and obey the Beloved, she asks for help. It is an act of obedience to get back under spiritual authority. Remember how He had told her to stay with the flock under the shepherds' tents? Doing what we know to do, or what has been previously instructed, is the right thing in the dark seasons. We may not know specifics yet, but we can read the Word, pray, and refuse the temptation to isolate from the body of Christ. Then seek and keep on seeking--you shall find. The specifics will unfold at the right time.

## Learning Obedience

The hope is that the absence of His manifest presence will cause us to seek. The difficulty sensing His presence reminds us of our great need for the Lord, especially in the problems we face (i.e., the night seasons). Diminished communion gives us an even greater desire for his presence and hunger for His righteousness. I am a lover and will arise and seek the One I love even though I still perceive areas of immaturity in myself. The voices from the enemy try to hinder me from seeking and will point out my flaws, but I must not listen. This juncture is critical: Will I run to Jesus or away from Him when He is not easily found?

Mike Bickle says, "Divine correction is not rejection."[5] The correction is drawing her back to Him. Discipline is painful, but it has a reward. Hebrews Chapter 12 tells us we are disciplined for our profit, "...that we may be partakers of His holiness" (v. 10). Jesus learned obedience through the things He suffered, even though He was already completely righteous. On earth, Christ learned obedience. From heaven, He *teaches* obedience to His disciples that we may become more righteous on earth. This experience in the night season is one of those times when the sachet of myrrh between the bride's breasts gives off its sweet fragrance. The fragrance is released by the heat of the battle. Obedience is often learned most effectively through the act of suffering.

Although the bride failed to obey and come away with her Beloved at first, she continues to call Him, "the one I love." Recall, she prayed in Chapter 1, "Draw me after you and we will run…." In Chapter 2 He answered and invited her into bridal partnership to run on the mountains, but she refused. She told Him to turn and go without her. Even in her weakness, her love for Jesus is still true. Even if our love for Him is imperfect, His love for us is not. He will continue to perfect us through His love, and we do not have to sink in the shame of our frailties and failures. He pursues us continually, nonetheless.

> It is God who arms me with strength, and makes my way perfect.
>
> He makes my feet like the feet of deer, and sets me on my high places.
>
> Psalm 18:32-33

We know Jesus, our Beloved, is like a deer and a gazelle, but this Psalm tells us that He wants to equip us with the same qualities. The little Shulamite maiden, a picture of the bride of Christ, shows us it is not too late to obey, even after we have messed up. She teaches us not to give up, even when we do not succeed at first. We must persist in our pursuit of the Bridegroom King. He has not given up His pursuit of us. Imagine His outstretched arms on the cross beckoning us near, even in the setting of our brokenness and failure. Make the decision to run to Him. He is not far away. Do you see the maiden's "I wills" in 3:2? Follow the valuable lessons they teach: Persistence, perseverance, and diligence.

In summary:

1. Never quit!
2. Arise!
3. Go seek!

**My Story**

I remember learning about the revival in Brownsville in 1995. A lady in the choir at First Baptist Church in Cookeville gave me a book her son had given her, *Feast of Fire*, by John Kilpatrick. He was the pastor at the Brownsville Assembly of God. I decided to go to Brownsville by myself in order to see what God was doing. It was during one of those seeking times which resulted in a life-changing moment for me. I had received the baptism of the Holy Spirit in 1972, and it was time for a fresh wind to blow. I am a God- seeker, and I was moved by John Kilpatrick's testimony. I stood in line all day with others in the hot August sun in Pensacola to get a seat in the sanctuary. People from all over the world had come to run to the altar and repent! The music was not the familiar Charismatic choruses, but a new sound given to Lindell Cooley; and we sang enthusiastically, "We will ride with You."[6] God was doing something new again.

*Help us, Lord, not miss the day of Your visitation!*[7]

Fresh fire was deposited in my heart in Pensacola as I sought the Lord. It was then that God began to reveal the groundbreaking paradigm of Jesus as my Bridegroom King, and that fire continues to burn in my heart until this day. This beautiful pattern in the Song of Solomon reinforces God's promise: When I seek Him with my whole heart I shall surely find Him.

Let's pray:

> *Lord, thank You for revealing Your heart to me.*
>
> *Your Word challenges me not to give up, but to seek You with my whole heart.*
>
> *I feel so inadequate. Help me never to quit seeking You.*
>
> *Help me not to miss the day of Your visitation.*
>
> *I want to be ready when You come.*
>
> *Give me the strength and courage to arise and seek when*
>
> *at first I don't find what You have set out for me.*
>
> *Let me have unwavering certainty of Your presence when*

*I encounter difficult times.*

*I will arise and seek the One I love and follow You to the mountains and hills.*

*Selah.*

*Amen.*

# 10

## Finding the One I Love

*I held him and would not let him go...*

(Song of Solomon 3:4).

Sometimes it takes awhile to realize we have veered off the path of our Bridegroom. The bride is learning the value of obedience. Andrew Murray said, "obedience to God is a heavenly art. Our human nature is so utterly unfamiliar with it." [1] The chamber of the Bridegroom makes the perfect classroom to learn obedience; as we learn to trust the Lord, obedience is easier and is a joy. I want to obey; "I delight to do Thy will."[2] The bride is a persistent seeker. She decides to obey, even after she has made wrong choices.

**She searches for Him!**

She had barely left the watchmen when she finds the Beloved:

> Scarcely had I passed them,
>
> When I found the one I love.

> I held him and would not let him go,
>
> Until I had brought him to the house of my mother,
>
> And into the chamber of her who conceived me.
>
> Song of Solomon 3:4

I found Him, the One I love! Her seeking is rewarded in full, and she declares she will "never let Him go." Throughout the rest of the Song, she fulfills this commitment not to let go. She has learned that the consequence of compromise and the fear of the mountains are not worth being separated from Him again. Even though it would have been easier to give up, she doubled down on her search instead. Continual pursuit and seeking in the night seasons are challenges! Remember that Caleb waited forty years to get his mountain after the wilderness wanderings.[3]

**Doing it His Way**

"I held Him and would not let…go, until I…brought Him to the house of my mother." The mother is a picture of the corporate church.[4] The maiden did it His way: She ran to the flock. Being under spiritual authority and the local church had been His first instructions. Many problems arise when we neglect the spiritual order of the kingdom of God. Likewise, we will avoid many pitfalls in the road and wrong turns if we obey even when obedience involves suffering and submitting--rather than running to "another lover" to satisfy the emptiness we are experiencing at the moment.

The bride is eager to share the good news with her family, the church, and wants them to "see" and know the Bridegroom King. She brings Him "into the chamber of her who conceived me" (Song 3:4). Later, in the Song of Solomon 8:2, we will find her bringing all people to Jesus.

**My Story**

As I mentioned in the last chapter, I experienced a fresh encounter with Jesus after going to the revival at Brownsville. I didn't know how to process what had happened, but I had encountered Him in a fresh new way; and I wanted everyone to know this wonderful Jesus.

I arrived in Brownsville on a Wednesday evening and stood in line to get into a building which had over one thousand seats. We had to sit in an overflow room and watch the service on a TV screen. The convicting power of the Holy Spirit was so real. After evangelist Steve Hill preached and gave the altar call, I wanted to run to the altar to seek a closer walk with Jesus. It seemed as if the whole congregation felt the same way; we had to knell in the aisles because the altars were full.

The next morning my eighteen-year-old nephew and I got into line in front of the Brownsville Assembly of God in Pensacola, Florida, at 8 in the morning. There were at least one hundred people already in line. It was the first week in August, and we stood in line all day in the hot Florida sun. There were no bathroom facilities except porta-potties across the way and no food except what vendors provided on the edge of the street. But the line grew longer quickly. People from many nations gathered in Pensacola that day to encounter Jesus. (This image reminds me of Naomi and Ruth setting out to return to Bethlehem to get bread. They certainly encountered more than they could have imagined in the fields of Boaz.) We stood in line until 6 p.m., found seats in the back of the balcony, and saved seats for other members of our family.

I had heard the "new sound" of the worship music before I had gone to Brownsville, but it had not appealed to me then. When Lindell Cooley and the worship team began, however, the air was electric with the presence of the Holy Spirit. We praised and worshiped for an hour and a half and didn't want to stop. Steve Hill preached a rather short, but power-packed, message calling us to go deeper with Jesus; and it seemed again as if the whole congregation responded. We went down for prayer. A prayer team wearing identifying badges, along with the evangelist Steve Hill, John Kilpatrick, and other men and women of God, prayed for us. We received an impartation which powerfully impacted and equipped us to carry the seeds of revival back to our hometowns. Needless to say, it was wonderful! At midnight the lights signaled it was time to go home, and I remember the red fluorescent lights on the Krispy Kreme 'Hot' sign during the trip back to the condo. We stopped to get a hot doughnut (yum!). But, it was still not as nourishing or enjoyable as the Bread of Heaven filling us up on the inside. After a few days we started the trip back to Tennessee. My nephew drove my car, and his younger brother rode with us and listened as I read Lindell Cooley's book aloud. They were All-American boys who had just been touched by God, and we didn't even listen to the radio! Instead, they soaked in what their aunt was reading about Jesus!

The following Sunday morning at First Baptist Church in Cookeville, where my husband and I attended, I sang my heart out in the choir during the early service. First Baptist was not like Brownsville at that time, and I respected that; but it did not stop what was going on inside of me. Meanwhile, our daughter was helping lead worship at First Baptist in Algood (later to become Church on the Hill, where we now attend). She was singing the special music later that same morning, so I headed down the road to their church when our service was over. I visited their church occasionally because of the affiliation of my son (who was the sound man) and daughter (who sang on the worship team). This church was open to the new things the Holy Spirit was doing. As I pulled onto the ramp of Highway 111, I heard the still, small voice inside me say, "I have a message for you to deliver at First Baptist, Algood today." My stomach sank. I did have a word to give occasionally in a service, but this was not my home church; and I hardly knew the pastor. I had the revival music in my CD player, and tears were streaming down my face as I drove down Highway 111 worshiping Jesus. I wanted to obey, but I didn't want to be out of order or violate any boundaries. I feared I was making up this impression in my head. The words formed in my mind, and I knew what I wanted to say. I felt as if the Lord said, "Just go in and sit on the back row." That sounded doable! The worship team sang the songs from the Brownsville revival, and I was a wreck weeping before the Lord. Enjoying the worship but still unsure what He wanted me to do, I thought the Lord said, "Just walk down to the front, and the pastor will direct you."

From past experience, I knew there was a risk of being turned down by leadership when I felt I had a word to share. Remembering it takes faith to please God, I obeyed. Sure enough, Pastor Chris Harrell approached me and said, "Do you have something?"

"Yes."

"What is it?"

I told him briefly what I thought the Lord had impressed on my heart to share:

> I have just returned from Pensacola, Florida, and the revival at Brownsville. People were standing in line in the hot Florida sun from 7 in the morning until 6 in the evening, waiting for the doors to open at Brownsville Assembly of God so that they could get a seat for the evening service. I was in line with people from all over

the world. People were coming from all nations to spend their vacation standing in line all day to attend the revival. Many fell on the altar in repentance after worshipping and hearing a message asking them to seek more of God. It was wonderful.

This morning the Lord reminded me that in recent history (1906) He had chosen a Baptist Church on Azusa Street in Los Angeles to pour out His Spirit. This Baptist Church was not open to a new move of God and rejected the message of Spirit-filled men. The men bringing the message then found a store-front shanty on Azusa Street and sought the Lord. It was in this place on Azusa Street that God poured out his Spirit, and a great revival began. It was raw and messy, but it was the birth of what we now know as the Pentecostal Church--and it was happening at other places in the United States at the same time. This was a fulfillment of what foretold in Joel 2 and Acts 2 where God said He would pour out His Spirit upon all flesh in the last days. (No Pentecostal denomination existed until that time. We take it for granted now because it is what we have known.)

I ended by saying,

This morning [the second or third Sunday of August,1996] God is coming to a Baptist Church here in Algood, Tennessee, to ask you, 'Will you receive the move of My Spirit?'

That was it.

I went home and cooked lunch for our family as I usually did on Sunday. The enemy began to attack my thought and accuse me, telling me how stupid I had been to believe I had heard from God. How could I deliver a message to a church where I wasn't even a member? However, that afternoon two of the leading men of the Algood congregation called me to affirm the message I had delivered. Their calls of encouragement and affirmation were so refreshing.

It is now over twenty years later, and First Baptist Church, Algood, has become Church on the Hill. It is where we now attend, and our son Paul Ramsey, Jr. is the pastor. It is a Spirit-filled Baptist church in good standing in the Southern Baptist Convention and has impacted many lives over the years. Praise the Lord!

When we seek, we will find. It may seem like it's taking a long time, but God is always on time. Hallelujah!

**"Do Not Disturb"--A Place of Rest**

The bride is a seeker, and she found the One she loved. After this time of seeking, the "Do Not Disturb" sign is hanging out again! Our God is good, and His plans for us are good. His plan includes time to rest.

> I charge you, O daughters of Jerusalem…
>
> Do not stir up nor awaken love until it pleases.
>
> Song of Solomon 3:5

The Holy Spirit speaks the phrase "I charge you…." three times in the Song of Solomon (2:7, 3:5, and 8:4). God has a plan: He is in control of the bride. "Do not stir up or awaken love until it pleases." She is right where the Beloved wants her, in a season of rest. Jesus commands rest by saying:

- "Come to Me all you who labor and are heavy laden, and I will give you rest" (Matthew 11:28).
- "Since a promise remains of entering His rest, let us fear lest any of you seem to have come short of it" (Hebrews 4:1).

God's presence is the rest. He told Moses, "My presence will go with you and I will give you rest" (Exodus 33:14, NIV). Sometimes resting and waiting go hand in hand. "Learn from me," Jesus said (Matthew 11:28). We have to learn to rest and wait on the Lord. Don't try to do it on your own or find your own way. Being called to both seeking and resting--what a paradox!

David understood this challenge of seeking and waiting in Psalm 27: seeking "one thing," meaning His face, or presence, and waiting for Him.[5] We don't have to live without the presence of God. The little Shulamite shows us how to address this challenge. Seeking and waiting produce seasons of rest. Selah (Pause, and think about that)! The paradox is a wondrous part of the journey.

Are you relating to this message? Let's pray.

*O Father, thank You for this beautiful pattern of searching and resting.*

*I come to You.*

*I seek Your rest.*

*Help me to run to You and not away from You in crises.*

*Help me to stay with the flock and close to spiritual authority.*

*Draw me close to You.*

*I will wait upon You.*

*Help me find the Way.*

*Amen.*

Sarah Ramsey – The Bridegroom's Song

## 11

### Coming Out of the Wilderness

*Who is coming out of the wilderness?*

Song of Solomon 3:6

**New Season--New Questions--New Revelation**

Times of rest do not last forever. In the journey to a more intimate relationship with our Bridegroom King, the season of rest transitions into a new season; and a new scene unfolds. He will forever be our place of rest, but we will be called to new things. As the old season evolves into the next, we will find King Jesus to be a safe, trustworthy Savior. He continues to reveal to us His ability to care for us, and our confidence in Him begins to grow. This new season begins with another question. Questions are a key throughout the Song of Solomon.

>Who is this coming out of the wilderness?
>
>Like pillars of smoke,
>
>Perfumed with myrrh and frankincense,
>
>With all the merchant's fragrant powders?

> Behold, it is Solomon's couch,
>
> With sixty valiant men around it,
>
> Of the valiant of Israel.
>
> They all hold swords, being expert in war.
>
> Every man has his sword on his thigh
>
> Because of fear in the night.
>
> Song of Solomon 3:6-8

A smokescreen obscures the view of this person and raises the question, "Who is this?" This wording is a rhetorical question. It is much like David's question, "Who is the King of glory?" in Psalm 24. We see in the next verse that the King is coming out, and He is compared to pillars of smoke. It is not smoke but it's very similar. Smoke indicates the presence of holy fire. Mt. Sinai was covered with smoke because the Lord descended on it in fire. It is also the smoke of the incense which contains the prayers of the saints ascending before God, as described in Revelation 8:4. Smoke is a manifestation of God's holy presence and, in this passage, speaks of the glory of God. This passage presents a picture of the King coming out of the wilderness victoriously.

Jesus, our King of glory, is familiar with the wilderness. He knows what we are going through, and He knows how to bring us out victoriously. Mike Bickle says, "This uniquely qualifies Him to bring us to a place of safety because He understands the perilous journey. He too has traveled through the wilderness."[1] We are yoked with the One who conquered the wilderness, and in Him we, too, will be conquerors! The smoke is perfumed with myrrh and frankincense, references we frequently see in the Song. Myrrh, as has been previously mentioned, is a spice used to bury the dead and represents Jesus' suffering and the finished work of the cross. He is surrounded by the fragrance of death, the sweet fragrance of the cross, as He comes out of the wilderness. Frankincense represents intercession and prayer. Jesus intercedes as High Priest for the saints.[2] The wise men brought myrrh and frankincense after the birth of Jesus[3] to prophetically declare His ministry. The women close to Jesus also brought myrrh to anoint Him in burial.[4] In the Tabernacle of Moses, the golden censer was filled with frankincense, myrrh, and coals from the brazen altar.[5] The fire released the sweet fragrance before the mercy seat of God.[6] Myrrh, though it is a spice with a bitter taste, releases a sweet, aromatic fragrance when burned. The smoke surrounding the Bridegroom King is the smoke from the golden altar as Jesus our High Priest appears. Hallelujah! Jesus forever lives to intercede for us![7] We share with Him in the ministries of suffering and intercession, which often coincide; but He has made the way for us to come through the wilderness seasons of life victoriously.

**A Royal Seat**

The wilderness scene changes; and the question, "Who is this?" is answered as His provision is revealed.

> Behold, it is Solomon's couch,
>
> With sixty valiant men around it,
>
> of the valiant of Israel.
>
> They all hold swords, being experts in war.
>
> Every man has his sword on his thigh because of fear in the night.
>
> Song of Solomon 3:7-8

The KJV calls this chariot a *couch*. It is the "bridal car," the Amplified Bible says. According to the Oxford Jewish Bible, it is a *palanquin*, a mobile throne on a litter, upon the shoulders of men. Another description is a portable chair, enclosed with curtains on poles and carried by royal attendants. The marriage palanquin is symbolic of Jesus' work on the cross to provide for His bride. The King died to give His bride her life seated next to Him. He paid for it with His blood and then presented her on it. What a beautiful picture! *Thank you, Lord Jesus, my Beloved.*

This royal chariot was used for a queen-to-be on her wedding day. A royal palanquin was very luxurious and comfortable and long enough to recline inside and could be of varied size and splendor depending upon the wealth of the king. The Beloved King provided this comfort for His bride on her long journey through the wilderness. She can find safety and rest in her seat beside Him. His bed, the bed she was previously afraid to leave, has moved to the throne. Isn't that just like Jesus, asking us to leave the place of rest so that He can take us to an even better place? He sometimes asks us to turn loose of comfortable things so that He can give us something of higher value. My fear is valid in the night hours—it is the wilderness, and the sword of the Word of God is needed to ward off fear. On our journey through life, scary places often envelope us; but Jesus tells us, "Do not be afraid." Fear is a real enemy, but He has given us a safe place to dwell in the secret place beside Him. Jesus said, "Peace I leave with you, My peace I give to you. Let not your heart be troubled, neither let it be afraid" (John 14:27).

**The Safe Savior**

The King's couch is surrounded by sixty valiant men holding swords, experts and experienced in war. In the Eastern world a bride on her wedding day was carried on the palanquin by strong men. In Revelation 19 Jesus' bride is by His side on their way to the eternal wedding ceremony. The valiant men in the Song of Solomon 3:7 give the bride ultimate protection. Jesus wants us to know we do not have to be afraid of surrendering all to Him. *He is the safe and secure Savior*. Nothing escapes His notice, and He is able to care for us in *all* of life's circumstances.

This revelation (seeing Jesus as trustworthy and safe) prepares her heart for the great turning point in her commitment in 4:6-16, when she believes that her heart will be safe. She is no longer afraid of leaving the comfort zone. She knows and trusts that obedience will bring life and not death. Following in obedience produces power in the inner man, and the inner man is empowered and filled with life.

At times we have to embrace the death of our old selves and let the fragrance of myrrh surround and fill us. We must hit our knees in intercession on many occasions and allow the incense to ascend before the throne of grace and ask for help in time of need. The fire of trial and suffering can release the sweet fragrance of myrrh. When we die to our flesh and pray, He makes the bitterness in our hearts sweet. His bitter suffering on the cross can make our harsh circumstances sweet. It is hard to die to ourselves when we don't pray and keep in touch with Him. Jesus prayed when He faced death. He wasn't excited about facing death. He prayed, "Not my will--Your will, Father."[8] We can embrace suffering and run to his merciful embrace in our time of need and cry out to the Lord of Glory.

The smoke, so easily dispersed, does not indicate weakness but a pillar of strength (Joel 2:30). The power of the Holy Spirit helped Jesus suffer and die, "who through the Eternal Spirit offered Himself" (Hebrews 9:14, KJV). We need this same power to help us die to our flesh. When we have confidence in the safety Jesus has provided, we can resist fear and trust Him to lead and guide us. He overcame death; and we, too, can overcome the death of our flesh (old selves) in this life.

As we identify with Christ in His death and yield to the death of our flesh, myrrh's fragrance of His life is released in and around us. We can rightly say, "I am crucified with Christ, I can do all things, not I, but Christ in me" (Galatians 2:20-21). Jesus overcame the wilderness so that I, too, can overcome (Matthew 4:1-11). He has made a place for us. Jesus talks about this place in John 14, just before the cross, and again in John 17, when He tells the Father He wants us there with Him. We will experience this place when He calls us to heaven, but He also wants us with Him now. He is calling us away *now* to be seated in heavenly places[9] and has made the way for us to experience Him in this life also.

**The Language of the Tabernacle**

Jesus came out of the wilderness with a place prepared for His Bride. Jesus came out of the grave with victory.[10] He opened the Holy of Holies[11] so that we could come in and be seated with Him in the heavenlies.

**The Heavenly Life**

We have this heavenly life in the secret place, the place of abiding in Christ. He came to earth and made Himself the way for our glorious and luxurious salvation. He became sin that we might become the righteousness of God in Christ and receive the gift of grace. "For if by one man's offense death reigned through the one [referring to Adam], much more those who receive abundance of grace and of the gift of righteousness will reign in life through the One, Jesus Christ" (Romans 5:17). His salvation is a place of rest, a place of victory, and there is a seat for me beside Him. The exceeding greatness of His power raises us up together so that we may sit in the heavenly places.

> Who is the King of glory?
>
> The LORD strong and mighty,
>
> The LORD mighty in battle.
>
> Lift up your heads, O you gates!
>
> And the King of glory shall come in.
>
> Who is this King of glory?
>
> The LORD of hosts,
>
> He is the King of glory.
>
> Psalm 24:8-10

David describes Him in this Psalm as the LORD of hosts,[12] referring to the LORD of the armies of Heaven, The Lord mighty in battle--The King of Glory. When I lift the gate, He *will* come in. It's a sure thing. He is victorious over principalities, powers, and rulers of wickedness in high places (Ephesians 6). No enemy can rob His victory because mighty men of spiritual strength surround the place He provides. I can be free from the fear of the night season. I can endure the wilderness, die to myself (myrrh), and run to prayer and worship (frankincense); and He will give me power to overcome and have victory. There are two "coming-out-of-the-wilderness" passages in SOS. Here, King Jesus, King of Glory, emerges; and in Chapter 8 the Bride comes out leaning on the Beloved.

The wilderness is part of the journey into intimacy. After His baptism Jesus was immediately led into the wilderness by the Holy Spirit. (Matthew 4:1-11). It is often a place where we are tempted (as Jesus was approached by the devil) and our convictions tested (refined by the Lord). Our temptations come from the enemy. Our testing and refinement come from the Lord. These should not be confused. The children of Israel and Moses went through with wilderness and gave us examples of how to live in the wilderness (1 Corinthians 10:6) and, on some occasions, perhaps how *not* to live. This fallen world is a "wilderness," and we will encounter places we have to go through and fight to come out on the other side. When the Israelites were delivered from Egypt, the Lord never intended for them to remain in the wilderness. Jesus made this wedding seat available to us, and we have the provision of being seated next to Him throughout the "wilderness" experiences. *Thank you, Jesus.*

**The Lavish Provision**

> Of the wood of Lebanon
>
> Solomon the King
>
> Made himself a palanquin.
>
> He made its pillars of silver,
>
> Its support of gold
>
> Its seat of purple
>
> Its interior paved with love
>
> By the daughters of Jerusalem.
>
> Song of Solomon 3:9-11

In these verses, we are told who made the vehicle and what materials are used. This description is a picture of Jesus' gift of salvation. As the lavish provision comes into view, it reveals the luxurious wedding palanquin where the bride's seat is provided beside her King.

Wood is symbolically used to describe Jesus' earthly life, and the wood of Lebanon was the finest available. Throughout Scripture, silver represents redemption.[12] Pillars of silver are symbolic of eternal redemption. Pillars of gold are symbolic of purity and royalty. The seat of purple was the color of royalty and was paved with love by the daughters of Jerusalem. The beautiful poetic language of the Song of Solomon describes the luxury of the King. Solomon himself made this palanquin, just as Jesus made the wedding palanquin for us. He didn't ask someone else to do the work. He bought us back on a wooden cross and redeemed us to become royalty. He finished the work.

**The Divine Exchange**

The knowledge of the finished work of Christ motivates me to become all He intended. There is much that comes with this divine exchange at the cross and firmly establishes my identity in Christ. It is worth reviewing the specifics mentioned back in Chapter 4:

1. Jesus was punished that we might be forgiven (Romans 5:1).
2. Jesus was wounded that we might be healed (Isaiah 53:4).
3. Jesus was made sin with our sinfulness that we might be made righteous with His righteousness (2 Corinthians 5:21).
4. Jesus died our death that we might share His life (Hebrews 2:9, Romans 6:23).
5. Jesus was made a curse that we might receive the blessing (Galatians 3:13).
6. Jesus endured our poverty that we might share His abundance (2 Corinthians 8:9).
7. Jesus bore our shame that we might share His glory (Hebrews 2:10, 12:2).

8. Jesus endured our rejection that we might enjoy His acceptance (Isaiah 53:3, Ephesians 1:6).
9. Our old man died in Jesus that the new man might live in us (2 Corinthians 5:17).[13]

You will never find any reason you deserve this exchange. It is the outworking of God's sovereign grace. It is the expression of His measureless love. He is the Safe Savior Who extravagantly provides. His provision is too good to be true, but it is TRUTH! Accept His love.

The Shulamite maiden has accepted that she is the bride and is seeing her identity. She is truly seeing Him, who she is in Him, and who she was created to be. This recognition empowers her to call the daughters. This is her first dialogue with the body since 1:6. Her personal experiences from 1:7-3:3 have been only with the Lord. The greatest feeding is alone with the Lord. You can be stirred by teachings, but you will be fed more as you get alone and turn the Word of God into dialogue with God.

**The Glad Heart of the King**

> Go forth, O daughters of Zion,
>
> And see King Solomon with the crown
>
> With which his mother crowned him

> On the day of his wedding,
>
> The day of the gladness of his heart.
>
> Song of Solomon 3:11

She calls the daughters to do two things:

1. Go forth.
2. See the King with His crown.

She sees Jesus and shares what she sees. Come with me and see the King with His crown! She is telling them, "Come look at the finished work of Jesus--the lavish provision, the luxurious redemption." He is crowned with many crowns: King over Heaven, King of the angels, King of Kings; but it is the crown He receives on His wedding day that makes His heart glad.

**Voluntary Lovers**

This crown comes from a willing, voluntary heart. He won't make us crown Him. His voluntary lover crowns Him and makes His heart glad. What a happy thought--the glad heart of the King!

*O Jesus! As I gaze on You, I see You in this new way as my Bridegroom King, not just as the Great Shepherd or the King at the table of provision. Your desire is for me, and You have given me this great desire for You. I see Your glory, Your splendor,*

*Your authority, the security of being in You.*

These new perceptions cause the bride to want others to see Him, too. "Go forth! Awake, arise, and behold your King!" She encourages the daughters to go forth, see the King crowned by the church on His wedding day, and make Him King in their lives as well.

When I locate my treasure, I locate my heart--a restatement of Matthew 6:21.

Wherever you are, seek. Don't stop, because in seeking you *will* find. Keep on asking, seeking, and knocking. Go forth. See the King of Glory. He wants to reveal the glory of you, who you really are.

Let's pray:

> *Thank You, LORD of glory, King of Kings, for bringing us into a new season.*
>
> *You're pressing us into a new place.*
>
> *You reveal the safety of Your presence*
>
> *And the lavish provision of Your salvation.*
>
> *You came and endured the work of the cross and*

Sarah Ramsey – The Bridegroom's Song

*prepared*

*the wedding palanquin.*

*Thank You for considering me worthy of royalty.*

*Open my eyes to see this wonderful, heavenly life.*

*I want to make Your heart glad!*

*By faith I come and take my seat beside You,*

*And I find rest for my soul.*

*Amen.*

Sarah Ramsey – The Bridegroom's Song

# 12

## A Place for Us Beside the King

*God has raised us up and made us sit together in the heavenly places with Christ*

(Ephesians 2:4).

Chapter 3 of the Song ends as the bride encourages her friends, the daughters of Jerusalem, to come and look upon the glad Bridegroom King. Chapter 4 opens with the Beloved's description of His fair one. He details her characteristics as He prophesies and proclaims who she is in the first five verses. Then in verse six the bride, obviously deeply moved by the King's words, makes her commitment to go to the hills and mountains with Him. Her response causes another beautiful stream of prophetic words from the Beloved's lips as He once more beckons her to come. He describes where they will go and pours out encouragement and affirmation upon her. He challenges her to separate herself for Him alone and uses still more intimate terms to address her. We see the bride move into her heavenly position. The bride yields and cries out for more of the wind of the Spirit as Chapter 4 ends, and we are nearly halfway through the journey of the Song!

She had not heard His voice since she sent Him away. She was afraid to surrender one hundred percent, and in 2:17 she disobeyed. The Beloved requested two things of His chosen one: (1) to rise up out of her circumstances, and (2) to go along with Him in His circumstance. Remember that in Chapter 3 she arose and found Him; but she did not go with Him initially. She was bound by a mindset from the past. Finally, she did arise and diligently seek; and He revealed Himself as the safe Savior. It is in this setting of seeing Him come out of the wilderness that He addresses her again. So chapter 4 begins.

**I Am the Favorite**

Listen! The King with the glad heart speaks.

> Behold, you are fair, my love!
>
> Behold, you are fair!
>
> Song of Solomon 4:1

Words are so significant! God created by speaking, "Let there be light"; and there was light (Genesis 1:3). Jesus tells us in Luke 6:45, "For out of the abundance of the heart the mouth speaks." Matthew 12:37 teaches, "For by your words you will be justified, and by your words you will be condemned." And so the

Bridegroom speaks, "Behold, you are fair, my love! Behold, you are fair!" Jesus, the Creator, has come to plant seeds of prophesy (words of promise) from His lips and release the creative power to equip her as His bride.

## The Voice of the King

Since first departing without her, the King speaks. He is not angry or condemning. These words bring a calming peace and assurance of His love and acceptance. He announces, "You are beautiful, My love." These words disarm her defenses and allow her to hear and receive. His life-speaking words bring maturity, causing her to rise to His vision. These are the kisses of His mouth we requested earlier. Jesus is nourishing and cherishing His bride as she is able to look into the mirror of His words.

> Behold! I am beautiful to my Bridegroom King. I am beautiful to Jesus!

Don't hesitate to confess it out loud. Say it aloud so your own ears can hear!

> O, Jesus, I am your favorite! I am!

I love what Mike Bickle has said: "God is so full of love, each of us can truly be His favorite...A God uniquely able to love individuals to the utmost."[1]

Jesus speaks prophetic words over her even though she is not fully mature. The same is true for us. His words declare and create His bride. Jesus blesses and prophetically calls forth what He sees. He declares eight budding virtues in her:

1. Her eyes
2. Her hair
3. Her teeth
4. Her lips
5. Her mouth
6. Her temples (cheeks)
7. Her neck
8. Her breasts

He calls things that are not as though they are in the present (Romans 4:17). He is the "God who brings the dead back to life and who creates new things out of nothing" (NLT)--the "God who gives life to the dead and calls into being what does not yet exist" (Berean Study Bible).

He sees who she can become. He begins with her eyes.

## Sarah Ramsey – The Bridegroom's Song

Behold, you are fair, My love!

Behold, you are fair!

You have dove's eyes behind your veil.

Your hair is like a flock of goats,

Going down from Mount Gilead.

Your teeth are like a flock of shorn sheep

Which have come up from the washing,

Every one of which bears twins,

And none is barren among them.

Your lips are like a strand of scarlet,

And your mouth is lovely.

Your temples behind your veil

Are like a piece of pomegranate.

Your neck is like the tower of David,

Built for an armory,

On which hang a thousand bucklers,

All shields of mighty men.

Your two breasts are like two fawns,

Twins of a gazelle,

Which feed among the lilies.

Song of Solomon 4:1-5

**Unlocking the Code**

One of the fun things about the Song of Solomon is unlocking the code, the poetic love language! Throughout the Song the human body is used symbolically, beginning with the head and moving downward. Eight characteristics are mentioned here, each with spiritual meaning. These are eight areas that reveal God's beauty in us. These eight areas make God's heart glad and my heart glad! The Bible is its own best commentary and reveals the symbolism of these Scriptures. This is going to require some diligence--make a decision to hang in there. This is for you, my sweet friend! You will want to come back later to meditate upon and memorize these features.

**The Budding Virtues of the Maturing Bride**

1. Eyes--Jesus begins with her eyes. Eyes speak of spiritual discernment, understanding, and wisdom (1 Corinthians 2:13-16).

Our spiritual eyes have the ability to see things in the Spirit. The eyes are the most prominent feature in spiritual maturity. The Bridegroom also referred to her dove's eyes in 1:15.

If you will recall in review:

- A dove is a picture of the Holy Spirit, beginning with Noah when he released the dove from the ark. When Jesus was baptized in water, the form of a dove was seen (John 1:32). The Holy Spirit illuminates and gives revelation (Ephesians 1:18).
- A dove does not have peripheral vision. Its focus is clearly set. Dove's eyes cannot focus on two things.
- Doves are faithful to one mate for life; even if one dies, the other will never mate again.

Her eyes are "behind the veil." She doesn't reveal all she sees. She is discerning and does not speak flippantly about the things God reveals.

2. Hair--Hair speaks of consecration and dedication.

As a vow of dedication to God, Samson was never to cut his hair. When he compromised and broke the vow, his power and strength were lost. Submission and spiritual covering are also represented by a woman's hair, as is her beauty (1 Corinthians 11:5-6, 15; 1 Peter 3:35). He sees my desire to be dedicated. I desire to be subject to Him.

3. Teeth--The teeth are the instruments used to eat food.

Teeth chew food, which nourishes the physical body. Each one has a "twin," indicating the maiden's ability to discern the word of truth and balance the food she consumes. For example, grace and justice balance each other, as do truth and righteousness. "Mercy and truth have met together; Righteousness and peace have kissed" (Psalm 85:10).

Babies don't have teeth. The bride is not a baby. She is able to eat meat, the Word of God. Her teeth are like a flock of shorn sheep. Sheep are clean animals in the Old Testament, permissible for consumption. Wool speaks of fleshly zeal, and the white speaks of her purity. She is balanced in her assimilation of God's Word, not with natural ability (wool), but she is cleansed and washed by the Word. She is shorn and dependent upon the Holy Spirit to appropriate truth. She can take in the Word and chew up the spiritual food He provides for nourishment. She can eat the fish and spit out the bones, so to speak!

4. The fourth feature is her lips. Lips are spoken of throughout the Song.

Lips and the mouth are used differently in the Song. This feature is distinctively her lips, not her mouth. Lips communicate, and the mouth gives kisses. Throughout the Song, lips refer to speech. Lips are the vehicle for expressing what I have received from God. She speaks the Word of God "like a thread of scarlet," symbolic of the blood of Jesus. Rahab put outside her window a scarlet cord which indicated redemption (See Joshua 2:18, 21; 6:23, 25). The bride's words/lips are under the authority of the King, anointed and covered by the blood of Jesus. Her words are redeeming words. The bride's lips also pray, worship, and encourage others. Let your lips be filled with grace.

5. Her mouth is mentioned fifth. The mouth is the symbol of intimacy.

As the lips express and give voice and access to what God says, the mouth speaks of her communion with Jesus. She requested the kisses of His mouth. Just as the lips relate to the speech, the mouth is about the kisses, or intimacy. These are the deep things of God.

The lips commune with people in the world and give praise, etc. The mouth, however, is not as superficial a term. The mouth, in its wholeness, is lovely to God. "Let the words of my mouth be acceptable in Your sight, O Lord" (Psalm 19:14). "Your mouth is lovely" (SOS 4:3).

6. The sixth trait mentioned is her cheeks or temples. The cheeks reveal countenance and emotions.

Her cheeks are sweet to God, like a rosy pomegranate full of juicy, sweet seeds. Like her eyes, they, too, are behind a veil hidden for God in genuine modesty and tenderness. She is on display within the veil for an audience of one, behind closed doors! Cheeks are like windows, revealing positive or negative emotions and indicate beauty. The pomegranate symbolizes fullness of life, plenty of seeds, and emotions open and exposed. But they are veiled. Emotions often cripple the children of God and how we approach Him. Even though God created us as emotional beings, He does not want us to be hindered by our emotions.

7. The neck. In Scripture, the neck represents the free will of man.

The neck can be either stiff or submissive. Her free will submits willingly and has become part of her spiritual warfare. "Like the tower of David," it is built for an armory with war prizes hanging on the wall-- "a thousand bucklers, all shields of mighty men." Instead of considering submission of the will as a dreaded requirement, it has become a weapon of freedom, a defense and protection against the enemy to prevent stiff-necked rebellion. No wonder the enemy wants women to believe they need liberating. God's ways truly set us free. The bride is learning how to bow to the Word of God without a stiff neck and accept His authority structure. Her submissive will is a defense against enemy attack; the shields of mighty men hang there. Acts 13:22 says David did *all* God's will. Her neck is like a tower, straight and tall, a place that gives vision in times of war. These are sweet mysteries. They are revealed in the light of David, the warrior, with his armory holding an arsenal of weapons.

Submission also reveals humility, which releases grace. "God resists the proud but gives grace to the humble" (James 4:5).

9. The last of the eight characteristics is the two breasts.

The breasts represent maturity in the bride. As we said, the bride is not a baby. She is a young maid with budding breasts. They are the seat of passion. A fawn is young, not fully developed. Two gives balance, like the teeth, as we also saw earlier. We are not to go to the right or to the left but should stay along the narrow path which gives life. "Narrow is the way that leads to life" (Matthew 7:14). Once the breasts are formed, she is equipped with passion and is ready to reproduce for her Beloved Bridegroom King. Young breasts are full of passion. Breasts also have the ability to provide nourishment for babies; she is able to nurture the pure and innocent. The bride is a maker of disciples. As she matures, we will see her breasts described as clusters of grapes (i.e. the new wine) to nurture and edify others.

**An Enemy Ready to Devour**

Wow--that is a mouthful! Oh, that we could see and believe who God says we are! He made us in His image and wants us to have a full revelation of who we are created to be. The enemy is forever telling us lies and making accusations contrary to the words we have just read. He gets into our faces and minds and attempts to lure us as he did with Eve by questioning, "Hath God said?" His tactics are still the same. He discredits the Word of God. He even attempted to do so with Jesus during the wilderness temptations. The devil said to Jesus, "If you are the Son of God…." He wanted Jesus to doubt Who He is, and he wants us to doubt who we are. The enemy does not want you to know who you really are. You are the bride, created and chosen by God for His Son. It is a sort of divinely pre-arranged marriage. He constructed the plan (palanquin), built it, and finished the work of redemption so that we could sit beside Him on His throne (Ephesians 2:6). Selah!

Please, as the Apostle Paul says, I *beseech* you to "walk worthy of the calling for which you were called" (Ephesians 4:1); and do not let these words fall to the ground! Read these first five verses again from Chapter four and soak in the fullness of the words, recovering your identity in Christ.

**Agree with Jesus, Not with the Lie**

The enemy is a thief. He continually tries to steal my identity. He does not come, "except to steal, and to kill, and to destroy" (John 10:10). The enemy accuses me day and night (Revelation 12:10). But Jesus sent the Spirit of Truth which dwells in me. He is saying, "Behold, you are fair my love--Behold, you are fair!" That is the report I choose to believe. We have a choice and must decide. Which report will you believe? Can you recognize the difference? The lie promotes deception and says we are ugly or unwanted. It does take faith to believe the words He speaks, especially about ourselves. Without faith it is impossible to please God (Hebrews 11:6), so let's just go ahead and believe and not have an evil heart of unbelief (Hebrews 3). The Beloved loves me! That is the truth. I have decided!

God has a plan for your life. Remember back in Chapter 1 when He said, "We will make you…"? God sees the end of the thing before it begins (Isaiah 46:10). When I agree with Him, I can speak prophetically into my own life. My words contain power! With my mouth I confess unto salvation, Romans 10:9-10 says. Now it's time for my part. Look into the mirror (James 1:21), and speak back to yourself the words He has just spoken about you. This is who I am, changed from glory to glory. This is what you will find:

> Behold, you are beautiful, my love,
>
> Behold, you are beautiful!
>
> You have dove's eyes behind your veil.
>
> Song of Solomon 4:1

Practice this by saying it aloud, and continue on with the characteristics you have just learned:

Behold, I am fair,

Behold, I am fair!

I am your love! The fairest.

I am beautiful to You, my Bridegroom King.

Isn't God's tender and affectionate heart towards His weak people beautiful? God sees us with hands raised and hearts abandoned. *O God, I guess I am beautiful to you. I'm just going to have to accept it.* Selah.

Let's pray together:

*Thank You for this beautiful Scripture that tells me who I am.*

*Thank You, Lord, for eyes to see and for helping me consecrate myself.*

*Thank You for teeth to chew the Word, for lips to declare what You say, and for a mouth that lets me enjoy intimacy*

*with You, my Beloved.*

*Thank You for emotions and for a veil to help me be*

*modest and discreet.*

*Thank You for helping me break my will and become*

*submissive to Yours. I love the necklace You give as I bow*

*to You.*

*Let my neck be lovely and yielding. Help me resist a stiff*

*neck.*

*Thank You for the passion and ability to nurture babies,*

*even babes in Christ.*

*I am passionate for You.*

*O God, thank You for opening my eyes to see. Help me to*

*believe!*

*It seems too good to be true, but I see it in Your word; so*

*I choose to believe.*

*I bow to you my Lord, willingly, and yield my soul to You.*

*Amen.*

**13**

**I Will Go**

*I will go my way to the mountain of myrrh and the hill of frankincense…*

(Song of Solomon 4:6).

**She Says Yes**

      Until the day breaks

      And the shadows flee away,

      I will go my way to the mountain of myrrh

And to the hill of frankincense.

Song of Solomon 4:6

The bride is finally saying "yes"--receiving His words and changing her mind and response. She repents and bows her neck in submission and declares, "I will go." The words of the Beloved are alive and powerful. They divide between the soul and the spirit. They are sharper than a two-edged sword. His words are able to judge the thoughts and intents of the heart (Hebrews 4:12).

**Commitment to Obedience**

This decision is a total commitment. She is saying, "I will go with you *all* the way." Mike Bickle says there are two parts of the cross. The first part is what Jesus did for me. It is a gift I accept by faith. He did the work and paid for it. I receive His gift. The second part is denying myself and taking up my cross to follow. This part is where I "do" something. I embrace the cross and all its splinters. At this place on the journey she commits to trust Him and embrace whatever following Him entails, as Philippians 3:10 says, "so that I may know Him...and the fellowship of His sufferings." My way here won't be exactly like someone else's way. No one else can do it for me. It's a personal call to obedience, and it involves a deliberate decision. Climbing the mountain of myrrh to embrace suffering is radical obedience. It reminds me of Abraham's climbing Mount Moriah in his total commitment to offer His son Isaac on the altar (Genesis 22).

The commitment to go all the way also involves the hill of frankincense. Frankincense is symbolic of prayer. Notice that it is a hill and not a mountain. A little prayer goes a long way. "Let my prayer be set before you as incense" (Psalm 141:2, AMP). Revelation 5:8 tells us the incense around the throne of God comes from the prayers of the saints. The bride chooses to embrace a life of prayer and commits to joining Jesus where He is now, interceding for the saints. *He is* the Golden Altar of intercession and worship.

**My Story**

The call to prayer in my life was a process. After I received the baptism of the Holy Spirit, one of the first things I wanted to do was pray. I immediately went to my teacher, Jim Massa, and told him, "Jim, I want to pray." Jim was a very thoughtful man and not quick to speak. He was a leader and spiritual father to my husband and me. After a few moments he said, "How about Saturday mornings at 5:30 here at First Baptist Church?" At that time our children were one, four, and eight years old. The commitment was real, and the price was high; but I remember it as a joyful time. As I continued learning how to pray, resources became available. We began learning to pray the scriptures. Through books like *Prayers That Avail Much* by Germaine Copeland and books by Andrew Murray, E.M. Bounds, and others, I was brought further into the ministry of prayer. "Lord, teach us to pray," was the cry of my heart.

Just like the little Shulamite maiden, I learned that prayer is a process. As I look back and remember, it has been a wonderful journey up this hill. I encourage you, at whatever stage you find yourself, to say "yes"--just for today. God is leading you, or you would not be reading this book. Just do it, and don't rely on your own understanding or feelings.

**Just Do It**

I could see how I needed to stop talking and just go and do it-- not just hear, but *do*. The closer I am to Him, the more the lingering shadows in me are visible; and I realize the need for His cleansing blood. I was reluctant to leave the comfortable place I was in with the Lord, but I went anyway. In the throne room I receive mercy and find grace, the unmerited favor of God, so that I may embrace times of suffering "...until the day breaks and the shadows flee...." He gives me the same ability to die to myself that He gave Jesus to finish His work on the cross.

This choice is also a commitment to endure "...until the day breaks and the shadows flee...." Praying through the night seasons is difficult when we feel alone and the darkness surrounds us. We can't see in the dark. We can't see the outcome, the answers to questions, the immediate impact of our prayers. The commitment is real when we say, "Lord, where are You? I can't see you through this darkness, but I will stay until this night season passes and the shadows flee."

This place is a place of sacrifice, just as the hilltop of Mount Moriah was for Abraham. I must embrace the death of my flesh. It is not the brazen altar; but it is an altar, a place of sacrifice and offering--the golden altar. I come with my priestly garments of salvation, righteousness, humility, and praise to come away with Him and pray by His side. Climbing this hilltop is intentional and means no longer sitting idly by. I am walking this out day by day.

**Come With Me**

"Come with me, come with me": The Beloved repeatedly entreats the Shulamite to come to the heavenly places, the high places of myrrh and frankincense. The invitation is to the King's chamber where Jesus is on the throne. He is no longer on the cross, at the brazen altar. Our great High Priest is receiving our prayers and interceding at the golden altar. He is holy, righteous, safe, undefiled and separated from sinners--higher than the heavens (Hebrews 7:26). My call is to get up, get out of bed, and accept His way by faith.

She has seen Jesus as Lord of the mountains and hills, the Lord of the wilderness who skips on hills and conquers them. The mountain of the Lord is the place of His holy habitation. But mountains and hills are also symbolic of obstacles that hinder faith and obedience. Remember that she did not go when He first called her. She knows the pain of life without Him. She knows she is identifying with Jesus in His death and embracing suffering until the day breaks. With this understanding when the Lord of glory calls, she obeys. My Beloved *is* the Lord of hosts, the Captain of all the angelic armies.

**Jesus' Love Language**

She has responded, "I will go," with the intent to obey; and Jesus makes known what delight and pleasure this brings Him. They haven't even started up the mountain yet, but the Beloved is overwhelmed! Jesus said, "If you keep my commandments, you will abide in My love" (John 15:10); "He who has my commandments and keeps them, it is he who loves Me...and I will love him and manifest Myself to him" (John 14:21). Obedience proves my love for Jesus. Obedience is His love language.

His prophetic words empower her to yield to suffering and prayer. We see the perfect picture of such yielding in the Garden of Gethsemane when Jesus submitted Himself to suffering. He prayed for us in His greatest time of need before yielding Himself to the pain of the cross. It was the greatest act of obedience and the greatest act of love. Gethsemane, translated, means "olive press." Luke 22:44 says, "...and being in agony, He prayed more earnestly." Reflect on that before you continue.

**Pleasing the King**

> You are all fair, my love,
>
> And there is no spot on you.
>
> Song of Solomon 4:7

The bride's response brings praise from the Bridegroom King. The "yes" in her spirit and mouth is so sweet; and He immediately responds, "Now! Just look at you! You're so beautiful to me! There is no spot in you. There is no area in which you are not yielding. Thank you for saying 'yes' to Me!" At this point in the Song He has called her beautiful and fair eight times, but notice here that He adds "*all* fair." Do we believe His words yet? Let's recap these eight utterances.

1. If you do not know, O fairest among women (1:8)
2. Behold, you are fair, my love (1:15)
3. Behold, you are fair! (1:16)
4. Rise up my love, my fair one, and come away (2:10)
5. Rise up my love, my fair one, and come away (2:13)
6. O my dove, in the cleft of the rock…(2:14)
7. Behold you are fair my love! Behold you are fair! (4:1)
8. You are all fair my love. (4:7)

Whew! I need to hear that over and over--just as I need to hear "I love you" from the ones I love.

When He says I am beautiful and fair, I need to meditate on His words and confess them aloud until I believe them. She is willing to embrace the cross in her life because she is so aware of His love. This growth does not mean that she has no sin or that she is fully mature, but that she is dearly loved in each stage of growth. She is--and I am—"all fair." *We* are all fair. There is no spot in me because His blood blots out my sin. Let's receive His love in our hearts. It is His love which equips and enables us to make the commitment to radically obey, even if we are reluctant. It's decision time. "I will go away with you, Jesus." Won't you?

Let's pray:

*I will go.*

*Holy Spirit, come.*

*Illuminate me.*

*Help me believe God's perfect and true love for me.*

*Help me open to you and receive.*

*Pour your love into me so that I can love you in return.*

*Give me the will to obey, and help me say "yes" even in*

*the night seasons.*

*Give me the strength to endure and embrace Jesus*

*through suffering.*

*Help me to come away with You when you call.*

*I want to go with You. Take me away with You. Amen*

## 14

### A Call to the Mountains

*Come with me...my spouse*

[Song of Solomon 4:8]

The little Shulamite maiden has matured. She is the bride of Christ. The next part of her journey is wonderful as He calls her "my spouse" for the first time. Some versions say "my bride." But let's take a deep breath. For when He calls her "my spouse," or "my bride," He is calling her to war. He tells her the destination and some of the risks involved. Her night season prepared her for the real deal--war! She has committed to go to the mountains to pray and war with the Beloved for the Beloved's purposes to be fulfilled on earth. She passed basic training and is now a ready soldier. The bride of Christ is a worshipping warrior. She is a lover of Jesus, and she now has a heart to war for His desires. The bride says, "I will go"; and the Beloved quickly responds, "Come with me...With me!"

**Another Invitation**

Come with me from Lebanon, my spouse,

> With me from Lebanon.
>
> Look from the top of Amana,
>
> From the top of Senir and Hermon,
>
> From the lion's dens,
>
> From the mountains of the leopards.
>
> Song of Solomon 4:8

He says, "Come with me...With me," repeating the entreaty, emphasizing His strong desire. He calls her to the fragrant heights of Lebanon, the heavenly position. He does not address her as His "sister" or "immature maiden," but as His "spouse." She is the bride. The cross has given God the Father a family, redeemed sons and daughters. Jesus' work on the cross provides a bride, the church, composed of individual believers like you and me. **Life begins at the cross--it does not end there**. His work of providing a way of salvation is finished, but He is not on the cross anymore. He is on the throne and wants us there with Him. O happy thought! In Revelation 4 Jesus says, "Come up here"; and in Song 4:8, He essentially says the same, "Come with me and look from the tops of the mountains." He wants to give us a different view, a heavenly perspective.

He tells her where they are going. Lebanon is a large mountain range in Israel. This mountain range has three peaks: Amana (which means truth), Senir (which means protective armor) and Hermon (which means victory). Israel could see the promised land from these mountaintops. Moses longed to see Lebanon

(Deuteronomy 3:25). Lebanon's mountains were dangerous but were noted for their beauty and strong, fragrant cedar trees. The glory of Lebanon is mentioned in Isaiah 35:2, filled to the brim with fragrant flowers (Hosea 14:6 and SOS 4:11). Jesus' countenance is also like Lebanon (SOS 5:15). Watchman Nee said, "The high mountains of Scripture indicate our leaving the earth level to move up to a heavenly position--being in the world but jutting far out of it into the heavenlies. The call which comes to the maiden here is one of ascent into heavenly elevation."[1]

**Position (Ascent into the Heavenly Position)**

It is impossible to perceive correctly without proper position. The maiden is now in proper relationship with Him--beside Him, seated in the heavenlies. She is in position. She now wants to be with Him more than she desires to be comfortable and pampered. She trusts Him for protection. Like David, she is a worshipping warrior. She is a lover of God and a warrior in partnership with God. The wars in the heavens are influenced by our prayers, and we are called to intercede so that the purposes of God come to fruition on earth. Jesus taught and commanded His disciples to pray this way, "Kingdom of God come. Let Thy will be done on earth, as it is in heaven." We are called to Lebanon (the heavenly places, the secret place, the throne room) to pray and usher God's will to earth. How overwhelming! He wants her to look from the peaks of Lebanon with Him. In the matter of spiritual warfare, two prerequisites must be addressed: position and vision. Once we get into *position*, we have *vision*.

**I'm in the Right Place**

When we presume and try to solve our problems using earthly and natural means, we can become frustrated. Frankly, we can miss the mark entirely. But we are learning. He is teaching us. In our heavenly position, on the mountain with the Beloved, we are in close proximity to malignant powers (cancerous; spreading; difficult to control) as well--represented by the lion's den and the mountains of the leopards. When we are in the "hot" (like a crucible or refining fire) areas of our lives and facing the struggles of daily life, the last thing we want to do is climb a mountain. Don't we really just want to stay in bed and hide? This stagnant place is an alert that we need discernment the most. Provision to overcome arrives by faith *when we begin to climb* the mountain. Then heavenly elevation brings discernment and gives a spiritual, eternal perspective.

This call is a great and demanding one for a weak and delicate maiden. The journey is treacherous. I see the truth when I am in the mountains with my Beloved--not in continuing to sit at the table, or in continuing to eat raisin cakes and apples (or assorted chocolates, for that matter) in bed. We must be mindful of the enemy, and we can see him better from this heavenly view. The enemy's habitation is very close. We are entering enemy territory when we commit and take our position in the heavenlies. The Beloved brought me here to have spiritual eyes so I might be victorious! Hallelujah!

In your seat beside your Beloved, the King of Glory, you can inquire of the Lord: "Am I seeing clearly? Should I pursue? What's going on here?" When John was leaning in closely on the breast of Jesus at the Last Supper, it was his position which caused Peter to ask John to say, "Jesus, who is the one who will betray You?" Jesus did reveal the secret of His betrayer's identity to John, the disciple in the most intimate position with Him. He was positioned to receive. Our true enemies become more obvious the closer we come to Jesus, and He reveals details of our lives we may not otherwise see. It's time to get into position--the mountain of the Lord, i.e. Lebanon.

**Vision**

The second prerequisite is vision. Not only do I have position from this vantage point, but I can also see and know the truth. This knowledge and preparation arm me for victory! He brings us to Amana, Senir, and Hermon (truth, protective armor, and victory, respectively). He is the Lord of Hosts. The hosts are the armies of heaven. Without vision, it is impossible to see the enemy's movement or perceive his true nature and his strategies and win victory.

"Concerning heavenly things, one must stand on heavenly

ground to discern clearly the issues of heavenly character."[2] Standing our heavenly ground enables us to learn about wrestling with principalities, powers, and the rulers of the darkness (Ephesians 6). Lindell Cooley tells of being in a hotel room in New York City. He was on a high floor with windows overlooking the parking lot. From that height, he could see into the parking lot from a different perspective. Now, imagine a thief trying to break into one of the cars. One could see the thief more clearly from higher ground: his directions coming and going, his mechanism for breaking and entering, etc. The view from the vantage point of the hotel room is much different from the view of the parking lot at ground level, where one could more easily be caught off guard. This call is not to a ground war. It is to an air war, and we are equipped for victory from a mountain-top position.

**The Enemy's Habitation**

The Bridegroom's exhortation to come and look enables her to see the enemy's camp, "the lions' dens, the mountains of leopards" (SOS 4:8, KJV). Scripture identifies these enemies. Peter tells us the lion's roar will fill us with fear and terrify (1 Peter 5:8). The Bible also speaks of the leopard's ability to devour and destroy by attacking swiftly (Habakkuk 1:8). The lions' dens and the mountains of the leopards are regions represented in the heavenlies. One reason He wants us to come up is to see the enemy's hideout. From the height, we can see what we are up against. But this is out of my comfort zone!

We are not wrestling flesh and blood during this fight, but demonic and spiritual principalities and powers.

However, we have the equipment needed, the spiritual weapons: belt of truth, breastplate of righteousness, helmet of salvation, shield of faith, shoes of peace, sword of the Spirit, and praying always in the Holy Spirit (Ephesians 6). My weapons are not the weapons of the world. I am fighting a spiritual enemy. We do not have to fear when we remain dressed and protected in His armor.

Has the body of Christ failed to be more successful in spiritual warfare because we are reluctant to totally surrender and go to the mountains? It seems the Lord will not allow us to engage in very intense spiritual warfare until we have committed and surrendered--so that we can be protected in the palanquin, the safe place. The more one abides in light, the more one recognizes darkness! The more mature a believer becomes, the more he or she will recognize areas of inward immaturity. The closer we get to Jesus, the bigger He becomes, just like walking to the mountain.

**My Story**

One morning as I was thinking about these scriptures, the words from the 1970s series, *Mission: Impossible*, began to form in my mind: "If you choose to accept this assignment...." I realized that, without my being in my position in Christ, this warfare really would be mission *impossible*. When I abide in Christ and dwell in the secret place, I come into this heavenly position; and I have the victory I desire. When *you* decide to accept this assignment, it then becomes mission *possible*!

When my sister and her husband were in Israel, they climbed these mountains in Lebanon. After they returned, we were talking about this part of the Song of Solomon. My sister told me how far she could see and that she had witnessed the sun breaking through the clouds on Mt. Hermon. What a beautiful illustration! Beni Johnson's book, *The Happy Intercessor*, teaches that we are not on the defensive. We have the ball. We will win this battle. The sun will break through the clouds and bring victory! Truth, armor, and victory are indispensable in our battle against the enemy. Paul tells us about being in the heavenlies in Ephesians 1.

> The eyes of our understanding are being enlightened to know what is the hope of our calling to see the riches of God's inheritance in us--and to know the exceeding greatness of His power to us who believe--which He wrought in Christ when He raised Him from the dead and seated Him at His own right hand in heavenly places!...He made us alive together with Christ...and *raised us up together, and made us sit together in the heavenly places* in Christ Jesus, that in the ages to come He might show the exceeding riches of His grace in His

kindness toward us in Christ Jesus! (Ephesians 1:18, 20 and 2:5-7)

**Victory Over the Enemy**

We cannot defeat the enemy from an earthly position or in the flesh. We must come to the heavenlies equipped with His weapons. We are well able to take this mountain—our mountains. The angel Gabriel said to Mary, the mother of Jesus, "For with God nothing will be impossible" (Luke 1:37). We destroy strongholds in the mind when we agree with what God says about us. The lie holds us in bondage, but the truth sets us free.

We want complete victory over all strongholds--anger, fear, unforgiveness, the traditions of men, etc. If the enemy is witchcraft or rebellion (which the Bible names Jezebel), it must be utterly defeated. From my heavenly position on Mount Amana, I know the truth and can see my spiritual inheritance. I can recognize the strategies of fear, double-mindedness, rejection, pride, etc. These enemies have devouring appetites, like leopards, and want to consume my inheritance. I receive insight and revelation on Mount Senir, armor to defeat the enemy's strategy. I will be victorious on Mount Hermon and triumph over the powers of destruction.

We want the enemy under the feet of Jesus. We want to keep the gate closed. God has called us to intercede for complete victory whether the enemies are inside ourselves or whether we are resisting the enemies' effects on behalf of others. I am who He says I am; He is the maker of the heaven and earth! I have found God's ability. He is going to tell me what to do; and as I obey, I will be successful wherever I go. I find grace at His throne to help in my time of need and am letting go in faith!

This reckless abandon leaves me speechless. Are you speechless? It's time to talk little, listen much.

## My Story

The Holy Spirit is such a wonderful teacher. Jesus said He would teach us all things (John 14:26) and that we would find treasure and mysteries through His word. This truth began to unfold as I began to take this journey into a more intimate place with Jesus. When I came to places I couldn't understand or began to doubt what the Holy Spirit was saying to me, God would send me a teacher. I was also sensitive to letting my thoughts and actions be judged by older and mature women in the faith when God brought them into my life at these pivotal moments. I have found security in coming under the authority of these godly voices, including my pastor and husband. As I had questions, then, God led me to answers. I want to share a few words from Watchmen Nee and John MacMillan. I hope they inspire you, too.

**Authoritative Intercessors**

Watchmen Nee's little book on Ephesians, *Sit, Walk, Stand,* explains a clear pattern throughout the book of Ephesians. The bride has learned to sit with Him (Ephesians 2:6) and to walk with Him (Ephesians 4-5), and now she is able to stand and war with Him (Ephesians 6). Sit before walking. Walk before standing. And then when we have done all to stand, we put on the whole armor of God. From this standing position, we wage war from the mountaintop. Watchman Nee also wrote *Song of Songs*, which has become one of my handbooks for the Song of Solomon. He lived many years ago, 1903-1972, but he knew how to sit in the heavenly places and have an intimate relationship with Jesus. More often than not we have not learned to sit in the dwelling place and, therefore, do not have the patience as we walk the walk. God likes order, and maturity is a process.

In *The Authority of the Believer*, John MacMillan writes that God delights to delegate His power to man--when He can find believing and obedient servants to accept and exercise it. God is endeavoring to train workers for a future and a mighty cooperation with His Son. The bride is a co-laborer with Jesus.

MacMillan has had great influence over my life as an intercessor. He continues teaching the methods of the Lord and of learning the secret of taking hold of the power of God in this excerpt:

> It's true also that the Lord is demanding a closer adherence to His appointed methods.

> As the individual believer matures in the Christian life, he often finds greater difficulty in maintaining spiritual victory. He had expected opposition to decrease, or at least to be more easily overcome. But he discovers that God is laying upon him heavier burdens and testing him for larger ministries. In like manner, as the age is advancing, the church is being prepared for the final struggle by being taught lessons of individual responsibility that in the past were the property of advanced saints only. All believers might have known them for they are revealed in the Word of God, but only the few pressed on to their attainment.

> For the greater struggles of our day and the thickening atmosphere into which we are entering, the church needs intercessors who have learned the secret of taking hold of the power of God and directing it against the strategic advances of the enemy. She needs those who have understanding of the times to know what ought to be

done amid the crashing down of old standards and the introduction of that which is uncertain and untried.

God is waiting for those whom He can trust and use, who will have the discernment to foresee His steps and the faith to command His power. Authoritative intercessors are men and women whose eyes have opened to the full knowledge of their place in Christ. To them, the Word of God has become a battle chart on which is detailed the plan of campaign of the hosts of the Lord. They realize that they have been appointed by Him for the oversight of certain sections of the advance, and they have humbly accepted His commission. Deeply conscious of their own personal unworthiness and insufficiency, they yet believe God's statement concerning their identification with Christ in His throne power.

Increasingly they realize that heavenly responsibility rests upon them for the carrying forward of the warfare with which they have been charged. Their closet becomes a council chamber from which spiritual commands go forth concerning matters widely varied in character and separated in place. As they speak the word of command, God obeys. His delight is in such coworking. They have caught His thought concerning the method of advance of His kingdom. Through them He finds it possible to carry forward purposes to fulfill promises that have been long held back for lack--not of human laborers, or of financial means--but of understanding spiritual fellow laborers.

Whew! Goodness gracious. *Lord, this is the place where I want to be found faithful. Help me hear Your voice and obey Your commands.*

**He Delights in Such Co-working**

What is this excerpt saying to us as it describes the warring bride who is seated beside her Bridegroom in heavenly places? He called us to this seat in the heavenly places to intercede and co-labor with Him. The bride is on earth in her prayer closet, perhaps in the morning while in her bathrobe or in the dark hours of the night; she has the Word of God in her mouth and declares into the earth what she has heard from the throne room in heaven. She speaks things that are not as though they are, thus finding an open portal for delivery of heaven's desires into the earth. Let us remember that the bride is gender neutral throughout the Song of Solomon. All believers are sons of God, as we are all the bride of Christ.

We must grow up, mature, and hear the bridal message. The Lord is not calling us to the "easy street" but to an overcoming life that is in partnership with the Bridegroom. Even to this day I am still learning how much He loves me and how to respond to such intimate love. He is equipping me for the next stage in my life, which is to rule and reign with Him. These measures of equipping are "big-boy pants," or "big-girl panties." They are not for a child. The call is to maturity so that we may be useful for His plans. The call to "press in" is loud and clear.

When we identify with Christ, we humbly and powerfully know our position. Our eyes become enlightened to see who we are in Christ, which gives us the confidence by faith to assume this position. We are the hope of His calling, co-heirs to the throne. Everything which belongs to Christ belongs also to us. It has nothing to do with our merit but everything to do with His finished work.

- Our appointment is by Him.
- He is the hope of our calling.
- We are His inheritance.
- His mighty power is the delivering agent.

We need to realize that the Lord has appointed for the oversight of certain parts of the battle and accept our assignments in His kingdom--assignments unique to the individual believer. When we choose to believe God's statement about our identification with Christ, we know His ability can secure any victory. We may go forward in the war of the ages, and our "closet becomes the council chamber" from which spiritual commands go forth. As we agree with Him and speak the word on command, God responds and obeys His Word. Hallelujah! O God, seal my heart--stamp it again!

**The Bride has Moved to the Mountains!**

This ascension to the mountain and hill is a hidden mystery. Paul the apostle explains:

> To me, who am less than the least of all the saints, this grace was given, that I should preach among the Gentiles the unsearchable riches of Christ, and to make all see what is the fellowship of the mystery, which from the beginning of the ages has been hidden in God who created all things through Jesus Christ; to the intent that now the manifold wisdom of God might be made known by the church to the principalities and powers in the heavenly places, according to the eternal purpose which He accomplished in Christ Jesus our Lord, in whom we have boldness and access with confidence through faith in Him. Therefore I ask that you do not lose heart at my tribulations for you, which is your glory.
>
> Ephesians 3:8-13 (ESV)

Do you see what's happening? We are fellowshipping in this mystery! And the manifold wisdom of God is being revealed as He uncovers His treasures to us. He made us alive and raised us up to sit in heavenly places!

- We were dead.
- He raised us alive with Christ.
- He raised us up together.
- We sit together in the heavenly places with Jesus Christ.

**The Challenge**

The call to come away is not a call from conflict but to confront this conflict. It is a call to embrace suffering (myrrh), and it is a call to intercede and worship (frankincense). Have we been ineffective in prayer because we have been unwilling to accept this mission? We are the channels He has chosen to release his supplies. Maturity requires that we eat meat and be strong. The trials push us to places which require us to rise up. Let's press on to maturity and clothe ourselves for the battle! "You...have clothed yourselves with Christ" (Galatians 3:27, NIV).

Let's pray together:

*I come to sit beside You and receive my assignment, Lord.*

*I accept my position.*

*Reveal the truth--equip me to war--give victory in the heavenlies.*

*Make me a portal on earth to usher in Your purposes from heaven.*

*I choose to accept this mission, though it seems "mission impossible."*

*Lord of Glory--Lord mighty in battle,*

*I will ride with You.*

Sarah Ramsey – The Bridegroom's Song

## 15

### The Ravished Heart of Jesus

*You have ravished my heart...with one look of your eyes...*

(Song of Solomon 4:9a).

The bride's commitment to go with the King elicits an overwhelming response! After He reveals the mountainous destination, the Beloved expresses His delight once again. He does not leave her with uncertainty or misunderstanding about His feelings. He openly expresses His love and adoration:

> You have ravished my heart
>
> My sister, my spouse;
>
> You have ravished my heart
>
> With one look of your eyes,
>
> With one link of your necklace.
>
> Song of Solomon 4:9

Once again he uses repetition for emphasis, "You have ravished my heart, my sister, my spouse; you have ravished my heart."

The bride is becoming sensitive to the Holy Spirit bringing pleasure and satisfaction to the King's heart. In the previous chapter we saw Him call her His spouse for the first time. Now He calls her "My sister." His Father is her Father. The lifeblood that is in Him is in her. But she is still His fair one, His bride; and He affirms the spouse role again. She is aware that the Beloved not only loves her, but that He is also *in* love with her. He calls her His sister and His spouse/bride, emphasizing this importance seven times in the Song.

Here are two powerful realities:

- Human nature was necessary. The *sister* designation emphasizes His identification with us in our human nature and His willingness to bear all our sufferings. He could not identify with us in the sibling role prior to the incarnation. Partaking in human nature was necessary in order for Jesus to become our brother.
- The *spouse* designation emphasizes His desire for bridal partnership. The cross was necessary in order for us to become His worthy bride.

This knowledge further expands her identity: She is His sister, and she is His spouse. How different is the love for a sibling from the love for a spouse? I am both to Jesus, and a recipient of both of those kinds of love. This combination should not seem contradictory given Jesus' roles to believers and is not the same as incestuous love. His love for me is bridal love; but we are brought into the kingdom as co-heirs with Him, which denotes a brotherly or sisterly position. Scripture tells us Jesus is not ashamed to call us brothers and sisters (Hebrews 2:10-11). He declares my love is better than wine--it is intoxicating to Him. This declaration is suggestive of a more intimate or passionate spousal relationship but should not interfere or disagree with the brother/sister delineation which comes from the order of God's kingdom.

**The Process**

Another way to look at these dual roles would be to visualize how we grow as individual believers in a progressive nature. We are born again into the kingdom of God as new believers, babes in Christ. We grow from babies into children of God and assume a sibling role with other believers in Christ. Jesus, who came as the Son of Man to take our place on the cross, is our Savior but also our brother and co-heir, sharing the inheritance of the Father. Ultimately, however, He desires the deeply intimate, spousal relationship in which we unabashedly surrender our souls and wills entirely in a relationship which transcends anything formerly known with Him. It hardly seems possible--that I could attain this type of close association and detailed knowledge of my Lord, one in which we are both totally smitten and daily laying down our lives for the benefit and joyful affection of one another, but it is true!

God is love. We would not even know how to love if He had not first given us the capacity to love. He is the source of our love (Romans 5:5). His love far exceeds our love for Him. We have a drip; He is the ocean. We feel His exceedingly precious love, yet we comprehend little the precious reality of His love. When man is drawn to the love of God, it is a response to God's invitation through His Son. When God loves through us, we (His creation) become an extension of the eternal, pre-existent (Creator); and His manifest presence comes to earth. In order for us to know God, He must reveal Himself to us. The Song of Solomon brings revelation about this magnificent attribute of God, and He longs for us to be partakers of His nature.

**Lifting My Eyes, Bending my Neck,**

**Giving my Beloved Pleasure**

The bride ravishes His heart with the singleness of her eyes. The spiritual perception of her eyes and the affirmative response of her neck give him much pleasure. Throughout the Song we have seen the eyes as a prominent feature. The necklace adorns her yielded neck. It is not what you have done (your ministry) or who you know; but you, His fair one, His spouse, can ravish the heart of God with your singleness of vision and submission to His desires. Her single eye, the surrendered will, represented by the necklace, brings this response. Each individual act of sincerity towards Him is one link of this golden chain as first mentioned in 1:10. Every move (link) of her dedication moves His heart. Isn't the Word of God wonderful? Each act of obedience is pleasing to the Lord. If one glance moves His heart, what will a fixed gaze do to Him?

**Unshared Love**

This unshared love is reserved for Him alone, the jealous love of God that seals our heart (SOS 8:6). As James 4:5 states, "...do you think that the Scripture says in vain, 'The Spirit who dwells in us yearns jealously?'" This verse is speaking in the context of prayer and warning us against becoming adulterers and adulteresses (or friends) with the world. We see the same message in the Song of Solomon and James, in the Old Covenant and the New. It is a love story preparing the bridal response, "I will not give my heart to another."

This is the "how to":

- set your gaze
- set your eyes (Acts 13:9)
- set your mind (Colossians 3:2), and
- set your heart (2 Chronicles 11:14)

Sitting in meditation brings revelation. Prophesy to yourself: I am loved! I am the fairest! I am accepted in the Beloved. I am the Beloved's and He is mine. Keep focused! Maintain the gaze! Submit to His plan, and ravish the heart of your Bridegroom.

Selah! Just take a deep breath and rest in this truth.

**Revealing and Awakening**

The Holy Spirit is revealing the lovesick heart of God and awakening this love in His people. God's emotions are stirred. Remember, obedience is the outworking of our love for God. Jesus knew God the Father loved the church as much as the Father loved Him. We see this specifically as Jesus prayed in Gethsemane, "You have sent Me, and have loved them as You have loved Me" (John 17:23). Faith will come as we hear, believe, and confess His words. Reading and knowledge alone will not cause these truths to be effective.

- We need the Holy Spirit's help.
- We need to cooperate and agree with Him.
- We need "the light bulb to go on" (i.e., the Holy Spirit's illumination).
- We need to hear what He is saying.
- We must be doers of the Word (Matthew 7:24).
- We need to meditate like Joshua (Joshua 1:8) and David (Psalm 1:2) and chew on these truths as a cow chews her cud as it grazes the field.

Jesus' words in John 17:23 reveal that (1) the Father loves us as He loves the Son and (2) Jesus loves us as God loves us. Speaking to His disciples He said, "As the Father loved me, I also have loved you" (John 15:9). Jesus is saying, "I want to tell you something. Come lean on My breast and let your ear hear what I am saying: *Father God loves you just like He loves Me.*"

God makes Himself transparent and vulnerable to His bride when He says, "You have ravished my heart, my sister...my spouse." The extravagant passions of God are uncovered in this passage, giving us a picture of true intimacy. Bob Mumford defines intimacy as this: "Into me He sees." Say that aloud and hear how it sounds. We serve a God with deep feelings and are made in His image. Our deep feelings and longings originate from Him, and can, therefore, be completely fulfilled only by Him. Many counterfeits distract and get us off track. The key is keeping our eyes single and yielding to His authority.

**O, How He Loves Me So**

The Bridegroom continues to reveal how He enjoys and desires her with these words:

> How fair is your love,
>
> My sister, my spouse!
>
> How much better than wine is your love,

> And the scent of your perfumes
>
> Than all spices!
>
> Song of Solomon 4:10

We all learn by rote--by hearing things over and over--just as children learn the Alphabet Song. Isaiah teaches that we learn through repetition, "For precept must be upon precept, precept upon precept; line upon line, line upon line; Here a little, there a little" (Isaiah 28:10, KJV). The Bridegroom reinforces her identity and the beauty of her love by telling her over and over that she is His heart's desire. Once again, He affirms her as His sister and spouse. His heart is filled with delight as He repeats the words she spoke to Him in SOS 1:2b, "How much better than wine is your love." The wine of this world offers a cheap counterfeit to the love God desires to pour into our hearts. Our love refreshes Him and makes Him glad. It fills the atmosphere with the fragrance of Christ; the scent of her perfume is better than all spices. Spices and perfumes were expensive aromas indulged by royalty. Our love refreshes Him and makes Him glad.

We are beautiful in the sight of God. Our love is better than wine. His words continue to reinforce this truth.

> Your lips, O my spouse,
>
> Drip as the honeycomb;

> Honey and milk are under your tongue;
>
> And the fragrance of your garments
>
> Is like the fragrance of Lebanon.
>
> Song of Solomon 4:11

Recall, "Your lips," refers to her speech (4:3). Her words are as sweet as honey and as nourishing as milk. Words are formed by the tongue. He compares her words to the milk and honey of the Promised Land. Honey is sweet and strengthens weakness. Milk provides nutrients to feed the young and build up the tender. She speaks slowly, like sweet honey dripping from a honeycomb, rather than gushing forth like a torrential stream from a fire hose. Her garments are fragrant and represent the righteous acts of the saints. In Revelation 3:18 Jesus counsels us to buy from Him "white garments." "And to her [His spouse/the church] it was granted to be arrayed in fine linen, clean and bright, for the fine linen is the righteous acts of the saints" (Revelation 19:8). I love how Scripture interprets Scripture!

> I will greatly rejoice in the LORD,
>
> My soul shall be joyful in my God;
>
> For He has clothed me with the garments of salvation,
>
> He has covered me with the robe of righteousness,
>
> As the bridegroom decks himself with ornaments,

And as a bride adorns herself with jewels.

Isaiah 61:10


Jesus gave us the garment of praise for the spirit of heaviness (Isaiah 61:3). Garments are seen from the outside--they cover nakedness. Although she is in the world, she has His fragrance on her attitudes and behaviors. The white garments referenced in Revelation clothe us to cover our shame (nakedness). Shame is the result of sin--the awareness of our shortcomings. Rather than hide our nakedness in darkness, Jesus provides robes of righteousness (bridal clothes) when we are cleansed with His blood. Scripture also instructs us to clothe ourselves with humility (1 Peter 5:5) and put on the armor of light (Romans 13:12). We "put on" Christ (Romans 13:14) and are covered with the sweet fragrance of Christ.


Fragrance is invisible and is discerned by the sense of smell. A special spiritual fragrance is released as a believer moves in the anointing of the Holy Spirit. It is distinctive and hard to describe. You just want another "whiff" of that fragrance. The bride's fragrance is enticing to the Bridegroom, subtle and lingering, which draws Him closer to inhale her sweet scent. Mary of Bethany anointed Jesus, and the house was filled with the fragrance of the oil (John 12:3). Second Corinthians 2:15 says, "...we are to God the fragrance of Christ among those who are being saved and among those who are perishing."


This fragrance is obtained from sitting close to the

Bridegroom—intimacy with Him. It gets onto a person. It is not the ointment itself, but the uniqueness of the fragrance as it blends with her own natural scent that is so alluring to Him. She smells like Jesus. It is like hugging someone and having their fragrance—like perfume, smoke, or food—linger on you. It is the fragrance of God on His bride, and she smells good to the Bridegroom. Fragrance is also released when words reveal the thoughts and intent of the hearts. "Out of the abundance of the heart the mouth speaks" (Matthew 12:34). Her words and her heart agree. She is still on earth, but her garments have a heavenly fragrance. She is in the King's chambers, and His fragrance penetrates her clothes like smoke rising from incense. He enables me to bring the fragrance of heaven to earth as I sit and soak in Him.

The bride is filled with His love, and it makes the Beloved's heart full of joy. Isn't it wonderful to be able to provide this pleasure for your King and to have the aroma of His anointing oil upon your life?

Let's pray together:

*Oh, Lord, I ravish Your heart with one look of my eye;*

*It is my delight to do Your will.*

*Oh, let me set my gaze on You, My Beloved.*

*Help me believe these extravagant words about myself.*

*Holy Spirit, help me focus. Help me gaze intently.*

*Draw me, Lord.*

*Draw me and lavish Your fragrance on me!*

*Amen*

## 16

### The Garden Enclosed

*A garden enclosed is my sister, my spouse…*

(Song of Solomon 4:12a).

The discourse continues as the Bridegroom prophesies and affirms His love for the bride. He acknowledges her fruitfulness and begins to describe her life as a fragrant garden.

> A garden enclosed
>
> Is my sister, my spouse,
>
> A spring shut up,
>
> A fountain sealed.
>
> Your plants are an orchard of pomegranates
>
> With pleasant fruits,
>
> Fragrant henna with spikenard,
>
> Spikenard and saffron,
>
> Calamus and cinnamon,

> With all trees of frankincense,
>
> Myrrh and aloes,
>
> With all the chief spices--
>
> A fountain of gardens,
>
> A well of living waters,
>
> And streams from Lebanon.
>
> Song of Solomon 4:12-15

## A Garden Enclosed, a Spring Shut Up, a Fountain Sealed

The bride's deep devotion to Jesus is described as a private garden. She has yielded to the discipline of being a disciple, and the Bridegroom proclaims that she is His private garden. She is not available or open to the spirit of the world. The NASB calls this a "locked" garden. Her heart is locked, and only the Beloved has the key. His affirmation of His bride in this way is exceedingly powerful and beautiful. These words are His confession of the bride. Her heart is not just a garden, but an enclosed garden, hidden away for the pleasure and delight of the Bridegroom King. The bride's heart is now accessible to the King alone.

The purpose of this garden is not for the growing of crops, but for the pleasure of the owner. Wow, what a thought! The beauty and fragrance of the plants are for the King's enjoyment, and it is to this place He goes for respite and refreshment. God began His good work in a garden in Eden. The bride says, "I am His garden, delighting and satisfying the Lord who planted me!"

This enclosed garden is supplied with springs and fountains from within. The figurative language implies privacy, walled and protected from public access. She is sealed and set apart for Jesus. She keeps herself chaste and pure. This enclosed garden is supplied with springs and fountains from within. In contrast, a public well is open and vulnerable to pollution and disease. The "springs" and "fountains" are sources of water within the bride and represent the Holy Spirit and the different ways He impacts her heart. Water is symbolic of the Holy Spirit throughout Scripture.[1]

Jesus' words in John 7:37-39 confirm this symbolism:

> Anyone who is thirsty may come to me! Anyone who believes in me may come and drink! For the Scriptures declare, 'Rivers of living water will flow from his heart.' (When he said "living water," he was speaking of the Spirit, who would be given to everyone believing in him. But the Spirit had not yet been given, because Jesus had not yet entered into his glory.) NLT

These Scriptures clearly teach the "living water," which Jesus said would flow from our hearts, refers to "the Spirit." Why does Jesus liken the Spirit to water? Water conveys life and vitality. Without it, life on Earth would be extinguished. By referring to the Spirit as "living water," Jesus is saying the Spirit is the very essence of life.[2]

The Lord ascended into heaven to usher forth the release of the Spirit. Jesus said to His disciples, "Nevertheless, I tell you the truth; It is expedient for you that I go away: for if I do not go away, the Comforter will not come unto you; but if I depart, I will send Him unto you" (John 16:7, KJV). All the spiritual refreshment and irrigation which flows into the lives of believers today is the outflow from the Spirit of life descending from the throne room of heaven. Jesus ascended (Acts 1) and released the river (John 7) and gave us the gift of the Holy Spirit, the promise of the Father (John 16:7). Ah, Selah!

**The Fruitful Garden**

> Your plants are an orchard of pomegranates
>
> With pleasant fruits,
>
> Song of Solomon 4:13a

A garden full of fruit glorifies the Father. A garden is planted with the purpose of bearing much fruit and is not meant to be unproductive or desolate. "By this My Father is glorified, that you bear much fruit," (John 15:8).

> Fragrant henna with spikenard,
>
> Spikenard and saffron,
>
> Calamus and cinnamon,
>
> With all trees of frankincense,
>
> Myrrh and aloes,
>
> With all the chief spices.
>
> Song of Solomon 4:14

The symbolism here is magnificent! Nine spices are mentioned--in particular, all the *chief* spices. The nine spices referenced represent the nine-fold fruit of the Holy Spirit Paul describes in Galatians 5:22: love, joy, peace, longsuffering, kindness, goodness, faithfulness, gentleness, and self-control. Can you see the correlation of these fruits with the individual spices? In his book, *Song of Songs*, Watchman Nee refers to this representation as "…the finished work of Jesus."[3] Jesus anoints His bride with the Holy Spirit and produces a garden filled with fragrant fruit and spices.

## Water Within, Water Flowing Out

Not only is her garden full of the fruit of the Spirit, but there are also sources of water nourishing and flowing within her garden:

> A fountain of gardens,
>
> A well of living waters,
>
> And streams from Lebanon.
>
> Song of Solomon 14:15

The Holy Spirit manifests Himself as water in her enclosed garden. We saw this allusion previously in the "spring shut up." Here, the Bridegroom mentions the fountain again and expounds upon the water concept with "a well" and "streams." The well-watered garden stays green and produces fruit; it glorifies Jesus and blesses His people. Streams or rivers are flowing and are consistent within God's plan. They surge and are not stagnant.

The river concept should not be overlooked here. The Bible begins and ends with rivers; and in the middle of the Word, Jesus speaks of rivers during his earthly ministry. The Song of Solomon, once again, connects the pieces and forms a bridge between the Old Covenant and New. We first see rivers in the

Garden of Eden (Genesis 2:10), where God placed man. Mankind fell in the original garden. Jesus spoke of rivers during the Feast of Tabernacles, a feast symbolic of the restorative plan of mankind for God's people. He went up to the temple and taught, stood, and cried out, saying, "If anyone thirsts, let him come to Me and drink. He who believes in Me, as the Scripture has said, out of his heart (belly) will flow rivers of living water. But this He spoke concerning the Spirit, whom those believing in Him would receive" (John 7:37-39). It is exceedingly significant that Jesus made this bold claim during observance of this particular feast (also called *Sukkot*), which celebrated a time of restored fellowship with the Lord. Revelation 22:1 says the river of God flows from underneath the throne of God in heaven. We will encounter another river in heaven when redemption has been made full.

The process of becoming an enclosed garden is a lifelong progression--line upon line and precept upon precept, through many acts of obedience. The believer bears fruit on the Vine. Jesus said, "As the branch cannot bear fruit of itself, unless it abides in the vine, neither can you, unless you abide in Me. I am the vine, you are the branches. He who abides in Me, and I in him, bears much fruit; for without Me you can do nothing" (John 15:4-5). Fruit will abound in the life of the bride as she is dependent upon the Holy Spirit, allowing Him to water her garden. The bride is the branch connected to the vine of Christ, which produces much fruit bringing glory to the Father.

We saw the Bridegroom come from the wilderness with words of affirmation. He is now sowing seeds back into His garden. He returns to His enclosed garden looking for fruit and is very pleased with what He finds. This passage in Chapter 4 is such a powerful one. As always, His affirming words bring even greater release, equipping her for more.

**Come Spirit, Come and Blow**

At this point she is willing to relinquish control with confidence and faith that her position in Christ is sufficient. She asks for more and calls for the wind of the Holy Spirit to awaken and come. The "Welcome, Holy Spirit" sign is hung outside her garden.

> Awake, O north wind,
>
> And come, O south!
>
> Blow upon my garden,
>
> That its spices may flow out.
>
> Song of Solomon 4:16a

She invites the Holy Spirit's participation to blow at His will. "Come north wind or come south wind," is saying that she trusts the Holy Spirit to choose and designate the wind needed to accomplish His purpose in her life. She knows she is well equipped and able to continue. Such times occur in our lives when we refocus and desire more of Jesus. She bids Him, "Let my Beloved come to His garden and eat its pleasant fruits."

**Food for Thought**

As we seek more and move into the heavenly places praying for God's kingdom to come to earth, we embark on an ambitious journey. The blustering forces often begin to blow upon our lives just as we requested. The south winds are warm and refreshing, and we welcome them. They carry the heady scent of spring and the balminess of summer. The north winds, however, often take us by surprise. They are invigorating, but cold, brisk, and penetrating. The fragrance released over the spices by the lung-tingling north wind is completely different from the fragrances brought by the south wind. She welcomes the Spirit to choose and indicates she will cooperate with Him, no matter which direction the wind blows.

The Lord deals with us in different ways during the various seasons of our lives. Times of planting and fruitfulness come in the spring and summer seasons, and we rejoice in the abundance of growth as we anticipate the harvest. The south winds stir up the fragrances of our fruitfulness as we reap the rewards of our labor. When the harvest does come, it is again making way for a new season. Winter arrives and with it a time of cleansing and barrenness. The north winds are cold and harsh but release an exhilarating fragrance from deep within us that the gentle winds from the south can never reach.

The bride relinquishes control when she invites the Spirit to choose the direction from which He will blow. She is saying, "Have your way with me, not my will but yours." She is maturing and trusting her Beloved to choose the circumstances which will bring the most growth in her life. She welcomes both the fruitfulness of the growing season and the emptiness which follows harvest, knowing both are needed for a healthy garden.

**Putting it Into Practice**

Many times on my journey it seems I have been backed into a corner and have had to choose to believe God. During one of those seasons, I began to learn to keep the gate closed when fear comes knocking. One day, this verse in the Living Bible came alive to me and illuminated my mind as I read,

> We need have no fear of someone who loves us perfectly; his perfect love for us eliminates all dread of what he might do to us.
>
> If we are afraid, it is for fear of what he might do to us and shows that we are not fully convinced that he really

loves us.

So you see, our love for him comes as a result of his loving us first.

1 John 4:18-19 TLB

Trusting in His perfect love is the lesson the maiden is learning at this point in the journey. It is vital for us to learn this lesson as well.

Making the choice to believe in the dark what is learned in the light is a real decision of the will. Sometimes we are pressed into battle so God can teach our hands to war. A warrior who has never practiced combat will be ill-equipped on the front lines of battle. It is scary and overwhelming, but when we know we are loved we can surrender our wills and yield to His leadership-- "thy will be done." When we know we are loved perfectly, we can endure--we can resist giving up and trust His ability for the courage to fight the good fight of faith. Our God is the Lord of Glory, the Lord Mighty in Battle, and He is well acquainted with the enemy. He is not surprised by what is in the dark. In Him, there is no darkness at all. I have learned and am still learning to stand my ground and not run away in fear when I open the door and a (spiritual) "bear" jumps out of the closet. Hallelujah!

In Psalm 24 David teaches that when we open the gates and lift up the doors to the King of Glory, He *will* come in. When we make our abode in Him, we have what we need for victory.

Remember that we have the full armor of Christ. We can get dressed, cover our nakedness and vulnerability to sin, and be prepared to embrace the north wind when it blows. This battle is one which requires perseverance and diligence in order to stay focused and keep the shield of faith in place.

The Lord began to teach me some of these principles as I prayed over some situations I was facing. "Holy Spirit, brood over the darkness and let there be light." When the light came on, I was surprised when it revealed a "bear" growling back at me. Often enemies are hiding where we are unaware, but the Lord knows they are there. He wants to expose them and calls us to war against them. The north wind appears out of nowhere, it seems, and howls and hisses, hitting us head on. When we surrender that place to the Lord, His sweet fragrance can be found even in difficult situations. We are more than conquerors and have the victory! Let's run together in the full armor of God and stay connected like a well-formed army and overcome the coming battles!

Let's pray:

*It is my desire, Lord Jesus, to be a garden enclosed.*

*I desire to yield to the wind of the Holy Spirit.*

*I can take courage and pray with the maiden,*

*Awake O north wind,*

*And come O south!*

*Blow upon my garden,*

*That its spices may flow out.*

*Amen*

## The Garden Party

*Let my beloved come into his garden…*

(Song of Solomon 4:16b)

**The Turning Point in the Journey**

We have reached the halfway point in the Song of Solomon. The bride has approached an important turning point in her life with the Beloved. This time is one of transition in her journey. By inviting both the north and south winds to come, the maiden has welcomed the Holy Spirit to come and take over. And now she bids her Beloved,

Let my beloved come into his garden

And eat its pleasant fruit.

Song of Solomon 4:16b

## **The Garden**

(Paraphrased) "Come, my Beloved, into Your garden and eat": Her desire is that He finds pleasure. She is saying, "Lord Jesus, enjoy what the Holy Spirit has produced in me." What she previously described as "my garden" (v. 16a) is now referred to as *His garden*. Her complete subjection to His possession of her assets is implicit in this simple statement. She invites Him to enter the whole garden of her inner life, and the fruits found therein are for His delight. The bride's response denotes her intent to glorify God through unconditional surrender and a rededication to His purposes.

Watchman Nee wrote:

> This was the Lord's garden. From this statement we learn that He had not always frequented it, but has come only in response to special entreaty. Let us remember this solemn lesson, that though a first dedication may make us truly the Lord's, yet only many and constant dedications can ever persuade the Lord to come into His garden in this manner. He will come only when there are fruit and spice to satisfy. Let us take heed lest self-satisfaction beset our souls in supposing that all is well

enough simply because we belong to the Lord. Many, many times this fact ought to come to us as a repeated warning, and again and again we should entreat the Lord to come to us and find what He wants. Or else, in a moment all unawares, you may discover that the Lord has not really come into His garden at all."[1]

## My Story

As I worked on this chapter, a friend of mine gave me a plaque to go into my garden: "Welcome to Sarah's garden." This gift caused me to reflect and remember that it was not my garden, but His all along. I want to be His garden. I began to recall a time in my life when I was learning to devote myself to seeking God more intimately and learning how to pray. During this time I was told about a group of people who prayed at Belmont Church in Nashville, Tennessee, which is about eighty miles from my home Cookeville. I desired to be effective in prayer. So I drove to Nashville by myself at least once and sometimes two times each month to pray and learn more about prayer. I continued the commute for several years until prayer grew in Cookeville. I was hungry to seek God and felt led to pursue a deeper prayer life. We went to the state capitol and prayed; we went to the Ryman Auditorium and prayed, as well as to other prayer venues in Nashville. But many times it was just ten or twenty of us gathered in a room at Belmont Church praying. We didn't know each other; but we had a connection through the Holy Spirit Who united us. We were learning to focus upon and emphasize the purposes and plans of God in our lives, the lives of our families, and the cities of the regions represented. We were tending God's Garden and bringing Him pleasure through our obedience. I began to consider embracing prayer, not as merely one of the spiritual disciplines, but as my assignment from God.

During this time, I became more aware of trusting God's will to come to earth as it is in heaven and of calling His will down from the heavenlies. I began to receive a deeper understanding of the power of declaring and proclaiming God's will into the earth. The power of my words spoken out loud began to carry more weight as I gained a greater revelation of how I was created in the image of God. Man is the only creature given the creative power to speak life and death into situations. This Scripture quickened me and became alive in my spirit (Proverbs 18:21, NAS)[2]. Declaring God's Word aloud in prayer helped me turn loose and trust God's will for me, my family, God's family, the nation of Israel, my city, my nation, and the nations of the world. It was a specific time I chose to say, "Come, Wind, blow upon my garden; Spirit of God, You choose north or south winds." In a real sense, I was learning to yield my garden to become His.

**Jesus Comes to His Garden**

The bride has issued an invitation, and the Beloved's response is quick and enthusiastic:

> I have come to my garden, my sister, my spouse;
>
> I have gathered my myrrh with my spice;
>
> I have eaten my honeycomb with my honey;
>
> I have drunk my wine with my milk.
>
> Song of Solomon 5:1

Jesus' response reveals the value of repeated and continual recommitment as we grow and mature in bridal love. The bride shows us how to communicate continually our desire for the Lord to come and have total access in our lives by declaring, "I am Your garden. I am Yours! I am my Beloved's."

"I am Your garden": Is this your confession? Say it out loud a few times.

The bride gives her Beloved a "full cup." He had planted and cultivated this garden. Now He comes to enjoy the harvest. He is not afraid to declare that she belongs to Him, not in a domineering way, but in a joyful proclamation that she is His treasured possession, greatly valued and worthy of celebration.

The Beloved is quick to take possession. There are nine "my's" in verse 1 and four "I have's":

1. My garden,
2. My sister,
3. My spouse,
4. My myrrh,
5. My spice,
6. My honeycomb,
7. My honey,
8. My wine,
9. My milk.

**The Garden Party--By Invitation Only**

Oh, My! What a day! "I have come to enjoy my garden in you, My sister, My spouse," is the Beloved's quick response. He identifies the bride in numerous ways and begins the conversation by acknowledging the suffering she endured (the myrrh), the sweetness developed slowly over time (the honey), the wine to make the heart glad, and the milk to nourish the young. None of this has gone unnoticed by the Beloved. "I have gathered My myrrh and spice, I have eaten My honey and honeycomb, and I drink My wine and My milk." She is cherished and acclaimed.

"I have come," the Beloved says, "to gather, to eat, and to

drink." Jesus accepts full ownership of her garden. Mike Bickle says, "This is her turning point in her progression of maturity in this love song. Jesus is greatly enjoying His bride. He begins here to enjoy His inheritance."[3] What an awesome day! Jesus has come into my garden at my invitation, announcing once more that I am His sister in Christ and spouse. He has just spoken over me words full of power and life, words which empower me to make the commitment to go to the mountain of myrrh and hill of frankincense once again. I agree with His Word and set my will to believe the power of His words. No word of God will ever fail (Luke 1:37, NIV); with God, nothing will be impossible (Luke 1:37, NKJV). He is able to accomplish what He speaks, and He has declared what I am; therefore, I will go. "Be it unto me according to Your Word" (Luke 1:38).

When Jesus is invited, *He comes*. Do not overlook this precious bit of insight. He went to the wedding in Cana and performed His first recorded miracle. He went to Matthew's house. He went to Zacchaeus' house. When Jesus is invited into the garden of a life, He comes. The garden is provided as a place for Jesus to have fellowship and communion with His bride. In the beginning, God took the man and put him into the garden of Eden to tend and keep it. God enjoyed uninhibited fellowship with man in Eden before the fall. Jesus desires to have uninhibited fellowship with us in the garden of our hearts as He redeems and makes us whole. When we offer our hearts, He quickly accepts the invitation and sees there is much to share.

Eat, O friends!

> Drink, yes, drink deeply,
>
> O beloved ones!
>
> Song of Solomon 5:1c

He extends the invitation for others to eat and drink with generosity. It is time for a garden party! The bride has the fruit of the Spirit hanging on her branches for others to enjoy. She is an exceedingly abundant and fruitful vine! Jesus gathers the fruit of the Holy Spirit in her life and partakes, tasting her sweetness--and He wants His friends to enjoy the fruit her life has produced. She has much to share. He is ready to celebrate and wants everyone to enjoy His bride.

When I trust my Beloved, it makes Him so happy that His heart is ravished. It makes my heart leap to think He is happy with me--that I could be the source of His pleasure and delight. It is beyond my comprehension; but He wastes no time gathering, eating, drinking, and bringing His friends to celebrate His love for me. It is truly a timeless tale of love. Selah!

When I ask for the kisses of His mouth, I receive his loving affection. Intimacy has produced a garden the Beloved can call His own. We can prepare a table for Jesus when we allow the Holy Spirit to fill us up, overflow, and produce fruit in our lives. When we drink deeply of the new wine, He does more than we can ask or imagine. He knows the desires of our heart, even before we ask. I'm so glad He chose me so that now I can freely choose Him in return. Won't you join me? What a day! What a party!

Let's pray:

*Come to Your garden, my Beloved.*

*I am an enclosed garden, a fountain sealed and set apart for You.*

*The fragrance of Your spices flow out and the scent of your Spirit is heavy upon me.*

*Streams of living waters nourish me from within.*

*Awake, O north winds. Awake, O south winds and blow.*

*I trust You, my Beloved with the directions of the winds.*

*You know what my garden needs to be fruitful.*

*Come to Your garden, my Beloved.*

*The fruits of Your Spirit are plentiful.*

*Taste and find delight, divine pleasures evermore.*

Sarah Ramsey – The Bridegroom's Song

## 18

### Another Challenge

*Open for me, my sister, my love, my perfect one.*

*Song of Solomon 5:2b*

**The Party is Over**

I just want to open this chapter with a big, "WHEW!" The party is over! But what a wonderful time we had at the garden party!

In the last ten verses of Chapter 4 (vv. 6-16), many changes occurred. The bride committed to go to the mountain of myrrh and the hill of frankincense with the Beloved. She believed the Beloved's words of affirmation and surrendered her enclosed garden to Him. She desired to go deeper in bridal intimacy and called for the wind of the Holy Spirit to come and blow. The acceptance of having the Beloved and His friends enjoy the fruit of her garden was overwhelming. Now the party is over, and the bride is ready to rest. She is winding down, and her body needs and finds refreshment; but her heart recognizes His Spirit brooding over her, even as she sleeps.

**The Voice of My Beloved**

The natural response after such a rewarding time with the Beloved and His friends would be to rest; but the scene changes yet again before she has scarcely had time to catch her breath.

> I sleep, but my heart is awake;
>
> It is the voice of my beloved!
>
> He knocks, saying,
>
> "Open for me, my sister, my love,
>
> My dove, my perfect one;
>
> For my head is covered with dew,
>
> My locks with the drops of the night."
>
> Song of Solomon 5:2

As she sleeps and is at rest, her heart is awake to the voice of the Beloved. He knocks and makes the simple request, "Open for me." He seeks *her*—He takes the initiative. Her heart is fully awake to spiritual things, with no conscious areas of compromise. During this address to the bride, in typical form, the Beloved once again conveys His pleasure with affirming words, which are becoming easily recognizable as His choice terms of endearment. He sees her commitment to be His one and only and acknowledges her pledge. She exalts Him above all other beloveds. Four times His voice reassures her saying, "You are mine!" His words impart volumes: "My sister, My love, My dove, My perfect one."

"You are mine"--this declaration has fourfold meaning here:

1. My sister--He tells her, "We have the same Father!"
2. My love--He reminds her again that she is His favorite, the fairest.
3. My dove--He considers her eyes, focused on Him alone.
4. My perfect one -- "Perfect" also translates as "mature," indicating her heart's response is completely towards Him and is no longer easily swayed by distractions.

**Opening to a New Revelation**

The Lord has come to reveal Himself in another dimension to His loved one as He stands and asks to come in this time. He portrays Himself in a new way through this request and demonstrates His desire that she would completely open herself to Him. Consider what may be implied when you read this intriguing, almost foreboding, description: "for my head is covered with dew, my locks with the drops of the night."

Watchman Nee says it this way:

> So we find the Lord saying, 'Open to me,' implying a new call to His loved one to open the heart still further to Him and to receive Him now as one covered with the drops of the night....[1]

The bride has drifted asleep, only to hear the voice of the Beloved call her to a deeper place. She could linger here in a time of rest. However, the Lord comes seeking an open door for a new revelation. We have not yet seen Him in this light. It seems almost out of character until we realize the implications of His appearance. His head is covered with dew--with the drops of the night. He has been interceding into the wee hours, with beads of dew like perspiration on his crown. She is about to learn that He is inviting her to a different place, one with anguish in the intimacy, like one marked by the indelible suffering experienced in the Garden of Gethsemane.

She cannot fully understand His pursuit here. It reminds me of the disciples in the Garden of Gethsemane on the night Jesus was handed over to the Roman soldiers. He told them to watch and pray while He anguished in prayer deeper into the Garden. They could not even stay awake long enough to keep watch with Him and, while Jesus prayed, drifted to sleep only hours before His crucifixion. They nodded off even as Jesus was sweating drops of blood in anticipation of the cross He would endure on their behalf.

**The Reluctant Bride's Response**

She responds to His call to open with the question, "How can I... How can I?" She asks, not just once but twice:

> I have taken off my robe;
>
> How can I put it on again?
>
> I have washed my feet;
>
> How can I defile them?
>
> Song of Solomon 5:3

She wonders why she needs to get up when she has just taken off her robe and washed her feet. It sounds as if she is ready to sit back, prop up her feet, and relax. She is no longer wearing her own robe but has put on the robe of His righteousness and the garments of His salvation (Isaiah 64:6, 61:10, Zechariah 3:5). She is aware of the daily cleansing of Jesus in her life. When her Beloved comes and asks her to arise during a period of rest, she expresses a moment of hesitation by responding, "How can I... How can I?" Even though she does not understand and her heart still has questions, she turns to hear His call.

Great challenges often follow great victories. Have you noticed? This perilous pause leaves the Lord outside in the night! Being willing to change is necessary for progress. Spiritual complacency prevents us from being positioned to receive from the Lord and indicates our refusal to be motivated to a higher calling.

Sometimes obedience is required without understanding. In this place we are asked to leave our understanding at the door and simply trust. God often asks us to sign a blank sheet of paper that He will fill out later; but rest assured--His intentions towards us are always good. Trusting God does not always require our "knowing" what comes next. We can't always see what's down the road, but He can. Could it be that we wouldn't go down the road if we knew exactly what lies ahead, whether or not it is for our good? Maybe He conceals at times so that He may later reveal when we are ready to receive what is in store for us.

**My Heart Yearns**

Previously, the Shulamite's commitment was, "I will go to the mountain of myrrh." (Do you remember the sachet of myrrh between her breasts in Chapter 1? Myrrh is the burial spice that covers the stench of death.) Just what is He asking her to do?

The Beloved has arrived during a time of rest after this tremendous party and is calling, "Open for Me." Even though He is loving on her, His head is covered with dew; and His locks are wet with the drops of the night.

> My beloved put his hand
>
> By the latch of the door,
>
> And my heart yearned for him.
>
> I arose to open for my beloved,
>
> And my hands dripped with myrrh,
>
> My fingers with liquid myrrh,
>
> On the handles of the lock.
>
> I opened for my beloved,
>
> But my beloved had turned away and was gone.
>
> Song of Solomon 5:4-6

My Beloved put His hand on the latched door. As I feel His hand on my heart, I yearn for Him and arise to open. I love the hand of God, gentle but firm. The hand of God was on Elijah, Judah, and Ezekiel, as well as the apostles, as they prospered, prophesied, witnessed, and turned others to the Lord (1 Kings 18:46, 2 Chronicles 30:12, Ezekiel 1:3, Acts 11:21). Among several requests in a prayer, including a plea for the Lord's blessing so that he might be a blessing to others, Jabez nobly asked for the hand of the Lord. The Lord responded and increased his territory (1 Chronicles 4:10). We will learn later in this chapter that the hands of the Beloved are pure gold. They are kingly and divine, strong with intent and purpose.

*O God, let your hand be on the latch of my heart!*

The touch of His hand awakened in the heart of the bride a yearning which motivated her to arise and open--even to the possibility of suffering without understanding. This call is distinct and carries directive. It is a call to open and suffer with Him and for Him. It is a deeper place of intimacy she has not yet fully experienced. Note that the Beloved's hand is on the latch; but the door was *locked* until she arose and gave permission for Him to enter. The Beloved never forcefully takes us to the Garden of Gethsemane. We must go willingly, as He did. His hand causes her heart to yearn for Him; and although His hands are dripping with myrrh and she first responds with reluctance, she ultimately arises to go.

**Choosing to Arise and Open**

As she chooses to rise and open the door for her Beloved, she grasps the handle; and her hands likewise drip with myrrh, spreading from the lock He had just touched. She is moving into a place where she is palpably able to identify with where He has been. She sees now what He is asking of her. Goodness! When I put my hands where His hands have been, my hands become lathered and softened in His liquid myrrh. We identify with Christ when we begin to experience the bitterness of sufferings and betrayals.

Myrrh trees produce sap which is harvested for its aromatic qualities. Liquid oozes from the myrrh tree when it is pierced and the skin of the tree is broken. The sap which drains from the fresh wound in the tree is bitter and raw. This image symbolizes the intensity of Jesus' suffering in Gethsemane and the wounds He suffered upon a tree. These wounds bring a spiritual sweetness and healing balm when applied to our lives. Liquid myrrh symbolic of the droplets of blood which flowed from Jesus' hands. His suffering was for a purpose, as our suffering is always for a purpose. He never asks us to do anything He has not already been willing to endure. Having been found in Christ, the Apostle Paul recognized the purpose of suffering for the Lord. His words in the letter to the Philippians eloquently describe the losses and gains which accompany this faith relationship "...that I may know Him and the power of His resurrection, and the fellowship of His sufferings, being conformed to His death" (3:10). Suffering is necessary so that we may come to know Him more and be transformed into His likeness. Have you ever prayed for God to reveal Himself to you more powerfully, only to encounter painful struggles and heartaches ahead? Be careful, therefore, how you pray; and be willing to allow your circumstances to mold you into His image, as painful as it may seem.

The bride is choosing to open the door to a new sphere in her relationship with God—suffering on behalf of and for the good of others. He gives us two indications that this season involves hardship to be endured--dew on His head in the night and myrrh on His hands. When His hand is on the latch, her heart yearns for Him. She chooses to arise and open, an indication that she trusts opening the door to Him. His hand will sustain and empower her to do His will. As I choose to arise and open the latch of my heart, I am released to trust open-armed, dripping with His fragrance, and to walk boldly the path set before me to Gethsemane.

**He is Gone!**

The bride opens the door for her Beloved, but no sooner has she done so than she finds He has gone. Oh, she never wanted to be away from Him! She had already experienced the terrifying prospect of being without Him, and she does not want to go that way again. She learned through her previous reluctance to rise and go. The Lord has promised to be with her (and each of us) always, even to the end of the earth. However, she wants His *manifest* presence, the tangible assurance He is there. She is finally willing to walk the walk, but she has no intention of doing it alone. Why, then, does it seem as though He disappears again so quickly?

If you can set yourself in the place of the maiden for a moment, imagine the decision before you. Have you ever entered such a time when confusion and doubt wanted to settle in and make you wonder where on earth the Lord must be? When I find myself at this juncture, I have a decision to make. I can choose to go back to bed or move forward. Certainly, the thick scent of His lingering myrrh reminds me of the suffering ahead, and the only sure victory will come through laying down my life. He has gone ahead of me to Gethsemane. I stand resolute and know the only sure path is forward to meet Him there.

He already knows what is in my heart, but the alert has been issued. The buzzer is going off. "This is a test! This is a test!" This is a test to reveal *to me* and to the daughters of Jerusalem (other believers around me) what is truly in my heart. Now here I stand ready, my hands swathed in myrrh, but He is gone. My heart yearns. I cannot live without Him! I must respond and open my hands to receive whatever this season brings. I would rather suffer with Him than go ahead without Him or remain behind alone. So I walk into the unknown and identify with Christ.

**Moses' Story**

This passage from Song of Solomon 5:6 reminds me of Moses in Exodus 32-33. You may already know those events, but let's refresh ourselves: Moses took a journey up Mount Sinai with Joshua; and God presented him with the Law, the Ten

Commandments. While Moses and Joshua were away on the mountain, the Israelites became restless because they thought Moses was taking too long to return. But because of their impatience the Israelites persuaded Moses' brother Aaron, who had been left in charge, to make an idol to worship in place of the God who had delivered them from Egypt. God revealed to Moses the error of the people's way, and he came down the mountain to a mess. In Moses' absence, the people flagrantly disobeyed; so much so that God purposed to destroy them and start anew with Moses. But Moses pleaded with God on their behalf (Exodus 32:11, 31); and the Bible says, "So the Lord changed His mind about the terrible disaster He had threatened to bring on His people" (Exodus 32:14, NLT). God then told Moses He would send His angel to deliver them, but He Himself would not go with them. Moses was unwilling to accept the offer of the angel of deliverance. He was after the very *presence* of God. In Exodus 33:12, Moses makes this great appeal to God:

> Then Moses said to the Lord, "See, You say to me, 'Bring up this people….' You have said, 'I know you by name, and you have also found grace in My sight.'
> 
> Now therefore, I pray, if have found grace in Your sight, show me now Your way, that I may know you and that I may find grace in Your sight…"
> 
> And He [God] said,
> 
> "My presence will go with you, and I will give you rest."

> Then he [Moses] to Him [God],
>
> "If Your presence does not go with us,
>
> do not bring us up from here.
>
> For how then will it be known that Your people
>
> and I have found grace in Your sight, except You go
>
> with us?"

*O, God! If You don't go with us, we don't want to go. Help us never to be satisfied without Your Presence.*

**The Relentless Bride—The Value of Seeking the Lord**

The bride of Christ is relentless! One thing we continue to learn from the bride is the value of seeking the Lord. She doesn't become angry or pout or go back to bed. She seeks Him. She diligently goes after Him and does not stop until she finds Him. The Word of God says, "And you will seek Me and find Me, when you search for Me with all your heart" (Jeremiah 29:13). The bride demonstrates to us the pattern of how to seek the Lord.

> I sought him, but I could not find him;
>
> I called him, but he gave me no answer.
>
> Song of Solomon 5:6b

I want to be relentless and follow the pattern the bride displays. I want to seek my Beloved. I love, love, love the presence of my Beloved! But can I still be faithful to Him when emotions fail and when I can't feel His presence? Can I stay fervent on His Word alone? Can I hold on when nothing else makes sense? What is in my heart? Will my anchor hold? Did His words from the last season take root enough to hold me until I can see what is in the next season? Do I know who I am? Do I know Whose I am?

> *Father, I am trying to accept Your absence and discipline.*
>
> *I seek You, Lord; help me find You! You know what is in my heart.*
>
> *This season will reveal to me what is in my heart.*

**The Lesson**

This is the lesson when I can't find Him: Seek! Seek Him with my whole heart! The enemy says, "It doesn't work--do something else. His promises aren't true," but the bride says, "Seek!" Perhaps not all discipline from the Lord occurs because we have done something wrong and are in need of correction. Sometimes we must discipline ourselves in specific areas simply to grow stronger. Hebrews Chapter 12 tells us we are chastened (disciplined) by the Lord that we might be partakers of His holiness. The Beloved is teaching her how to remain steadfast *in spite of* her contradictory feelings and how to believe in His Words when nothing else seems to line up. Jesus' feelings did not take Him to the cross. He endured the cross because of His submission to and belief in something greater than the suffering. He endured for the night season and brought many sons to glory. Now He allows us to partake in His holiness as we bear the crosses in our own lives.

When God hides His face, we must stand on His precious Word. Can I fully obey without knowing the next step? Can I fervently seek without immediate breakthrough? My Beloved turned away and was gone; my heart leapt up! When I sought Him, I could not find Him. I called, but He gave me no answer. Can you relate? This is not the time to quit. This is the time to engage and do the things you have been taught. Faith without works is dead (James 2:26). James also encourages us, "Be doers of the Word and not hearers only, deceiving yourselves," (1:22). Today—right now--is the time to arise, open to the Lord, and seek Him once more. Let's run together.

**My Story**

Opening myself to suffering was a challenge that came to my life when my husband was given an unexpected diagnosis of lung cancer. I was working on this verse and chapter when it was diagnosed. As I responded to the news, I felt the Lord say two things:

1. Surrender your husband to Me.

2. "Trust in the Lord with all your heart,

   And lean not on your own understanding;

   In all your ways acknowledge Him,

   And He shall direct your paths" Proverbs 3:5-6.

Many years ago, thirty-six years to be specific, during another time of suffering, the Lord challenged me to live one day at a time. The verse He gave me then was, "Therefore do not worry about tomorrow, for tomorrow will worry about its own things. Sufficient for the day is its own trouble" (Matthew 6:34). As we began this new journey with my husband's illness, He again reminded me to live one day at a time. My husband of fifty-five years died only months later. It was not the way I had thought it would be—God's ways were not my ways. The secret things belong to the Lord. This was a season of suffering with which I was not familiar. I surrendered, and I am thankful to pause and know that God knows what tomorrow brings and that I can trust Him with it. Selah!

We are opening to the unknown. I feel myrrh on my hands as I enter this journey. We don't see the way but we are led by his light and scent. We don't know where we are going or how to get there. But the One knocking, calling me to open, knows the end from the beginning. His ways are higher than our ways, and His thoughts are higher than our thoughts. He is the perfect leader, and I am thankful that, as we proceed daily, I am learning to lean on my Beloved and laboring to rest in Him. He is leading and guiding us into all truth, and we love the truth! Shine Your light, Jesus!

Let's pray:

*O God, thank You for Your Word.*

*Thank You for this beautiful pattern that encourages me*

*not to give up.*

*I will accept the challenge and seek.*

*Even when I cannot find You, I bow down, Lord.*

*If I have found grace in Your sight,*

*Show me now Your way, that I may know You,*

## Sarah Ramsey – The Bridegroom's Song

*And that I may find grace in Your sight.*

*Help me believe what Your Word tells me.*

*Your Presence will go with me, and You will give me rest.*

*Show me the way as I draw closer to You.*

*Draw me as I seek You in Your Word, through prayer, by Your Spirit, and through Your body.*

*I agree with Moses—*

*If Your Presence does not go with us, do not bring us up from here.*

*For how then will it be known that Your people and I have found grace in Your sight, except that You go with us?*

*I seek You first.*

*Help me, Lord, not to grow weary.*

*Help me, Lord, not to isolate from Your body.*

*I cry out to You, my God. I set my heart on You.*

*Show me the way, I don't want to go without You.*

*Amen*

## 19

### When God Is Silent

*Oh God of my praise,*
*Do not be silent.*
*Psalm 109:1 (NIV)*

**Equipped to Endure**

> I sought him, but I could not find him;
>
> I called him, but he gave me no answer.
>
> Song of Solomon 5:6b

In spite of its title, this chapter is wonderful. It may wind up being your favorite, so don't dread reading it. During this season when God is silent, I should not accept the devil's accusations but must keep my confession of faith. I *will* seek and find, and the door *will be* opened when I knock. Just like the bride, I commit: "I will, my Beloved." I answer the call to the fellowship of Jesus' sufferings.

> He (Jesus) began to be sorrowful and troubled. He said,
>
> 'My soul is overwhelmed with sorrow to the point of
>
> death. Stay here and watch with me.' Going a little

further, he fell with his face to the ground and prayed.

Matthew 26:38-39 (NIV)

In the Garden of Gethsemane, Jesus went to mountain of myrrh and the hill of frankincense.

> 'Father, if it is Your will, take this cup away from Me; nevertheless not My will, but Yours, be done.' Then an angel appeared to Him from heaven, strengthening Him. And being in agony, He prayed more earnestly.
>
> Luke 22:42-44 (NKJV)

I love that: *Being in agony, He prayed more earnestly.*

What did you learn in the last season? I *will* keep my commitment. I will get to the mountain of myrrh and hill of frankincense and remember what He's done for us. God told us to speak to the mountain. I will hold up the rod of authority.

> *Let the waters open, Lord. Get us to the other side. Lord, let the waters swallow up the enemy. Teach us Your ways, O Lord, that we may do in the light what we learned in the dark* (Matthew 10:27).

Jesus glorified God. He completed His assignment. "I have brought You glory on earth by completing the work You gave me to do" (John 17:4-26, NKJV). It brings God glory when we finish the work, complete our assignments. Our work is to do those things He has called, chosen, appointed, and anointed us to do. Endurance means we don't quit during the darker times. Jesus prayed and was strengthened in the garden and then prayed with even more diligence. We also must pray for the endurance not to quit on our toughest assignments.

**My Story**

When these times come--when the light turns to night--it is time to look to the scripture and practice what I have preached. The party is over. The vacation has ended. My default is to allow my feelings to dominate and cause me to get discouraged and isolate myself. The Word of God instructs us: The Word of faith is always near me. I must have faith and hold onto hope. What I need to do is to run to the secret place and sit at the Beloved's feet. I need to remember faith comes as I hear the Word of God. Faith is not passive. It includes putting the principles I am learning into action. I am equipped to finish the race! I find a quiet place--a favorite chair with a cup of coffee--often before the sun comes up or anyone else has gotten out of bed. Sometimes I go into the closet and shut the door. I follow the pattern I see in the Word of God. I confess what Jesus has done for me and who I am in Him like this:

*Lord, I've gotten up early for the express purpose of*

## Sarah Ramsey – The Bridegroom's Song

*seeking You.*

*I've done all I know to do.*

*My bones ache, and I feel the pull of discouragement.*

*But, Lord, I come to You; and I begin to say aloud,*

*"The Lord is my Shepherd."*

*(I remember what I stored in my heart as a ten-year old*

*as my Mother encouraged me to memorize scriptures.)*

*"I shall not want.*

*You lead me beside still waters.*

*You restore my soul."*

*This morning things are foggy, but I will not fear.*

*You are with me.*

*Though I walk through this valley, I will not fear, for*

*You are with me.*

*You never leave me or forsake me.*

*Your rod--Your authority, Your power-- comforts me.*

*Your staff reaches toward me and draws me near.*

*There is food on the table in the presence of my enemies*

*called fear and discouragement.*

*There is oil--fresh anointing--for my head, my*

*understanding.*

*I will dwell here in Your chambers, in the House of the Lord, forever.*

*I will trust in the Lord with all my heart, and I will not lean on my own understanding.*

*I sit in the secret place under the shadow of the Almighty and wait. Selah!*

**Continual Pursuit**

Seeking the Lord without spiritual breakthrough is a challenge, but this is no time to stop. When doors begin to close, keep on knocking—not to break doors down, but to see whether others will open. Sometimes even spiritual mentors or church leadership are unable to meet you in the place of your despair, and it seems everyone has abandoned you. The bride felt this alienation. God alone knows your most desperate needs and will meet you there.

The watchmen who went about the city found me.

They struck me, they wounded me;

> The keepers of the walls
>
> Took my veil away from me.
>
> Song of Solomon 5:7

"The watchmen… found me."

The watchmen represent those in spiritual authority. They struck me and wounded me and took away my veil. I can't feel God. I can't serve God. I stand naked for God and man to see-- vulnerable and transparent. There are times when leadership hurts me, intentionally or not. The question I must ask of myself is this: "Who am I in this journey for?" In these times, people are not the answer, and it is not time to play the blame game. The answer is found in seeking the Lord; so I must say, "It's just You and me, Lord, on this trek of the journey. You are my refuge, You are my strength, You are my present help in time of trouble." Seeking refuge in others at this juncture will only prolong the misery and delay my appropriate internal response. The answer is, "You are My Lord. You are my exceedingly great reward!" (Genesis 15:1). Hebrews 13:5-6 says, "For He Himself hath said, 'I will never leave you, nor forsake you.' So we may boldly say, 'The Lord is my helper. I will not fear. What can man do to me?'"

I stand before an audience of One. My faithfulness is to Jesus, whether or not I feel acceptance from the body of Christ. If all we see are the imperfections of human beings, we will resist life in the body of Christ. Fear, previous rejection, and other factors can deceive and tempt us into thinking we can do it alone. When I see Jesus as the head of His body, I realize I cannot disregard the body of Christ without disregarding the Lord. What do we do, then, when we find ourselves at this place? We follow the example the bride gives in the Song of Solomon. Continue to seek. (--sound familiar?) Seeking will produce results. It is so good of God to show us this pattern. We are not the first, nor will we be the last, to encounter these feelings and obstacles. It makes it easier to know He is giving me the opportunity to grow. He overcame so that I can be an overcomer.

**Seeking Help--Becoming Vulnerable**

In humility, she asks for help.

> I charge you, O daughters of Jerusalem,
>
> If you find my beloved,
>
> That you tell him I am lovesick! Song of Solomon 5:8

I charge you, O daughters of Jerusalem (immature believers). I humble myself instead of retreating in separation and bitter isolation. I stay with the flock. I feed the little goats. I stay under the shepherd's tent, under authority, even if I am rejected. I do not separate myself from body life (the church). Instead, I integrate and become incorporated in Him. I engage with others in humility rather than isolating myself. I am in fellowship and communion with the youngsters! She is not too prideful to ask even a less-seasoned believer for help. "O daughters of Jerusalem, if you find my beloved, tell Him I am lovesick!" I am not mad at God. I am not offended that He withdrew His presence, that His hand is withdrawn, that I am injured by leadership. I am not placing blame! He will use it all for my good.

There are times we have to make a conscious decision not to be offended by God, especially when those who represent Him make bad choices or simply do things we don't understand. We must learn to separate the imperfections of man from the intentions of God. His judgments (even when delayed) are just and righteous, and I cannot understand the inner workings of everything going on in the heart of man or the heart of God. Anger towards God about what He does (or allows) or does not do, as we think fit, does not produce the righteousness of God. Offense towards God is a slippery slope that can easily derail us into compromise and self-righteous attitudes. If you struggle in this area, ask the Lord to help you and forgive your incorrect presumptions about Him based on others' actions or responses (or lack thereof). This lesson is a vital one to learn at this juncture; and the sooner we learn it, the sooner He can deliver us from it!

### Lovesick in the Dry Season

This is not the first time the Shulamite maiden has sought and not found (SOS 3:2). This is not the first time she has confessed her lovesickness (SOS 2:5). But now things are entirely different. During the prior season, she had been in the midst of circumstances that promoted love. She was full of love and emotion.

Earlier in her journey, her lovesickness flowed from having drunk and been full, which is in deep contrast to this dry season when she continues to seek because she hungers and thirsts for the Beloved's manifest presence. Lovesickness is a necessary part of the progression. Now she is saying, "I am sick with love" in an adverse circumstance and is speaking to those who do not understand her heart. She feels wounded by the watchmen. She is left with immature believers and dried up emotions. Her soul is challenged at His withdrawal.

### Another Question

She has not hidden her feelings from the daughters of Jerusalem, but they do not understand. So they ask:

> What is your Beloved

> More than another beloved,
>
> O fairest among women?
>
> What is your Beloved,
>
> More than another Beloved
>
> That you so charge us?
>
> Song of Solomon 5:9

They ask the question twice to add emphasis. *What is your Beloved more than another beloved?* The way she has responded to her suffering has awakened love and fervent desire in the daughters. James said, "When you encounter various trials--rejoice--the testing of your faith produces perseverance." Her faith produces hunger in the spiritually dull and passive daughters of Jerusalem. This outcome is supernatural agape love. God is pouring His love into their hearts through hers. She has "put on," or clothed herself, in love. She is motivated by His love in all of her searching, and they find this curious. They do not ask *who* Beloved is, but *what* is He more than another. This is the question for us today--what is *your* Beloved? The daughters did not understand her passion for Jesus, but they were prompted to find out more through her example. Mike Bickle explains,

> The daughters had 'other beloveds' in their lives ahead
>
> of the Lord Jesus; such things as money, pleasure,

prominence, and the comfort zone. They actually loved these things more than they loved the Lord, though they were sincerely saved. They are saying, 'What is He more than all the other loves of life that He has so gripped you?' The 'beloveds' that have gripped the Body of Christ more than Jesus are numerous. We mature as He becomes the First beloved of our soul. Our goal is to make Jesus the prominent beloved in our life, not necessarily the only one. The Lord does not mind that we love other people and things. He wants to be first. He wants the first commandment to be in first place. The bride is not gripped by the things that grip the daughters.[1]

They wonder, "How can you be lovesick when everything is going wrong?"

**The Daughters' Question--The Bride's Response**

This question, "What is your Beloved more than another," from the daughters of Jerusalem is one of my favorite parts of the Song. It isn't prosperity and blessing that get the attention of the daughters. It is the bride's response in the midst of deep suffering. The daughters see something in the bride that makes them ask, "What is your Beloved?" It is the unique and marvelous relationship between the Shulamite maiden and the Beloved and her undying devotion to her King of kings. She is not hiding her circumstance, though the natural response is to hide, as Adam and Eve did in the garden; but the supernatural response is to stay in the light with the body.

Are you in a hard season? It is tempting to hide during difficult seasons, just to crawl under the rug. But there is a better way. Hiding often produces loneliness and depression. The bride teaches us to seek and stay plugged into the body, to ask her little sister. The bride seeks Him and seeks help to find Him.

This season reveals the bride's heart to the daughters and brings revelation to the bride about herself. Jesus knew what was in her heart. But this fiery trial is revealing the bride's faith to herself. The gold is about to shine. This is a test. Motives are tested. She is being faithful to Jesus without being controlled by overt emotions and stays committed to the body of Christ even when she feels mistreated.

**Sending a Message to the Beloved**

It is not her wisdom or ministry anointing that attracts the daughters. It is not her power in prayer that they find so appealing. It is her passion for Jesus. The lovesick bride is not offended with God. She displays humility and insatiable love. She resists the temptation to isolate and separate herself in her pain and asks the daughters of Jerusalem for help. She feels abandoned, and possibly betrayed, by other believers. But instead of being offended at Him for withdrawing His presence and allowing her to feel alone and mistreated by the body, she makes a request and sends Jesus a message. "If you find Him, tell Him I am lovesick!" She is not playing a game. She is admitting vulnerability. The daughters of Jerusalem see the bride's spiritual beauty but cannot understand why she continues to pursue the Beloved more than the other "beloveds." How can she still seek Him? Why would she continue? How can she be so assured of His approval and confident in His love? In her enduring quest she makes a key decision which makes her even more beautiful.

The decision is to refuse to pick up an offense. Offense is knocking at my door. The feelings of abandonment are bombarding my mind, but I will not open the door. I will possess the gate of this enemy. I accept this cup of suffering, as Jesus did. I set my eyes on You, my Beloved. I set my heart, my mind, my love. I will not try to figure this out. I will trust in You and not lean on my own understanding. I will not be angry with God for the things I perceive as injustice. I will rely on God's just character and holiness. I love you, Jesus, and I love Your people.

The daughters recognize and acknowledge her beauty, that she is "fairest among women." Their question is, "What is your Beloved, O fairest of women?" Why is He in first place with you? This question is the result of her seeking their help. The daughters enjoy her fragrance, which was produced as the north wind blew on her garden. It is not the blessing that is attracting their attention. It is the fragrance of myrrh around her neck, between her breasts, in the night season. The sweet fragrance erupting from her response to suffering envelops her, draws them, and creates hunger in the daughters. She is preparing them to behold the majesty of the King!

Let's pray:

*Dear Lord, sometimes I feel alone and abandoned.*

*Even when I seek You and seem to find no answer, I want to stay devoted to You.*

*When I feel wounded by spiritual authority, help me to seek more diligently.*

*When You seem to be nowhere in sight, help me persevere.*

*When my feelings betray me, I will believe Your Word and remember Your faithfulness.*

*Forgive me when I blame You and others.*

## Sarah Ramsey – The Bridegroom's Song

*Forgive me when I perceive You as unjust and uncaring.*

*You alone know my inmost thoughts and understand my Gethsemane experiences.*

*Walk with me through this night season so that when I emerge, others will ask, "What is your Beloved more than another?"*

*You are the first among all other beloveds.*

*Amen.*

**20**

**My Beloved Is**

*My beloved is...chief among ten thousand*

Song of Solomon 5:10.

The bride has been desperately searching for her Beloved. With a lovesick heart she responds to the daughters and answers their question, "What is your beloved?" In essence, they are asking, "Who on earth is this King Jesus?" Although they know the Beloved as the Kingly Savior, they have not yet experienced Him as the Bridegroom King. Despite her hurt, she reaches deep into her Spirit and reveals the splendor of the King as she boldly declares, "My beloved is...."

My beloved is white and ruddy,

Chief among ten thousand.

## Sarah Ramsey – The Bridegroom's Song

His head is like the finest gold;

His locks are wavy,

And black as a raven.

His eyes are like doves

By the rivers of waters,

Washed with milk,

And fitly set.

His cheeks are like a bed of spices,

Banks of scented herbs.

His lips are lilies,

Dripping liquid myrrh.

His hands are rods of gold

Set with beryl.

His body is carved ivory

Inlaid with sapphires.

His legs are pillars of marble

Set on bases of fine gold.

His countenance is like Lebanon,

Excellent as the cedars.

His mouth is most sweet,

> Yes, he is altogether lovely.
>
> This is my beloved,
>
> And this is my friend,
>
> O daughters of Jerusalem!
>
> Song of Solomon 5:10-16

Oh, she sees Him! She sees the King of Glory. "What is He?" the daughters ask. She has the answer. She thrills the daughters with the answer to their question. She describes the Beloved literally from head to toe in what I see as the most beautiful description of the King of kings in all of Scripture. She starts with His head and goes down His body revealing His beautiful attributes. Let's break down what she is saying. We can read through it quickly, or we can ask the Holy Spirit to reveal what He is speaking to us.

> *O Holy Spirit, uncover and reveal what You are speaking.*
>
> *Give me ears to hear what the Spirit is saying!*
>
> *Help me to respond to suffering and remain true,*
>
> *Even when your manifest presence is withheld*
>
> *And the body of Christ disregards me.*

She follows His example of praise using symbols of the body, terminology with which we are already familiar. Her anthem of praise is easy to remember because she begins with the Beloved's head and works down the body to the feet. She also begins and ends with statements incorporating His entire person.

To unlock this treasure box is most thrilling. Are you ready to dig for treasure?

**The Picture**

My beloved is:

- *My Beloved is white and ruddy, the Chief among ten thousand*! Other translations describe him as dazzling, or radiant, which expresses splendor. His reddish complexion (ruddy) denotes health coming from the inside. His physical and mental attributes and His personality are in perfect balance. The number *ten thousand* is a metaphor designating Him as the Chief among all things. He has no rival.

- *His head is like the finest gold.* His head represents His leadership. He is equipped to lead with divine, heavenly ability. "*The finest gold*" represents purity. He has the purest intents at heart and will make decisions which purify me in return. Gold represents divinity and royalty. He has kingly authority–something most costly.

- *His locks are wavy and black as a raven.* Hair is symbolic of commitment, just as Samson's uncut hair represented his commitment to the Nazarite vow. Hair is the wife's covering and is symbolic of her dedication to her husband's leadership. His hair is black with eternal vigor, not limp and gray. He is always in His prime. He does not lose His luster and never grows old. His commitment to me is forever young! Hair represents His dedication to me.

- *His eyes are like doves by the rivers of waters, washed with milk, and fitly set.* His focus is on me like doves' eyes. He sees things as they truly are with perfect clarity. He even sees the "yes" in my spirit when my failings cause me to question myself. His eyes are clean, bathed with milk, meaning He has purity in His motives; He sees and knows all things (omniscience). He discerns perfectly, with eyes fitly set, with nothing distorted. It brings me security knowing He sees and knows all things, creating an even greater atmosphere of trust.

- *His cheeks are like a bed of spices, banks of scented herbs.* His cheeks reveal His emotions, His passion for me. The love He feels is unhidden, and He is transparent about His feelings and expresses them. This fragrance is like walking through fields of lavender (spices). What a happy thought, indeed!

- *His lips are lilies, dripping liquid myrrh.* His lips are His Words spoken over me, creating my destiny and declaring my identity. They are pure, like lilies, and capable of helping me in suffering and crisis. He speaks with kindness and tenderness but deals precisely with areas which need correction and refinement in the bride. Liquid myrrh, the burial spice, shows how His words divide the soul, enabling the death of self, but tempering the process with sweetness and gentleness.

- *His hands are rods of gold set with beryl.* His hands perform His Word with divine purity and beautiful, Kingly authority. His hands work out in action my destiny spoken from His lips; both are marked with golden, pure purposes and are accentuated with fine jewels. Beryl is a gemstone known to be both hard and durable. These faceted gems can occur in a variety of colors and physical properties. His hands are firm, capable, and dependable, yet brilliant and intense, beautiful to behold.

- *His body is carved ivory inlaid with sapphires.* His torso, or belly, is the center of His tender compassion. He knows I am dust. Ivory is clean and white. It is expensive, rare, soft, fragile, and easily carved. He feels what I feel. The individual jewels, or sapphires, are inlaid in His body (the church) for reflecting His beauty.

- *His legs are pillars of marble set on bases of fine gold.* Pillars represent strength, dignity, orderliness, and endurance under pressure. These pillars are powerful and capable of getting me to His purposes. He finishes what He began and gets me where I need to be. His legs are enabled to fulfill God's plans. He won't fail or cave under pressure. He has the power to execute His Father's plans. His legs are like the marble pillars left standing in the ruins when all else is gone, withstanding devastation and destruction. His legs, too, are set in gold (the currency of the King), pure, divine, and royal. (Gold is used three times in this description of the Beloved.)

- *His countenance is like Lebanon, excellent as the cedars.* His face shines upon me. This image represents the impartation of God's grace and goodness upon His people--like the cedars of Lebanon--pleasing, strong, and fragrant. His countenance displays His glory, His brilliance. He imparts Himself to His people with the countenance of His face.

- *His mouth is most sweet.* The mouth is the vessel of intimate communion and is the most personal way intimacy is expressed. This intimacy is what she seeks; and His mouth is the final physical attribute, echoing her desire from the beginning of the Song when she cried out for the kisses of His mouth. The kisses of the mouth are deeper than the speech of the lips. His kisses transcend words and are our deepest desires. She sought His kisses, and she has found her life in the Beloved. Spiritual intimacy with our Beloved is the culmination of our existence and brings ultimate fulfillment to the human experience.

- *Yes, he is altogether lovely. This is my beloved, and this is my friend!* This final statement-emphasizes that He is more than a lover: He is a friend. Like the first statement (*Chief among ten thousand*), this is not a single attribute but a composite description. The Beloved is her divine Husband but can also descend to her level of humanity and be her friend. He is relatable at all levels. She speaks of Him with great urgency, passion, and longing. He is the whole package!

Don't you love how the Word brings life and how the imagery comes alive as we unlock the code? Do you see what's happening? Are you learning the language of the Song? The Shulamite maiden is embracing the light! We, too, can say, "Open the eyes of my heart, Lord. I want to see you!"

**Revealing Jesus**

The bride uncovers and reveals Jesus to the daughters. She paints for them a picture of Him, and they look at her with their mouths hanging open. She enables the daughters to *see* her Beloved. Her method, rather than rebuking them, reveals Jesus to them. She is not offended by them, nor is she offensive to them.

What a lesson!

- She has the answer to their question, "What is your Beloved more than another?"
- She lets light shine in this dark place.
- Instead of looking inward and feeling sorry for herself, she looks beyond herself to Him and gives an edifying answer.
- She places her focus on the King on the throne and rehearses who He is rather than taking offense at the way she is treated.

The daughters recognize her sincerity. When they ask the question, she overwhelms them with her answer. She does not expose or reveal their inadequacy and ignorance but answers their questions by revealing the beauty of Jesus. They see that she is suffering. They smell the fragrance of myrrh surrounding her.

What an example! Keep on gazing at the Beloved. This focus is our pattern. In times of difficulty and dryness or testing, remember your Beloved. Memorize His attributes. Say them aloud and back to Him. Let love awaken!

**To Behold by Revelation**

After years of walking with the Lord, David gave expression to his heart's longing and demonstrated this pattern. He ultimately concluded there was only one thing he truly desired, and only one thing would fully satisfy his purpose in life: to dwell in the house of the Lord all the days of his life, to behold the beauty of the Lord, and meditate in His temple (Psalm 27:4). David knew how to *see* his Beloved.

The Hebrew word for "behold" is *chazah*, which means "to see, behold, or select for oneself." It appears fifty-four times throughout the Bible and occurs in every period of biblical Hebrew history. *Chazah* literally signifies the ability to see "in a prophetic vision or as a seer in an ecstatic state."

*Chazah* is demonstrated through a prophet's vision. The oracle who hears the words of God and sees the vision of the Almighty has unveiled eyes to behold biblical promises. The sum of David's passion was captured in that "one thing," beholding the beauty of the Lord. His desire was to gaze upon His beauty and delight in His loveliness. The Psalms are expressions of David's experiential comprehension of the beautiful realm of heaven, not just a daydream of what it might be like.

Can we behold the King in all His beauty? May it be our chief desire to see, behold, comprehend, and explore the mysteries and infinite riches of the Lord's goodness and beauty. Gazing into His majesty, we discover the plans ordained for the unique times and hour in which we live. Through this revelation we begin to build our lives according to His appointed purposes. Ask the Lord to give you eyes to see!

**The Confessions of the Bride**

At this part in the journey, it is time that you make these confessions your own. Begin by going back to the bulleted statements describing the Beloved under the heading "The Picture." Start with the first attribute, and begin to memorize the scripture from the head down. It is much easier to memorize the order--head, hair, eyes, cheeks, lips, hands, body, legs, countenance, and mouth. Then just add the scriptural description of the Beloved for each body part. Perhaps read through the basic attributes a time or two. As the days go by and you remember what you have learned, go back to this pattern; and let it become a praise-and-picture manual. For example, let's take the first attribute referring to His head:

*Oh, Jesus, my Bridegroom King, You are the greatest leader.*

*Your head is like the finest gold.*

*You have authority and power as the King of Kings.*

*You are pure in Your Kingly intentions.*

*You will never lead me the wrong way. Your leadership is trustworthy and safe.*

*You always have my best interest at heart, and Your kingdom is eternal.*

As you learn that attribution, add others, one or two at a time, until you have the full picture of Jesus from head to toe. Then memorize the beginning and ending phrases describing the composite picture of Jesus as the Chief among ten thousand and His place as your lover and friend. Elaborate on these in a personal way. Your blessing will be much greater than the effort and price you pay to deposit these in your heart. These phrases will always be at your disposal. Your burdens will lift as you gaze upon the beauty of Jesus.

The bride has been transparent and has revealed what is in her heart. She is holding nothing back. She is genuine and has made it personal. He is my Beloved—my friend. Her focus is in the right place, upon Jesus, not upon her circumstances or other people. She does not blame or condemn. She gives us a beautiful example to imitate.

The knowledge of the beauty of Jesus empowers the bride to be an extravagant worshiper even during severe testing and equips her to endure in faith. When we see divine beauty, we are enabled to overcome and not draw back. For God has no pleasure in the one who shrinks back (Hebrews 10:38). Once we see His divine beauty, we cannot, we shall not, we will not draw back. His beauty protects us from offense. The decision to focus upon His beauty rather than to be preoccupied with disappointments and stresses will bring the believer into His presence.

**The Bride Seeks—The Bride's Armor Toolbox**

As we press in to seek God, the Holy Spirit reveals how to become intimate with the Beloved. These attributes are tools given to us by God. When we meditate upon His attributes, our souls embrace God; and we become equipped to penetrate the seasons of barrenness which inevitably come through tribulation and testing.

The bride's beautiful and eloquent answer pierces the hearts of the daughters of Jerusalem, and now they present another question. As the body of Christ watches closely, there is still no word from the Beloved; and they ask, "Where is your Beloved that we may seek Him with you?" Her response is making seekers of the daughters! They now want to seek Him, too!

Let's pray:

> *Oh, Lord, I desire that my heart would respond to Your beauty in such a way.*
> 
> *Give me the words to describe Your beauty when others ask.*
> 
> *Give me a seeking heart so that I lead others to desire the object of my affections, You!*
> 
> *Impress upon me the beauty of Your divine attributes.*
> 
> *Reveal Yourself to me in such a way that I can express You to others, especially in the midst of suffering.*

*Thank you for being the Lover of my soul, and also my Friend.*

*Amen.*

## 21

### Awakening an Earnest Desire

*Where has your beloved gone, O fairest among women?*

*...that we may seek him with you?*

Song of Solomon 6:1

The bride's beautiful description of the Beloved causes the daughters of Jerusalem to ask another question:

> Where has your beloved gone,
>
> O fairest among women?
>
> Where has your beloved turned aside,
>
> That we may seek him with you?
>
> Song of Solomon 6:1

**O Fairest Among Women**

The daughters of Jerusalem refer to the King as "*your* Beloved" (not claiming possession of Him for themselves yet), and they also acknowledge that the Shulamite maiden is the fairest among women. They even announce their desire to seek Him! The fragrance of the Lord is on her and is drawing others to the Beloved. The bride is a worshiper, and worshipers beget further worship from themselves and others. They have watched her and want some "how-tos" on where to find Him. Can you tell me how to find Him? They have been stirred to seek with greater passion. The daughters have made a decision to let go of their many less-significant beloveds and seek the true Beloved. The seed is coming up; the crop is budding, signifying the promise of harvest. They want to go with her--to run together. So they ask, "Where is He?"

An earnest desire for His love has been awakened in the daughters. Notice the transition of questioning from "What is your Beloved?" to "Where has your Beloved gone?" The bride is a seeker, and that quality is duplicated in the daughters as they ask questions. The bride's first question to the Beloved in Chapter 1 was "Where do you feed?" The daughters are asking her now: "Where can we find Him?"

Her passion causes them to hunger. The season of testing brings forth fruit. We, too, can find glory in tribulations knowing that it will produce perseverance, character, and hope; and have faith that it won't disappoint (Romans 5:3). This season of testing has become a season of harvest. Remember, it is her response to trials, not her prosperity, which brings about the budding faith in others.

Our deliverance is found many times in delivering others. As we bring the knowledge of Jesus Christ to others, our own spirits are refreshed. When the bride begins to declare the Lord's worth, she is spontaneously revived. Jesus called this "salt." He said, "You are the salt of the earth." In other words, "You make people thirst for me." The daughters are thirsty and seeking the Living Water. Although the daughters are unable to help her find Him, the bride's answer to her own question comes through inner revelation from the Holy Spirit.

**The Beloved is in His Garden**

The bride needed to be asked this question about her Beloved's presence. It pricked her remembrance. She had become so intent upon His absence that she forgot she already knew where He was. She suddenly had an "Aha!" moment. When the daughters ask the question, then, she readily responds:

>My beloved has gone to his garden,
>
>To the beds of spices,
>
>To feed his flock in the gardens,
>
>And to gather lilies.

Song of Solomon 6:2

This garden is figurative language for her life in Christ. He is living in her spiritual affections where He had been all along. Immediately her understanding is illuminated, and she realizes His presence is *within* her, indwelling her. The Beloved had not really left her, nor was it necessary to "ascend into heaven" to seek Him. She is where the Beloved is found! He is in His garden, and she *is* His garden.

When God created Adam and Eve, He placed them in the perfect garden of Eden. He walked with them in the cool of the day. The garden was His dwelling place, a place where He could be with His creation. We were designed to live with God in intimate fellowship. Jesus said, "In that day you shall know that I am in you" (John 14:21). The indwelling Spirit of Christ is within the maiden. He was and is always present in His garden. She is learning to live on the promise rather than to depend upon emotions.

It is easy to let emotions rule and neglect the steadfastness of God's Word. "He Himself has said, 'I will never desert you, nor will I ever forsake you,' so that we confidently say, 'The Lord is my helper, I will not be afraid. What shall man do to me?'" (Hebrews 13:5-7, NASB) He is in the midst of me whether or not I feel it. I find it especially significant that Jesus' last words were, "I am with you always, even to the end of the age" (Matthew 28:20, NASB). I believe He used those words at that time because He knew we would have a tendency to doubt His presence within us. Hearing His word cultivates faith. If I begin to doubt, I need to repeat His words to myself. The truth is that He has never left me, even if His manifest presence is not discernable. I don't even have to ask Jesus to be with me—I just need to thank Him for never leaving me. Sometimes I need to be asked this same question, "Where is He?" so that He can reveal the answer to me all over again.

**God's Manifest Presence**

God's manifest presence is not always easy to discern in difficult seasons, but the Shulamite had already given the Beloved unlimited access to her life. Recall the invitation she issued in Chapter 4:

> Awake, O north wind,
>
> And come, O south!
>
> Blow upon my garden
>
> That its spices may flow out.
>
> Let my beloved come to his garden
>
> And eat its pleasant fruits.
>
> Song of Solomon 4:6

What a lesson! Declare who He is to others. Then stand firm, and do not believe the lie that He doesn't care or that He has forsaken us. He is in His garden with the lilies, feeding and gathering in the midst of His people. In Revelation 1:12-17, Jesus reveals Himself in the midst of the church (the lampstands). Do you want to seek Jesus? Get with the body of Christ. His first instruction to her in Chapter 1 was, "stay with the flock" (Song 1:8). Perhaps she remembers the fragrance of the beds of spices where He feeds and gathers.

**A New Confession**

The Beloved has come to His garden to feed His flock and gather His lilies (Song 6:2). Remember that the lilies symbolize purity and also refer to the individual believer. The bride is called the lily. Jesus finds nourishment in the garden among His lilies. He feeds Himself, He feeds others, and He feeds me. As the bride matures, she begins to trust Him. As I mature in faith, her confession becomes my confession:

> I am my Beloved's, and my Beloved is mine.
>
> He feeds among the lilies.
>
> Song of Solomon 6:3

For the second time in the Song, she declares her identity. Developing maturity produces a reversal in the order of her confession. This detail is important and should not be overlooked. Previously in 2:16 she had said, "My Beloved is mine and I am His." Now she says, "I am my Beloved's and He is mine." By Chapter 6 she is growing, and her first desire is to be His. The emphasis is less about her possession of Him: It is no longer "all about me." Think about one of the first words out of a toddler's mouth: "mine!" Early in a believer's walk, the same is often the case. The focus is more about what the Lord can do for "me." The maiden's focus has shifted from me (or mine) to His possession of her. She now belongs fully to Him, first; and He is hers, second. Further on in Chapter 7, she will make a third declaration. We will see her filled with the acceptance that His desire is towards her. She knows who she is in Christ. She is His garden, and He is feeding among the lilies of her life.

Though feelings change, the covenant remains unchangeable, steadfast and unbroken. Faith, not feelings, brings results. Her earlier confession in 2:16 was founded upon emotions; this confession in Chapter 6 is based upon faith. John the Baptist understood proper focus in his statement, "He must become greater; I must become less" (John 3:30, NIV). Living in a fallen world is a mixture of joys and sorrows. Learning to rest in the storm is an essential part of the journey. I can lean into Him during such times, having confidence in His unchanging and eternal nature. Despite persecution or heartache, I can, like John the Baptist and the Shulamite maiden, magnify His name, lift Him up, and dethrone my self-seeking interests and wavering emotions.

## My Story

I remember learning during the 70's and 80's about being "in Christ." Kenneth Hagin's little brochure, *In Him*, taught me to recognize that, when a scripture says, *in Christ*, *in Him*, *in whom*, etc., it means I should personalize it. For example, the Bible says, "But now in Christ Jesus you who were once far off have been brought near by the blood of Christ" (Ephesians 2:13, NKJV). So, I say, "That's me!" and I say, "But now in Christ Jesus, Sarah Ramsey, who once was far off has been brought near by the blood of Christ." That is why I am here in the King's chambers. He has brought me near!

At a Community Bible Study teacher's conference during the 90's, I was reminded of Dr. Neil Anderson's book, *Living Free in Christ*. He incorporated a list of scriptures and confessions which served as a bookmark and helped me know who I am in Christ. As these scriptures took root in my spirit and not just my mind, I became acutely aware that I was more than just the King's "kid." I am the bride of Christ--along with you, beloved of God. God's Word is a "proceeding" Word. As we obey, the seed takes root downward and bears fruit upward; and it's not just all about me. I am my Beloved's, and He is mine. Selah!

## Jesus in the Midst

This truth motivates me: "I am my Beloved's and He is mine." My great love for my Beloved is rooted in His passion, desire, and enjoyment of me. He is feeding His flock and feeds among the lilies. He is feeding me as I minister to the daughters of Jerusalem. When we get with the other lilies, we receive the benefits of His nourishment; and ministry abounds. Remember, we run together. Some desiring deep intimacy with Christ leave the church to seek Him. Some of the mystics throughout church history have sought to hide themselves in caves to find deeper life in Christ. They neglect the principle of Jesus' being present in the midst of His gardens, the church. Solitude has its place in getting alone with Christ for personal growth, prayer, and study; but sustained absence from the body of Christ will cause the individual believer to wither from lack of nourishment from the Head.

**The Progressive Process**

The bride is growing and changing--line upon line, precept upon precept. God doesn't reveal everything to us all at once—we wouldn't be able to handle it. The children of Israel came out of bondage progressively and came into possession of the Promised Land "little by little." Slow and steady wins the race. God will not give us what we cannot maintain. We must occupy what He gives, and He will contend with our enemies until they are all destroyed. "I will not drive them out from before you in one year, lest the land become desolate and the beasts of the field become too numerous for you. Little by little I will drive them out from before you, until you have increased, and you inherit the land" (Exodus 23:29-30; see also Deuteronomy 7:22-23). Deliverance is a lifelong process made of up a series of battles. The Israelites chose wandering in the wilderness for forty years rather than making an eleven-day trek into a land of freedom. The enemies were not the problem. God's power was not the problem. Once they crossed into the plains across Jordan after their wilderness wanderings, God helped them occupy the land gradually so that the enemy wouldn't overtake them. They had to gain strength and learn to maintain their ground. As we learn to rely on His Word and not our feelings, the ownership of the garden changes. The maiden's garden has become His garden—she is submitting to the process.

Let's declare these truths aloud in prayer:

*Oh God, I am so inspired by the bride.*

*I am seeing the progression in her and declare that you are in me, too, Jesus.*

*I am Your garden, and You are here.*

*You will never leave me or forsake me.*

*Why should I fear?*

*Lead on, O King eternal.*

*Amen.*

## 22

### The Bridal Attributes

*O my love, you are as beautiful as Tirzah*

*Lovely as Jerusalem,*

*Awesome as an army with banners!*

Song of Solomon 6:4

### A New Level of Maturity

This season of suffering has revealed the bride's heart. The voice of the Beloved has not been heard since His knock in the Song 5:2. This period without communication with the Beloved has revealed a new level of maturity in the bride. She has remained diligent to seek the Lord and powerfully communicate His essence to those yet unable to see the fullness of His glory. She is lovesick. Her adoring description inspires the daughters to seek with her. When asked where He is, she suddenly realizes He is right where He said He would be--in the garden with His flock, gathering lilies.

## The Power of the Spoken Word

As the bride speaks about her Beloved, He speaks to her. In the midst of her confession, the bride hears the sound of His voice once again. Listening and learning to believe the words of the Beloved are key principles. Learning to believe is often the greater challenge. Hearing is one thing, but believing is quite another. The bride is being equipped to walk in mature partnership with Jesus, the objective being communion, beholding, and transformation.

"Jesus breaks His silence to reassure her of His great love for her in a season of testing," Mike Bickle says.[1] Take in His words of love:

> O my love, you are as beautiful as Tirzah
>
> Lovely as Jerusalem.
>
> Awesome as an army with banners!
>
> Song of Solomon 6:4

He verbalizes His view of the bride, beginning by confirming His affection for her. He always calls her "my love," an expression of His feelings about her. In another beautiful poetic analogy, He compares her to two great and powerful cities. This imagery identifies her beauty as both natural and spiritual. Tirzah was known as one of the most beautiful cities in the ancient world and became the capital city of several kings in the Northern Kingdom. The word *Tirzah* means delight. Jerusalem is God's capital city, the place of Solomon's temple, the center of worship where the Shekinah glory of God was housed. (*Shekinah* is "The majestic presence or manifestation of God which has descended to 'dwell' among men" (JewishEncyclopedia.com). Jerusalem represents spiritual beauty. The bride is beautiful in her earthly life (Tirzah), and beautiful in her heavenly life (Jerusalem).

**The Interceding, Warring Bride**

The bride's physical attributes are beautiful in the natural (Tirzah), even in the eyes of the carnal believer; and her inner spiritual attributes are beautiful to the Lord. She is equipped for war, as fierce as an army with banners displaying victory. An unfurled banner denotes glorious victory. She is the interceding, warring bride--lovely and exalted by her King but a force to be reckoned with among her enemies. She is following in the footsteps of her warrior King. "The Lord is a man of war. The Lord is His name" (Exodus 15:3). Have you noticed we are at war? Thankfully, we are equipped for the job! "Blessed be the Lord my Rock, who trains my hands for war, and my fingers for battle (Psalm 144:1).

The bride's progress has been a long, arduous process. In Chapter 4 she had come to Lebanon, to the mountaintops of Amana, Shenir, and Hermon. She came away to the mountain of myrrh and the hill of frankincense. The saints have union with Christ in the realm of the heavenlies (on these mountain tops), but it is also in that realm that they meet the real attack from enemy forces. When holy character is maintained, victorious warfare causes the enemy to retreat before our eyes. She gained her most recent victory in Chapter 5 of the Song as she battled and pursued in His absence while enduring harm from the body of Christ. The bride encountered and passed the two-fold test:

- She was first challenged to keep her eyes focused on Him throughout the trial (when His manifest presence was withdrawn).
- She remained steadfast when she was wounded.

Isaiah 55:8b says, "'My ways are not your ways,' says the Lord… 'for my ways are higher than your ways.'" This path is not the way she would have chosen, but she ended up right where she needed to be. Let this encourage us to rise, like the bride, take our seat beside Him in the heavenly places (Ephesians 2:6), assume the position of a warrior, and turn our faces to gaze into His eyes of fire. Pay attention as He continues the praise of the Shulamite's beauty in Chapter 6 of the Song:

> Turn your eyes away from me, for they have overcome me.
>
> Your hair is like a flock of goats going down from Gilead.

> Your teeth are like a flock of sheep,
>
> Which have come up from the washing;
>
> Every one bears twins,
>
> And none is barren among them.
>
> Like a piece of pomegranate
>
> Are your temples behind your veil.
>
> Song of Solomon 6:5-7

Throughout the Word of God, the singleness of the eye is emphasized--not a concept exclusive to this chapter in the Song (also seen in SOS 1:15 and SOS 4:1). Jesus said in Luke 11:34, "The lamp of the body is the eye. Therefore, when your eye is good, your whole body also is full of light. But when *your eye* is bad, your body *is* full of darkness" (emphasis added). The eye is the window to the soul. We have seen the bride maintain focus despite her feelings, and she has ravished the Lord altogether in the process. When He looks into the bride's eyes, He finds her focused upon Him alone after this season of suffering. He does not rebuke her because she was slow to open, nor is he angry with her for previous failings. This test is working for her good. Her dove's eyes are irresistibly beautiful! The King of all the earth, the Almighty, the One who created all things in heaven above and on earth below is overcome by the steady gaze of the obedient bride, so much so that He has to look away. It's almost too wonderful to imagine, but it is true of her; and the same can be true of you!

## Jesus Declares the Bride's Attributes

These descriptions are the same as those listed in 4:1-3, which were budding virtues at the time of His initial proclamation. He was able to see the end result, even as He spoke over her; and now His Words are bearing fruit. The spoken, imperishable seed sown into her heart is sprouting and developing into mature fruit.

- *Eyes...have overcome me*
  Her doves eyes were hidden and veiled in Chapter 4, but her gaze is now so intense and focused upon Him that He is swept away. "Your eyes have overcome me!" She has not only personally overcome, but she has also smitten the King of Glory and overcome Him with her steadfast gaze! Jesus is overwhelmed, proclaiming her beauty and hold on Him.

- *Hair like a flock of goats going down from Gilead*
  Her hair flows down like the promises of God. Her hair is the crown of her head-- her covering, consecrated, and dedicated. The physical head is the seat of one's honor. She is submitted to and under authority (1 Corinthians 11:5-6, 10, and 15. See also Nazarite vow in Numbers 6). Gilead is a mountainous region east of the Jordan in the Promised land. Gilead was the site of many well-known events in the Bible. When Moses climbed Mount Nebo, the Lord showed him the land below sworn to his

descendants through the Abrahamic covenant. Moses was able to peer into the land of Gilead from this vantage point. It was part of the much-anticipated land flowing with milk and honey, which would one day be occupied by the Israelites. It was also at Gilead that the peace covenant between Laban and Jacob had taken place (Genesis 31) after Jacob married Laban's two daughters, Leah and Rachel, and left the household of their father.

- *Teeth like a flock of sheep*
  She uses her teeth to eat the Word of God with balance. She can chew the food and make it digestible. She knows how to meditate on the Word and "chews on both sides"—for example, grace and truth (every tooth bears a twin, no missing teeth). She is washed and cleansed (shorn) as she eats the Word. She is a doer! Hebrews 5:14 says, "But solid food is for the mature, who by constant use have trained themselves to distinguish good from evil" (NIV). Wow! How she has matured!

- *Like a piece of pomegranate are your temples behind your veil.*
  Her cheeks are full of emotion, but she is not controlled by emotions. Like a piece of pomegranate, juicy and full of seeds, the cheeks emit emotion; but she has a veiled discretion and does not allow this unbridled emotion to override her actions. Her emotions are not repressed—she is expressive, yet her emotions are in check, not out of control.

We continue to learn the symbolic language of the Song as the Beloved paints a word picture of His bride. Her eyes remain focused and please Him. Her dedication (hair) remains faithful and endures. It flows like the promises of God. This dedication has produced good works like a flock of goats walking in stately order. Such dedication to God flows out of Godly wisdom rather than fleshly zeal. She has an abundance of good works—a flock, not just one or two. She is consecrated. She is able to eat the meat of the Word with a balanced set of teeth instead of subsisting on a babe's diet of milk, showing maturity of her faith. She is nourished with long, loving meditation in God's word. The excess is shorn off as she is washed in the Word. Her capacity to receive balanced teaching has been increased, and she correctly discerns the Word of God. Her temples, which reflect her inward beauty, are a hidden attribute. She glows like a bride.

**The Favorite**

The Beloved continues to set her apart as His favorite:

> There are sixty queens
>
> And eighty concubines,
>
> And virgins without number.

> My dove, my perfect one,
>
> Is the only one,
>
> The only one of her mother,
>
> The favorite of the one who bore her.
>
> The daughters saw her
>
> And called her blessed,
>
> The queens and concubines,
>
> And they praised her.
>
> Song of Solomon 6:8-9

She is unique, set apart completely as the object of God's pleasure. Mike Bickle says,

"This is the essential definition of what holiness means."[2] God Himself works this nature in us: "For it is God who works in you both to will and to do for His good pleasure" (Philippians 2:13). It is for His pleasure. His language singles her out as the favorite! There are many, but you are my dove, my perfect one, the only one. There is none like you, my darling bride!

The bride has developed royal characteristics. Queens and concubines represent different degrees in the royal court, but the bride is more than both of these. She is set apart by Jesus. The young women see her and called her blessed; the queens and concubines praise her; all recognize her identity is fully in Him.

There are daughters, queens, concubines/virgins; but you, bride of Christ, are the favorite. She has been the fairest all along. Jesus knew it, but it takes the brothers and sisters longer to see it. There is only one who fully satisfies the Beloved's heart--the bride. Can't you just imagine the great cloud of witnesses watching the maturing bride? The church's becoming the maturing bride has never before happened in church history. God is a finisher: He will finish what He has begun.

The Bridegroom and the church love seeing the bride mature as God bestows His splendor upon her. Ezekiel 16:14 says, "Your fame went out among the nations because of your beauty, for it was perfect through My splendor which I bestowed on you, says the Lord God!" As the bride is making herself ready, heaven and earth rejoice. The church is full of children of grace, but those who allow His grace to work its fullness to completion are rare.

**Make it Personal**

The words from the lips of the Beloved are a key in the Song of Solomon. As we study and meditate on this beautiful passage, the goal is to apply it in our lives individually. We, as the bride of Christ, are being ignited with His love so that we can love Him with single eyes. As I write, I am so happy to realize this speaks about me as an individual and about all believers corporately as we emerge as the bride of Christ. As you read and meditate on His words, repeat them and make the decision to believe what He says. "If you will not believe, surely you will not be established" (Isaiah 7:9b, 2 Chronicles 20:20). Are you having trouble believing you are the bride of Christ? He is speaking about *you*.

## A Stronghold of Unbelief

The bride is challenged to *believe* His Words and the praise He lavishes upon her. Do you struggle with a stronghold of unbelief? Alice Smith, one of my favorite authors, writes, "People who are struggling with a spirit of unbelief are constantly dealing with negative self-talk and convincing themselves that they are unworthy to be loved or receive from God." That lie takes up residence in the heart and becomes a stronghold which prevents intimacy. If you are dealing with a stronghold of unbelief (Hebrews 3), ask the Lord to open your eyes and then make the following declaration with me:

> *I renounce you, spirit of unbelief and spirit of lies,*
>
> *I command you to leave my life right now.*
>
> *I break all covenants, vows, and agreements with you.*
>
> *I decree and declare that I am no longer bound by your deception.*
>
> *I decree and declare that God's Son has set me free, and*

*I am free indeed.*

*In accordance with God's Word, I announce and proclaim that nothing is impossible with God; therefore, I am free to hear His voice and experience His love now.*[3]

Now, choose to replace unbelief with the truth. We need to love ourselves. Jesus said, "Love your neighbor as you love yourself." As we refuse to make the negative statements and replace them with what God says about us, faith grows and intimacy increases! If you feel inadequate, ask Him for help.

Jesus' completed work on the cross provided the grace needed for completion of His work in us. He has given us access to this throne of grace where we may come to receive help in our time of need. Can you hear the call to come up to the King's chambers to find grace and clothe ourselves as the bride of Christ? He is our provider, giving us both this grace and the clothing (robes of righteousness). The bride confessed who He is; then He declared who she is in turn. Let us hear, believe, and confess what He is declaring about us!

We can put these words into action by praying together:

## Sarah Ramsey – The Bridegroom's Song

*Lord, I agree with You above my mind, will, or emotions.*

*My eyes overcome You.*

*Thank you, Lord, that my steady gaze overcomes You.*

*You love my eyes being focused upon You.*

*I give you pleasure when I am totally committed.*

*Thank You, Holy Spirit, for confirming my maturity;*

*I am dedicated and able to eat the meat of Your Word.*

*I can rightly discern good and evil because of Your Word.*

*I am not ruled by my emotion but appeased by Your Spirit.*

*I'm settled down in You, my Beloved.*

*I am Your favorite,*

*I am praised and blessed because of You.*

*With all my heart I desire to honor You and give You praise.*

*All that is within me gives you praise.*

*All that I desire is in You!*

## 23

### The New Day Dawns

*But the path of the just is like the shining sun,*

*That shines ever brighter unto the perfect day*

Proverbs 4:18.

The Beloved has set the bride apart as the only one. She is His favorite and has become the favorite of the church also. Selah!

A new day dawns as the bride is revealed. However, this new day brings another question:

> Who is she who looks forth as the morning,
>
> Fair as the moon,
>
> Clear as the sun,
>
> Awesome as an army with banners?
>
> Song of Solomon 6:10

**The New Day Dawns--Another Question Arises**

As the bride is singled out and steps onto the stage, another question is posed, "Who is this?" Several questions have been asked and answered already. The daughters previously asked her in earlier parts of the Song, "Who is this (referring to the Beloved)?" "What is your Beloved?" and "Where is your Beloved?"[1] Now the question is a rhetorical one referring specifically to the bride, "Who is she coming forth as the morning sun?"

The morning breaking with the dawn is a new era of grace. There were references to this day in SOS 2:17 and 4:6 when she had refused to go with the Beloved and He had gone on without her. The phrase, "until the day breaks and the shadows flee away," is identical in these passages. The bride has moved into position in the morning light. In this early part of the day, the soft, gentle light of the moon reflects the light of the sun (or Son). We are the light of the world, as Jesus proclaimed.[2] She starts as a gentle light but gradually becomes brighter until she is a mighty force of war and brilliance in this world. We, as the church, are collectively on this same journey moving towards the noonday sun, free from shadows.

The bride is breaking forth like the dawn; shadows of compromise are conquered as the darkness gives way to morning. The light grows brighter, and the fairness of the moon gives way to the brightness of the sun. "Who is this?" What on earth is going on? She has been transformed; and the changes are becoming evident to those around her, provoking the question, "Who is she?" She is becoming unrecognizable as her former self fades away.

When the new day in the spiritual realm begins to emerge in the church, questions often loom on the horizon. Light comes into the world, and we see a day emerging without shadows. We are being transformed!

The Holy Spirit reveals four parts to this question:

1. Morning--The new revelation of the bride shines forth in this new day.
2. Fair as the moon--The bride reflects Jesus' light.
3. Clear as the sun--The bride will shine like the radiance of the sun. The dark night of the soul has passed.
4. Awesome as an army with banners--The bride is warring, carrying victory banners! She is effective and victorious over the powers of darkness.

The moon and sun symbolize the heavenly life of Christ. She has already been compared to earthly cities. Now she is being compared to celestial objects. The heavenly attributes developing in the bride's life raise the question, "Who is this bride who radiates as the morning?" The glory of the heavenly life is being revealed as she emerges from the night. She is shining progressively brighter just as the light of a new day grows more intense with time. She is also equipped as a warrior, having overcome with victory in her soul by gaining control of her mind and emotions.

**The Ultimate Makeover**

Jesus has given her a makeover. He is conforming her to His image. Isn't it funny how the world counterfeits whatever God is doing? We see makeovers everywhere showing the "before" and "after," but this is the ultimate makeover; and we have been given backstage access! In the "before," she was the little dark and lovely Shulamite maiden. In the "after," she has emerged as the beautiful and glowing bride of Christ.

The Beloved is revealing the victorious bride to His church, they--and we--see her in her wedding garments! Let's look at her: She is evangelistic--she wants others to have what she has. She is effective in the darkness of the fallen world. She looks forward as the day dawns. She is as fair as the moon, with the transparency of the sun, and is also effective at high noon in the height of battle.

God has imparted beauty to the bride through tribulations and suffering.[3] He is equipping and purifying her through testing. Jesus learned obedience by the things He suffered through (Hebrews 5:8). There is no better way to learn!

His declaration creates beauty. His Word creates foundation. In Genesis we see how God said, "Let there be light," and there was light. The knowledge of how Jesus loves the bride makes her even more beautiful. The manifold wisdom of God is revealed as the bride comes forth. It is the mystery of the fellowship of the bride and her Beloved Bridegroom spoken of in Ephesians:

> The fellowship of the mystery, which from the beginning of the ages has been hidden in God who created all things through Jesus Christ; to the intent that now the manifold wisdom of God might be made known by the church to the principalities and powers in the heavenly places, according to the eternal purpose which He accomplished in Christ Jesus our Lord, in whom we have boldness and access with confidence through faith in Him. Therefore, I ask that you do not lose heart at my tribulations for you, which is your glory (Ephesians 3:9-13).

We can look back and see the unfolding of God's plans and mysteries over time:

- God chose Abraham.
- God gave the law to Moses.
- God sent Jesus to make the way for us to draw near to Him.
- John the Baptist came wearing sackcloth and eating locusts and announced Jesus as the Messiah. The

transition from rough nature to grace was bumpy and difficult.
- The Father sent the Holy Spirit on the astounding day of Pentecost.
- Martin Luther nailed up the ninety-five theses on the Castle Church in Wittenberg, laying the groundwork for the Reformation of the church, a challenging time for the body of Christ.
- The Wesley brothers created a storm with their barroom songs converted into spiritual anthems as they preached sanctification by the Word of God.
- The Holy Spirit was poured out at Azuza Street in 1906. The Church was afraid of the emotionalism, and great conflict ensued.
- Many great evangelists rose up (Charles Finney, Billy Sunday, Billy Graham).
- Healing revivals with Oral Roberts and many others were released.
- The Charismatic Renewal touched millions with the outpouring of the Baptism of the Holy Spirit and the renewal of the gifts of the Holy Spirit; but that movement, too, was fraught with conflict and criticism, as seen in the great revivals of the 1990s in Toronto, Canada and Brownsville, Florida.
- Further illumination came through prophetic prayer and worship with emphasis on the Holy Spirit.

So, then, we should not be surprised as we are awakened and God opens a new day with the unveiling of the bride of Christ, and the question arises, "Who is this?" We are seeing the manifold wisdom of God, as mentioned in the Ephesians passage, reveal the appearance of the bride as prophesied throughout Scripture. It is becoming apparent that God is working to bring the church to maturity in preparation for His promised return. God wants us to remember what He has done, but He is on the move today!

In our study of the Song of Solomon, the bride is prophetically revealed. The King has brought her into His chambers, and He has been preparing her appearance for this great stage! In SOS 6:4-9, the power of the Beloved's words extravagantly impart the bridal attributes of beauty and holiness. It states repeatedly that we are set apart, corporately as the church and individually as the bride. God will finish what He started!

However, times of transition can leave us unprepared for new journeys. Jesus said, "'No one after drinking old wine wants the new, for they say, 'The old is better'" (Luke 5:39). It is *always* difficult to move from the old way into the new! It can be uncomfortable and unfamiliar. We are currently witnessing such a time of transition as the body of Christ is unveiled, revealing the bride of Christ, as prophesied in the Song of Solomon.

**The Proceeding Word**

God does not stay in the past. His ways unfold after giving us a "proceeding Word," as described in Matthew 4:4: "Man shall not live by bread alone, but by every word that proceeds out of the mouth of God" (NASB). The new day does not begin at noon. It is a gradual unfolding. We are seeing the curtain rise on what the prophets have longed to see. The bride's soul escapes like a bird freed from a cage, and she is carried away by the Beloved. The daughters will soon beg her to return just so that they can gaze upon her beauty, but they can't quite figure her out right now. She has grown from being the maiden who asks, "Where is He?" to this valiant, warring bride prompting others to ask in turn, "Who is *she*?" (emphasis added)

Do you know her? She is filled with hope concerning the future. She is in possession of the heavenly life of Christ. She is abundantly triumphant in relationships to her enemies and throughout life's circumstances. Her daily song sings of victory. She is valiant and strong with radiant beauty which reflects the fullness of His glory. Have you seen this maiden? Is this the image evolving from your own transformation? Are you in possession of this glorious life in Christ? Can't you just see her stepping into the light on stage as the curtain rises? I would like to be so changed by the revelation of Christ in me that people gasp, pause to look twice, and ask, "Who is *this*?"

Let's pray:

> *Lord, You are opening my eyes to see the bride of Christ emerging.*
>
> *I am thrilled at the hope of a new day dawning.*
>
> *Help me draw near and run together with You as we mature into the spotless bride.*
>
> *I need help. Please give me a desire for the new wine.*

*Let me rise like the dawning sun and shine like the midday sun.*

*May Your glory be manifested in my life.*

*Thank you, Holy Spirit, for leading and guiding me into all truth.*

*You teach me all things, and You alone can bring this to pass.*

*Amen*

## 24

### The Garden

*I went down to the garden…*

*My soul made me as the chariots of my people*

Song of Solomon 6:11-12.

The bride has matured, and her beauty has been unveiled. Earlier in the journey, the daughters had asked, "Where is He?" Their question prompted inner revelation within the bride, "He is in the garden!" Once she knows the answer to the question, she takes off to be with Him! I like that. I want to be with Him in His garden even if it means going down to the hard places! She answered the daughters' question and then went down to the garden to join Him as the bridal partner. As the daughters of Jerusalem contemplate the changes in the bride, she herself goes to see what is happening in the garden, where He resides.

> I went down to the garden of nuts
>
> To see the verdure of the valley,
>
> To see whether the vine had budded
>
> And the pomegranates had bloomed.

Song of Solomon 6:11

**Clothed with Humility**

She went *down* to see the hard places—the garden of nuts! Notice that the phrase "to see" is emphasized with repetition. She goes down *to see* the "verdure of the valley." Webster defines *verdure* as the fresh, vibrant greenness of flourishing vegetation. It is alive, growing, and flourishing.

We find hard places among the nuts, where outer shells need cracking before the precious fruit is enjoyed! This road is not an easy one. Breaking shells and prying out fruit require diligence and can be tedious work, but the bride is clothed with humility. Rather than basking in the praise of the daughters, she arises and goes to work alongside the Beloved. She is interested in what is happening in the garden. Are the vines flourishing? Are the pomegranates blooming? She is ready to roll up her sleeves and be productive. She is no longer lying on a blanket under the apple tree eating raisin cakes. Instead, she is going to see what He is doing and actively participate.

The bride pursues the garden. She wants to be in the midst of God's people and work with them. Community can be messy business, but she is willing to get her hands dirty. She commits herself to the whole church--nuts and all! (--and I'm sure we all know a few nuts!) We find all kinds in our surrounding circles, don't we? But fellowship within the body is a place that can also be rewarding. So often, while ministering to others, we find what our own hearts truly seek; and we experience the kind of spiritual fulfillment that comes only in surrendering our purposes. The inside of a nut is hearty and nourishing like meat, even if it takes longer to extract its goodness. Consider this analogy: when reaching out to those who can seem difficult—prickly or challenging to engage--in the beginning, her desire is to be like Jesus who said, "...I must be about my Father's business" (Luke 2:50). She has a willingness to invest in the budding vines, anticipating the harvest and God's visitation. Remember, the budding vines are prophetic signs that harvest will one day come and God will visit!

The garden is mentioned nine times in the Song. The first three references are to her garden,[1] and the last six references are to His garden.[2] This difference is of utmost significance: in the middle of the Song, at 4:16, a major transition takes place; and her garden becomes *His* garden.

The garden of nuts has three distinct characteristics:

- Verdure of the valley
- Budding vineyards
- Blooming pomegranates

These different stages of maturity are analogous to the

progressive maturation of the body of Christ. It is alive and green; then it buds and produces fruit.

## Progress and Victory

Song of Solomon follows the theme of a developing union with every forward step and Jesus equipping His bride to walk in mature partnership with Him.[3] She desires to see activity in the body of Christ, and she accepts the different levels of maturity found therein. This acceptance includes young ministers as well as the more experienced ones. She does not discriminate, which gives her another forward boost. The bride gives her heart to the whole body of Christ, the mature as well as the immature, and this inclusion empowers her on an entirely new level.

> Before I was even aware,
>
> My soul had made me
>
> As the chariots of my noble people.
>
> Song of Solomon 6:12

She is surprised by the sudden movement of her soul towards her noble people. Before she knows it, she is swept away like a swift chariot and becomes the vehicle to move the church forward. The chariot was the fastest mode of transportation in Solomon's time, much quicker than walking, running, or even riding a horse. She is equipped for her calling and becomes engaged in a love larger than she can fathom as she gets to work. She is overwhelmed and filled with fiery zeal for the whole end-time church. As she is maturing, the young ones and those with less understanding look up to her, too. Her task is not cumbersome. She is ready to embrace them and help them get established. She is not content with spending time only among those in her own spiritual arena. She is spreading wings. The comfort zone no longer restrains, nor is she hindered by the challenge of cultivating the lives of other people. She is fervent with self-sacrificing desire as her love for the church enthusiastically moves her. After realizing the Beloved is in the garden, she promptly leaves for the green valley of budding vines and blooming pomegranates to be with Him and becomes enveloped in His calling.

**The Challenge**

The bride's decision sparks among the daughters two different responses: a plea for her return and another question of the bride's character.

    Return, return, O Shulamite;

> Return, return, that we may look upon you!
>
> What would you see in the Shulamite--
>
> As it were, the dance of the two camps?
>
> Song of Solomon 6:13

This verse is the only place in the Song where the bride is identified as the "Shulamite." Shunem means "peace" and is a city in Israel. This word has the same root as Solomon's name, the person of peace.

Empowered by the Holy Spirit, she departs for the garden; and her friends cry, "Return!" The daughters appeal with a sense of urgency—not with just one plea, but with four cries--"Return, return, return, return!" They state their reason: "That we may look upon you." She is attractive to those with a sincere heart, and they are not ready to let her go. Several verses earlier (SOS 6:1) we saw the daughters request instruction on how to seek the Beloved. They wanted to seek the Beloved with her. Now they want to look upon her. The fragrance of Christ draws them to her; they love her ministry. They see Him in her and desire her leadership. The mature bride reflects the image of the invisible Jesus. They want to see Him through her because they do not yet have mature faith to see Him who is invisible. This description is not a criticism of the daughters. They are becoming seekers, too. In some respects, in the beginning, it can be easier to see the Lord through a mature believer than to seek Him on your own. The bride has given them a close glimpse of the Beloved, but she begins to move in a different direction.

As the daughters reach a new level of maturity, the bride is also advancing in Christ. Their growth creates a shift in movements: Although all are growing towards Christ, they are not altogether synchronous. The emphasis on "return" denotes a sort of desperation. The daughters desire the deeper spiritual things seen in the bride. In essence, they are calling for Christ's leadership through her. In other words, let us look at you! Be our teacher! Be our guide! This desire is not necessarily a bad thing. Paul wrote to the church in Thessalonica, "You became imitators of us and of the Lord…" Paul gave the early church a worthy example to pattern in their own lives just as the Bride is giving the daughters.

The daughters' enthusiasm is also met with another response, as seen in the second part of this verse. Bear with this more difficult portion of the passage for a moment. Glance back at the latter part of v. 13 on the previous page. (As an aside, particular verses can be challenging in the Song when the speaker is not easily identified. Some translations and interpretations vary in this regard. A case in point is v.13b.) Very clearly, the daughters of Jerusalem are speaking to the bride with the cries of "Return!" in the first portion of the verse. However, the speaker is not as obvious in the second portion of the verse. There is a hint of skepticism or perhaps even sarcasm in the later response, "What would you see in the Shulamite--as it were, the dance of two camps?" I follow the line of the teaching of Mike Bickle, which recognizes this question as the voice of the watchmen who previously wounded the Shulamite maiden.[4] A case could be made that the second portion comes from the bride herself as she questions what the daughters see in her. Perhaps the second response could be from other daughters who are not completely on board with her yet. No matter who the speaker is, the point at hand is that conflict arises over the bride, who is now completely "sold out" for Christ.

A wholehearted bride interrupts the agenda of a lukewarm church. This process is not without conflict. The "dance of two camps" distinguishes between those who say "Yes!" in their spirits and those who refuse to move on in the Lord. One camp sees her passion for the Lord and desires this type of intimate relationship for themselves. Another camp is uncomfortable in her presence and doesn't quite know what to think about her passionate love for her Beloved. The question begs an answer: "What do you see in the Shulamite maiden that we don't see?" They just don't get it (or want to get it). Misunderstanding of the bride breeds skepticism in the beholder. Wholeheartedness and passionate love are offensive to some parts of the church, but the bride is lovesick and has left tradition and religion far behind. She has found the real thing and won't let go despite persecution and offense.

**What Do You See?**

Do you see what I see? I see a bride who has fully satisfied the Lord:

- First, the Beloved admonishes her with new commendation (SOS 6:4-9).
- Second, the glory of her heavenly life is revealed (6:10) as a new day rises; her heavenly qualities (her identity) are bestowed. She is as awesome as an army with banners.
- Third, she is clothed with humility (6:11). Rather than basking in praise, her thoughts are concerned with others, and she goes to work. She is willing and unwavering. Her humility causes her to focus on what needs to be done rather than to rest in her revealed glory.
- Fourth, she makes great progress and obtains victory (6:12); she is willing and empowered as she receives supernatural ability. She is an overcomer, and the victory in her soul becomes a vehicle for the Lord's movements.

I see the bride victorious in battle, fully committed to her goal, and not a people-pleaser. I want to be like her! What do you see in her, precious one?

Let's pray:

*Oh, to have eyes to see and ears to hear what the Spirit is saying to the church!*

*The Spirit and the Bride say, "Come."*

*Help us Holy Spirit!*

*Gives us the willingness and the passionate desires of a sold-out Bride!*

Sarah Ramsey – The Bridegroom's Song

*Clothe me with humility.*

*I seek You in Your garden.*

*My garden has become Your garden.*

*Lead me according to Your ways everlasting.*

*A new day dawns, and I am running after You!*

*Amen.*

## 25

**The Daughters Bless the Bride**

*How beautiful are you...O prince's daughter!*

*A king is held captive by your tresses*

(Song of Solomon 7:1a, 5).

Throughout their relationship the Beloved has spoken encouraging words to His bride, always beginning with a description of her eyes. The daughters observe as the bride continues to mature, even as they cry for her return in the midst of conflict. Jesus has been continually sowing seed into the bride with His words. His words bring change from the inside out, from the head down. Jesus, by the power of the Holy Spirit, changes her first on the inside so that she is empowered to *be* holy on the outside. Now the daughters, representative of the body of Christ, see the fruit in her life and praise her.

Here in Chapter 7, the daughters' beautiful chorus begins with her feet because they see that which manifests outwardly—her words and her walk. In vv. 1-5, ten more affirmations are given to the bride. This is another passage in the Song of Solomon where there could be some debate about who is actually speaking the affirming words to the maiden. For the purposes of this study, I am taking the stance that the daughters of Jerusalem likely address the prince's daughter (the Shulamite maiden) in order to answer the sarcastic statement, "What do you see in her--the dance of two camps?" seen in the previous chapter. Don't get too hung up here in over-analyzing the dialogue. The overriding significance is in the meaning of the words and the prophetic description (given through the Holy Spirit), which can be applied to the individual believer. In contrast with the way the Beloved had previously addressed her, these verses begin with the feet and reveal her fruitfulness. They end with four attributes of her head, her inward qualities.

How beautiful are your feet in sandals,

O prince's daughter!

The curves of your thighs are like jewels,

The work of the hands of a skillful workman.

Your navel is a rounded goblet;

It lacks no blended beverage.

Your waist is a heap of wheat

Set about with lilies.

Your two breasts are like two fawns,

Twins of a gazelle.

Your neck is like an ivory tower,

Your eyes like the pools of Heshbon

By the gate of Bath Rabbim.

Your nose is like the tower of Lebanon

Which looks toward Damascus.

Your head crowns you like Mount Carmel,

And the hair of your head is like purple;

A king is held captive by your tresses.

Song of Solomon 7:1-5

The secrets found in the symbolic description of the bride are keys that open treasures from the bottom to the top:

- *How beautiful are your feet in sandals....*
  Feet speak of evangelism. Isaiah 52 says the feet of those who bring good news are beautiful to others. Sandals represent dignity and honor. The father put shoes on his son's feet when the prodigal returned home (Luke 15:22). The bride is equipped to walk in the fruitfulness of evangelism. She is an evangelist-- prosperous and powerful in her walk and in delivering the good news. Her feet are shod with the gospel of peace, and she is ready to walk (Ephesians 6:15).

- *The curves of your thighs are like jewels....*
  The thighs give power to your walk. The bride has been "working out" by doing the Word. These muscular

qualities are like costly jewels set by the hands of God. (Feet and thighs denote skills visible in the outer life.) She has on her running shoes--just look at the muscles in those thighs! She has strength and power in her legs to carry the good news of the Gospel. She has a good personal trainer and years of discipline and training under her belt. Her motivation is not of the flesh; she is the workmanship of God. Her strength comes as a gift from a skilled carpenter (Jesus) and not from her own fleshly efforts.

- *Your navel is a rounded goblet...lacks no blended beverage*
The navel represents the inner life. Foundational nourishment comes from the mother through the navel. The bride is spiritually prepared and able to impart life to the ones she births. The life she imparts is healthy and balanced. She gives nourishment from the ample supply from which she has already received. She has learned to partake of His life and sustenance and, therefore, is fruitful in the lives of others.

- *Your waist is a heap of wheat....*
The waist is symbolic of the womb that produces abundant harvest (wheat). Lilies are mentioned again. They represent the pure and innocent converts which Jesus brings to fill His garden. A "heap" of wheat means a lot of wheat. Wheat is used to make bread, which sustains life. The navel and womb speak of both attitudes and values seen in the inner life. She is a

nurturer and imparts an abundance of healthy life.

- *...Breasts...like two fawns, twins of a gazelle.*
  The two breasts like fawns represent passion and the ability to nurture others. She has matured and is ready to have babies of her own to nurture. She edifies and gives life, yet she does not lose her passion for the Beloved. She is maturing in contrast to little sister (mentioned later in SOS 8:8), who has no breasts. The daughters see her passion. Jesus sees her abilities to nurture and feed, as this attribute will be mentioned again in Chapter 8.

- *Your neck is like an ivory tower....*
  The neck is symbolic of free will. Her neck is described as an ivory tower. She is not stiff-necked, however, but yielding and submissive. A tower provides a vantage point from which to see and offers protection and strength for spiritual warfare. The tower of her neck is made of ivory, which is a soft material but costly and rare. Ivory is produced by the sacrifice of an elephant, which indicates a suffering process. Submission involves suffering--dying to your personal agenda. Submission to authority has made her a soldier, and she is ready to do war. She is humble. Because of her submission to the workings of God, her neck has become beautiful and supple with the quality of ivory. Earlier in SOS 4:4, her neck represented power like the tower of David, which was a kind of armory for weapons. Her yielded will, then, is not only beautiful, but is also powerful.

- *...Your eyes like the pools in Heshbon by the gate of Bath Rabbim.*
  Eyes provide spiritual insight and focus. She has clear revelation like the pools of Heshbon, abundantly clean. Her dove's eyes are open to the light of heaven, suggesting a pure heart open to God and free from the distractions of the flesh. The eyes always represent a discerning or beholding power, but this reference to the pools of Heshbon takes the meaning a step further. Here the eyes are likened to the deep places of the heart, dug by the very hand of God. Pools are filled with springs of water unearthed by digging deeply, much as we mine truths from the depths of God's Word. A pool of water, in and of itself, has no grandeur or power of its own accord, but it does have the ability to reflect the beauty of the surrounding universe. Think on that awhile.

- *Your nose is like the tower of Lebanon which looks towards Damascus.*
  Her nose is compared to the tower of Lebanon. Her nose has not been previously mentioned. It is symbolic of discernment. It allows her to "sniff out" the enemy. Damascus was Israel's greatest and fiercest enemy during the time of Solomon. From a tower, or heavenly vantage point, the bride's discernment guards and protects the King's property as well as the daughters and little sisters. She has a well-developed inner sense that can be trusted to discern truth, not by natural means but through supernatural guidance from the Holy Spirit. She is perceptive and can distinguish the subtleties between fragrances--good and evil odors. (Hebrews 5:14)

- *Your head crowns you like Mount Carmel....*
  The head represents leadership. She has leadership qualities and authority like Elijah displayed on Mount Carmel when he called down fire from heaven in front of all of Israel and the prophets in order to prove the falsehood of Baal (1 Kings 18). Mighty prayers were offered and answers received on Mount Carmel. The helmet of hope inspires and protects her thought life and keeps her pure. The head is one of the most significant targets in spiritual warfare. Satan's attacks usually begin with an assault against the thoughts. When our image of God is clouded and our hope is undermined, we are spiritually vulnerable. She has wisdom and power against satanic attack as she is enabled by the Holy Spirit to demolish demonic forces (1 Thessalonians 5:8). She is a strong leader backed by the power of God.[1]

- *The hair of your head is like purple; A king is held captive by your tresses.*
  We have established that hair indicates commitment and extraordinary dedication. Hair speaks of the consecration of the Nazarite vow (Numbers 6) and also covering and submission (1 Corinthians 11:1-16). This passage says the "king is held captive by your tresses," implying that her yielded spirit takes hold of the King's heart. Her hair is described as purple, representing royalty and the authority of the throne. Her commitment and dedication have a royal flavor in direct proportion to the influence the King has on her life. She is loyal to the King even under pressure. It is the "I will" in her heart. The King is

mesmerized by her abundant faithfulness as it flows from her head like tresses cascading down her shoulders.[2]

Isn't it fun to gain insight into God's Word? How inspiring! I love it! Oh, to be like her!

The bride has been walking out her salvation, and her good works have revealed Jesus to the daughters. They, in turn, describe what they see, beginning with her feet--shod with the preparation of the gospel of peace. Shulamite means "a person of peace." Jesus said, "Blessed are the peacemakers," and, "My peace I leave with you." She is like the Prince of Peace, her Beloved, and she has His nature. She is in union with Him. She is wearing her walking/running shoes and doing the Word of God.

I believe the Holy Spirit is speaking words of affirmation to the bride through this chorus from the daughters of Jerusalem, her peers. She is called the prince's daughter, suggesting that it is the daughters and not the Bridegroom speaking. Remember, the Beloved has been calling her "My love" or "My spouse," and the "prince's daughter" is a less-intimate term. Notice how this passage begins with her feet and moves up to her eyes. They are watching her walk as she keeps her dove's eyes focused on Jesus. Unlocking the language is once again a treasure being revealed by her walk and reflected in her eyes.

**The Chosen Generation**

The bride has matured. The love of the Beloved and the grace of God have surrounded her and enabled her to love the Lord with all her heart, soul, mind, and strength. As we come closer to the end of the Song, it's good to remember how we got here and to acknowledge that we, too, are a chosen and unique generation. The Holy Spirit is awakening love for the Bridegroom King. We, the church, are seeing our Beloved. He is bringing us into His chambers, and He is revealing Himself to us. We know our identity individually and corporately.

In review:

- In Chapter 4:1-5, the Beloved makes eight statements, six dealing with the bride's head.
- In Chapter 5, the bride describes how she sees Him and declares His beauty. The bride gives ten characteristics about the Beloved to answer the daughters' question, "Who is He?"
- In Chapter 6, the Beloved gives her more affirmation and declares that she is an awesome warrior whose eyes overcome Him. He also singles her out as the only one for Him.
- In Chapter 7, the daughters see her beauty in Christ and admire her fruitfulness. They shower her with ten statements of affirmation.

As the bride, we must sometimes hear something repeatedly in order to really believe it is true. I remember the first time Paul, my husband of fifty-five years, told me he loved me. I wanted to hear it over and over again, and I asked him again and again until I wore him out! That's how a bride needs to be cherished continuously. We never want our Beloved to stop repeating, "I love you". It is wonderful how He knows our deepest needs and continues to tell us how wonderful we are and how He loves us so. Can you believe that here in Chapter 7 He is still reminding the bride who she really is? I take comfort in knowing she needs to hear it as much as I do. In Chapter 1 his first words had been "O, my love," and throughout the Song he has continued. Now in Chapter 7 He is affirming her yet again, this time through the body of Christ.

My heart is stirred by the Word of God. Selah!

Let's pray:

*O Lord, You really do love me!*

*Thank You for continuing to affirm who I am.*

*You remind me how You see me as I truly am to You.*

*It's almost too much to believe You are held captive by me,*

*That I can captivate You with my attributes, character,*

*and beauty--*

*only because they are expressions of You.*

*You see in me the one You created me to be.*

*Thank You for loving me and giving me life.*

*I give my life back to You.*

*Amen.*

# 26

### Take Hold of Me, My Beloved...I Am Yours

*I will go up to the palm tree, I will take hold of its branches...*

*I am my beloved's, and his desire is toward me*

(Song of Solomon 7:8, 7:10a).

Throughout the Song Jesus continues to encourage the bride with words of affirmation and love. Aren't you glad He never tells her how poorly she is doing? This grace gives me much encouragement! In the next verse Jesus spontaneously interrupts the daughters' chorus with His own descriptive words. Let's look at His words as we begin this chapter:

> How fair and how pleasant you are,
>
> O love, with your delights!
>
> Song of Solomon 7:6

We can tell Jesus is speaking because this language is the same He has used to address her throughout the Song, "My love, My fair one, or My spouse." We need affirmation from our Beloved and He needs the same from us. To hear the Beloved Himself describe the bride's maturity is amazing. Knowing that I delight God gives strength to my heart and refreshes me as I am awakened to His love. The Beloved tells her how He feels about her; she is fair and pleasant and a delight to the King of Glory! She thrills the heart of God. Nothing is more delightful to Him than the heart of the bride overflowing to Him and His people. Our voices are sweet and our faces lovely to Him, even in our struggle to overcome sin. Can we dare embrace the concept of how much God loves us without letting our emotions overwhelm us? Would you dare believe this Word is for you, sweet follower of Jesus?

**Developing Spiritual Stature**

Jesus continues His beautiful Song.

> This stature of yours is like a palm tree,
>
> And your breasts like its clusters.
>
> Song of Solomon 7:7

"Stature" refers to her spiritual maturity. She is tall and straight. About the palm tree in the Song of Solomon, Mike Bickle expounds: "The palm tree grows very high and very straight because its roots go very deep. This is a picture of tremendous perseverance under pressure. The winds come, and the palm trees don't break. They find water sources way under the ground."[1] Palm trees are able to endure the dry seasons in the same way the mature believer digs deeper and develops stronger roots when outside sources seem to run dry. Interestingly, palm branches were used to usher Jesus into the city before He died on the cross. He was entering into the maturity of His greatest assignment. The Beloved is saying, "You're like a palm tree. You find the deep and satisfying waters underneath in Me. Your faith is not uprooted, and you don't move-during the storm. You are a sign of victory."

The bride is growing up. She is looking like Jesus--and looking like her Father. She has roots that touch the deep fountain of living water beneath her in the midst of the wilderness desert. We are believers living in a desert world and subject to fierce trials and testing from the constant storms. Yet a hidden union with God will produce blossoms and bear fruit under the most dire circumstances.

"Blessed is the man who trusts in the Lord,

And whose hope is the LORD.

For he shall be like a tree planted by the waters,

Which spreads out its roots by the river,

And will not fear when heat comes;

But its leaf will be green,

And will not be anxious in the year of drought,

Nor will cease from yielding fruit."

Jeremiah 17:7-8

Earlier in her journey, the bride had loved the passion but had little capacity to nurture others; now her ability to nurture is growing, and she has the capacity to satisfy hunger in others. The bride has matured not only in stature but also in ability. When we understand the deeper meaning of the symbolism, we see the beauty of these passages in a way that is not overtly sexual but is symbolic language to describe the maturity of the bride.

Let's take a moment to look more closely at the terminology the Beloved uses. He describes her breasts like clusters; She is maturing and her breasts are growing in kind, representing her ability to nurture and edify others in a larger capacity. "For whoever has, to him more will be given, and he will have abundance" (Matthew 13:12). Her breasts, previously described as fawns, began as small but full of passionate love and emotion for her Beloved (SOS 4:5). She was faithful in her passion but has now received an abundance to nurture with two full breasts. Passion for our Lord from within overflows into the lives of others. Both are important in our relationship with the Lord. The bride is becoming a mother nourishing her babes with milk! Breasts like clusters indicate that they are overflowing, no longer like budding fawns but full of power and sustenance and able to nurture and encourage others in the body with the new and fresh wine from the springs.

**Jesus Takes Hold of His Bride**

The bride is growing up in *all* things, becoming Christ-like. The Beloved is about to take hold of her. Listen to His words in verse 8:

> I said, "I will go up to the palm tree,
>
> I will take hold of its branches."
>
> Song of Solomon 7:8

The branches are where the fruit is produced and nurtured. Let's not forget the value of the parable; so simple, yet so complex! (Remember what you read about parables in Chapter 1.) In this picture the bride is a palm tree, and Jesus is taking hold of her and releasing His power into the branches and roots so that much fruit will come forth and be released into the kingdom. Apart from His power, she can do nothing. This dependence brings glory to the Father. We see the same picture in the parable of the vine and branches in John 15:1-8.

As the Bridegroom takes hold of her branches and releases the power of God, she will have attestation (evidence provided by bearing witness). God gave attestation to Aaron, or authenticated His power, when his rod budded (Numbers 17:8), designating him as God's choice as priest. Likewise, God approved and gave attestation to Jesus with signs, wonders, and miracles (Acts 2:22). Here, the bride receives attestation from God, and He is getting ready to empower her to move. Her contemporaries ask, "Who is she?" But, the Bridegroom King endorses her by answering, "I will go up and take hold of her branches!" He is saying, "*I will* show you who she is!"

**Commissioning the Bride**

Jesus continues by issuing three prophetic statements and commissioning her to nurture others in the power of the Holy Spirit as pictured symbolically by the vine.

> Let now your breasts be like clusters of the vine,
>
> The fragrance of your breath like apples,
>
> And the roof of your mouth like the best wine.
>
> Song of Solomon 7:8b-9a

He has said, "I will go up. I will take hold. He now says with a command, "Let now"!

- Let now...your breasts be full of passion and nurture--The bride's ability to nurture is enabled and supplied by the power of the Holy Spirit and not by her natural ability and body.

- Let now...your breath be like apples--Her breath is like the wind of the Holy Spirit, fragrant and refreshing. Breath comes from the inner life and, like apples, is nourishing and fragrant. Jesus breathed the Holy Spirit into the disciples (John 20:22). Jesus is likewise releasing the Holy Spirit from within her to refresh others.

- Let now...your mouth be like the best wine—Throughout the Song the mouth refers to her intimacy with Him. Jesus has saved the best wine until the end of the age (like the miracle of turning water into wine at the wedding feast). At such a time, He will bring the church into greater intimacy with Him. The roof of her mouth indicates the Holy Spirit is imparting fiery passion. Remember, the Song begins with the bride seeking the kisses of His mouth. He is answering her fervent prayer and imparting passion to her.

His prophecies (words) take hold of her and impart power to her for three unique purposes: 1) Nurturing others to maturity 2) Anointing her with the sweet fragrance of the Holy Spirit to release intimacy within the Body (the Church), and 3) Enabling her to enjoy the best wine and maintain intimacy with the Beloved.

**The Bride's Response**

Suddenly, the Beloved's words give way for the bride to commit to receive. The bride is anointed with the Holy Spirit (breath) to awaken others who are spiritual sleepers, and she accepts the assignment and declares:

> The wine goes down smoothly for my Beloved,
>
> Moving gently the lips of the sleepers.
>
> Song of Solomon 7:9b

Jesus never calls the bride "My beloved"; so we will consider that the bride is speaking here.

She is acknowledging to the Beloved that she is receiving His words eagerly and without resistance. She responds with obedience and fully accepts what He has for her. He is also receiving love from her. The intimate relationship between the individual believer and the Beloved is the best wine of all, and this nourishing drink goes down smoothly for the Beloved. I love this phrase. It indicates that her obedience to the Holy Spirit is rooted in a deep foundation of her love for Jesus. "This passage is a wonderful confession of faith in times when the Lord challenges us in a way that seems difficult.... It is a spiritually romantic and poetic way to declare our commitment to obey."[2]

Both the bride and the Beloved are enjoying this sweet union, and their mutual affection is intoxicating, to the extent that it spreads to the hearts of other believers. It's like watching two young lovebirds snuggling each other on a park bench. It revives young love in others. The Lord is now using the bride to awaken others who are spiritually sleeping and bring them to a life of worship and passion for Jesus. The more the bride fully receives from the Lord and gives of herself in bridal partnership, the more she is able to impact others. We are the generation being awakened to passion for Jesus and desiring to see others awakened alongside us.

**Stolen Identity Recovered**

My great love for my Beloved is rooted in the revelation of His passionate desire and enjoyment of me. His love for me is the source of my motivation to love Him more fully. My Beloved desires *me* the most—more than any other part of His creation. He desires me with His entire being. His unfathomable and undivided love has no end and reminds me of an anonymous quote which may help us relate: "For a mother is the only person on earth who can divide her love among ten children and each child still have all her love." Because He is perfect, He is able to love us all perfectly, equally, and completely. Each one is the favorite because He *is* love. He desires my fully surrendered heart in return for His love. Because we have all been loved imperfectly on earth, to some degree, our self-value is marred. However, I can allow my Beloved's value of me to define how I feel about myself and fill the hole the earth has left in us. Throughout the Song the daughters have spoken, the Beloved has spoken, and the bride has spoken. She knows who she is now--His favorite! Her identity has been restored, and we can rejoice with her and claim our identity in Him too:

> I am my beloved's,
>
> And his desire is toward me.
>
> Song of Solomon 7:10

We awaken spiritually when we know who He is and who we are in return. This truth makes me become aggressive in my confession and want to shout this out loud: "I belong to the lover of my soul and His desire is for *me*!" Can you see her progression from "He is mine" to "I am His and He *desires* me?" This word *desire* here brings a deeper and more personal meaning to His love, a sort of desperation implying that He will not be satisfied with anything less than *my* love. No matter how many come into the fullness of His love, He will not be content without me!

**Three Defining Statements in the Song of Solomon**

In this chapter we are focusing on the third of three defining statements found in the Song. This final culminating statement shows us how much she has progressed and is evidence of her maturing love toward her Beloved. Notice that none of these declarations are necessarily wrong, but the emphasis of her words reveals much about her heart at each stage in her maturity. Let's summarize her process and see how far she has come:

- In 2:16 she declares, "My beloved is mine, and I am his." In this statement the bride's focus is on *her* perspective. She says, in essence, "He belongs to me," and I have the rights to enjoy Him. Then, almost as an afterthought, she says, "but I am also his," acknowledging, "He does have some rights to me." This declaration immediately followed her refusal to go to the mountains with the Beloved. She was not yet fully devoted, although she felt secure in His love. As their relationship develops, she comes through the tight and hard places without abandoning faith and hope; and love grows.

- In 6:3 she confesses, "I am my beloved's, and my beloved is mine." This follows the glorious description of the Beloved to the daughters and the realization that He resides in the garden of her heart. The order has significantly reversed. He is now on the throne of her heart. She sees the Beloved as the center of attraction and is focused upon Him first above everything else. With eyes focused on Him, she is fully surrendered, even though she still has some secondary emphasis on herself.

- Now, here in 7:10, she exclaims, "I am my beloved's, and his desire is toward me." She is embracing His great love and understands that she is the object of His affection. She has given Him her whole heart, totally abandoned. She is fully His, and His desire is all she really cares about. She is no longer double-minded in her confession. This abandonment is not a pompous declaration but is confirmation that she has fully received Him as well. It is one thing to love someone; but love takes on another dimension when the love is a two-way-street, enjoyed mutually, given and accepted unconditionally by both. My Beloved's desire is towards me. Not only does He love me, he is *in love* with me. Selah!

The bride has learned not to rely on feelings but to rely on the trustworthiness of His words about her. Feelings change, but her covenant with the Beloved is forever unchangeable. It is built on faith in what He says, not on feelings; but erupting emotions affirm the truth about His love. The transition in the bride's heart has now fully taken place, and she is His—*completely* His. She understands and wholeheartedly acknowledges, "I am my Beloved's, and His desire is towards me." The Beloved was committed to the bride all along--from the beginning of time, but she is just now realizing it. It is a truly a love story of epic proportions.

We have discovered many powerful confessions in this chapter. The Lord wants to take hold of us in a powerful way and flow through our branches, and we are now able to embrace Him fully in return. Let's pray a few of these confessions aloud:

## Sarah Ramsey – The Bridegroom's Song

*I agree with Your words, my Beloved Bridegroom King.*

*Take hold of us, O God, take hold of us! Endorse Your church!*

*Take hold of me, my Beloved! Take hold of my branches!*

*You manifest Your power through my branches.*

*You are the Vine, I am the branch.*

*You will go up, Sweet Jesus!*

*You will go up and take hold of my branches and release Your power to make me fruitful!*

*Oh, take hold of me, Jesus!*

*Release the power of God in me through the branches of Your church.*

*Take hold of my husband and me.*

*Take hold of my family.*

*Take hold of the church where you have placed me.*

*Take hold of my community.*

*Take hold of my state.*

*Take hold of the country!*

*Take hold of us, my Beloved!*

*Oh, Jesus, You will take hold of me and anoint me to*

*love You and nurture others with sweetness.*

*Breathe on me, my Beloved! I love you, Holy Spirit, and thank You for saving the best wine for the bride! I am thirsty, and come to drink my fill of Your Spirit!*

*Let the anointing of the Spirit be released through me!*

*I am my Yours, Beloved, and Your desire is towards me.*

*You desire me the most, and I am fully Yours.*

*Yes, Lord!*

*Selah!*

*Amen.*

## 27

### Come, My Beloved

*Let us go forth...let us lodge...let us get up early...let us see…*

*There I will give you my love*

(Song of Solomon 7:11-13).

The bride has found her identity in Christ. The Beloved has announced His love and delight in the bride for all to hear, and He has chosen her as His favorite. The daughters have also praised her. The Beloved has taken hold of her and anointed her branches for fruitfulness. The wind of the Holy Spirit has filled her, and she is equipped and empowered with the fruits of the Spirit to sweetly and faithfully do the work of the kingdom. She has labored to rest. It is no longer "me," but "Thee in me." She has taken up His yoke, learned from Him, and found rest in her soul. Love is waiting in the vineyard. She is a voluntary lover and has the courage to invite her Beloved to come away with her. This invitation echoes the one He used to beckon her in the beginning of the Song. She is reciprocating His lovely request and paints a beautiful picture worded for us to enjoy:

She cries out:

Come, my beloved,

Let us go forth to the field;

Let us lodge in the villages.

Let us get up early to the vineyards;

Let us see if the vine has budded,

Whether the grape blossoms are open,

And the pomegranates are in bloom.

There I will give you my love.

The mandrakes give off a fragrance,

And at our gates are pleasant fruits,

All manner, new and old,

Which I have laid up for you, my beloved.

Song of Solomon 7:11-13

**Let Us**

Notice, "let us" is spoken four times in this passage. She is aggressively interceding and asking, "let us go forth" into Your kingdom and labor for rewards and prizes. We all enjoy being gifted rewards and prizes at the end of a great challenge. She has begun to value storing up spiritual treasures and is excited for the challenge ahead! They are in part her gift to Him. She says:

- "Let us go forth to the field;"--She acknowledges the harvest of the kingdom is accomplished in the fields. She knows how to till, plant seed, and wait for the ripening of hearts for the harvest. She knows her Lord is the Gardener who makes things grow. This is *work,* but she is not afraid to roll up her sleeves and get sweaty and dirty and is patient in the process. She wants to do this *alongside* her Beloved.

- "Let us lodge…."--She is not in a hurry and expresses her desire to "set up shop," so to speak. Whatever it takes, and for as long as it takes, she is willing to go the distance and stay in the villages of the people she is called to serve. She is getting out of her comfort zone again and going to the people on their home turf, so they have no excuse to not hear of and experience His work. She is no longer content to rest in the palace, even though she is fully secure in her royal position, as we saw in the previous chapter.

- "Let us get up early to the vineyards;"--She is ready to get up early and look for life and enter the days ahead with anticipation. Vineyards bring forth wine. She eagerly anticipates sharing the "new wine" with her Beloved. The suggestion of getting up early indicates her willingness to be prepared and sacrifice her own comfort. She dreams and makes plans for the journey together ahead.

- "Let us see if the vine is budded,"--She is eager to catch a glimpse of the tender grapes, even if they are not quite ready for harvest. She sees value in the process and progress, not just the final product. She is excited to see progress on the vine, which gives her encouragement for what is to come. She wants to share in the joy of seeing budding believers with her Beloved because they are the product of their union of love.

Can't you just see her confidence? Can't you see her grab the Beloved by the hand and run, saying, "Come, my Beloved...let us go, let us lodge, let us get up, let us see!" Can't you just see Him throw back His head in laughter and joyfully embrace her as they go? His heartbeat is as her own and lifts up her soul. Can't you just see the bride energized by His love and committed to His plan? She is eager to move and complete the harvest. She sees the sovereignty of God but also the responsibility of a believer united with Christ.

She wants to walk in the vineyard with her Beloved to see how things are developing. She is interested in the budding vine. She realizes fruit doesn't grow in a day. "Therefore be patient, brethren, until the coming of the Lord. See how the farmer waits for the precious fruit of the earth, waiting patiently for it until it receives the early and latter rain. You also be patient. Establish your hearts, for the coming of the Lord is at hand" (James 5:7-8). She values the bud but is patient and waits for the harvest. Plucking fruit before it is ripe spoils the sweet reward. She has great anticipation for what is ahead. She understands that this is a maturing process and that it takes time to meet the needs of the body, and she advances the purposes of God as she waits.

The Shulamite wants to explore among the budding vines with Him. This new growth in the crop promises a great harvest ahead but needs time to mature. She labors with Him to nurture the blossoms to come to full love (purpose). They observe the different stages of budding blossoms which will soon produce the juicy fruit of the pomegranate, a symbolic picture of the corporate church on the vine (the community of believers budding and individual pomegranates with all those juicy seeds.)

We can learn so much here as we compare this heavenly picture to an earthly marriage. The great mystery of Ephesians 5 describes this same unity in marriage. The husband and wife become one flesh, united, like Christ and the church. Each is fruitful when united. Marriage partners are an extension of one another. Husbands long for wives to respect them, to be eager for and supportive of their endeavors. Eve was created to come alongside Adam; and the husband needs support from his wife, just as she needs to be loved and cherished by him. Marriage brings mutual edification of each partner when it operates according to His designed plan. The union of man and woman also brings forth children. Jesus longs for the same willingness in our souls as we come alongside Him and are fruitful in His kingdom, reproducing heavenly rewards. Sometimes when I respond to Jesus spiritually, I find it easier to respond to my husband in the natural world. It's a beautiful picture, but it is a great mystery.

The bride is eager in her work, but her goal is to maintain

intimacy in the process. The challenge is to cultivate intimacy and be a lover of God in the midst of the immature (growing) body of Christ.

**Loving in the Midst of Labor**

Ministry flows out of union. The passage says, "*There*, I will give thee my love," (emphasis added) meaning in the fields, villages, and vineyards. She does not give Him love in isolation but by loving His people through laboring, warfare, persecution, and sacrifice. Working with Him is not a distraction from her love for Him. In earlier stages of her walk, work was the cause of estrangement. Now she knows she must love Him in the midst of laboring. As they work and fellowship together, she is no longer compelled by others to work. She is no longer working out of her own desire. This is *His* desire. True ministry flows out of union and does not compete with intimacy—it is a result of it! Faith and works have been united at last (James 2:14-18). Hallelujah!

It is easy to lose intimacy in the midst of the burden of ministry. In Revelation 2:4 Jesus gave admonition to the church in Ephesus to return to the priority of their "first love." The maturing bride knows the challenge of "keeping the main thing their primary goal" and actively works towards serving the Lord first, not the ministry. Her prioritization of allegiance to her Lord enables her to love openly in the midst of ministry, warfare, and persecution, not just in the privacy of the bedchamber. It is one thing to give Jesus our love in private with no distractions, but it calls on a greater depth of allegiance to love Him in battle when we are hurt, tired, mistreated or abused. Many emotions get stirred up in battle, and some of them may be unpleasant or difficult. Sometimes we are disappointed or misunderstood, and conflict or even confusion can set in. It is fierce on the battlefield, but He is with us in the trenches. When we keep our focus on Him, these hurdles are more manageable and don't derail the work of ministry. When we keep our focus on ministry our satisfaction wanes and we become burnt out. We can still work our tails off in the food pantry, Vacation Bible School, children's or men's/women's ministry, teaching, or on mission trips, etc., and maintain intimacy while loving Him extravagantly in the process. The goal is to stay in love with Him while doing the work. Intimacy and servant-hood go hand in hand, and one is not complete without the other. When I get my identity primarily from ministry rather than my Lord, I am vulnerable and the following can occur:

1. I may become defensive toward correction.
   Pride tells me that if I don't do it, it won't get done.
2. I may over-commit, and the work becomes more important than the Lord.
3. I may become overcome with fear and jealousy and driven to get the job done, even urging others to work/labor without developing the needed intimacy with the Beloved.
4. My purpose of ministry can become dislocated to myself, and perspectives about what others are doing or not doing become distorted.
5. I may become performance-oriented.

When my identity is in Christ, I share the affection of God's people. I am secure in my position. I can let go of perfectionism and accept my own mistakes as well as those of others'. I can allow things to develop in God's timing and simply be obedient to the tasks at hand. I pray more and talk less. I allow God to cultivate His gifts in others and am appreciative of what they bring to the table. I can sincerely celebrate in the ministry successes of others without comparing my achievements to theirs. I do not revel in others' failures. I can deeply enjoy intimacy with God in the midst of the labor and be content with my portion of work in His kingdom.

**The Fragrance of Love**

This intimate union produces a lovely fragrance and fruits which are sweet to taste:

> The mandrakes give off a fragrance,
>
> And at our gates are pleasant fruits,
>
> All manner, new and old,
>
> Which I have laid up for you, my Beloved.
>
> Song of Solomon 7:13

Mandrakes are purple-flowering plants which produce a beautiful fragrance, enticing one into intimate love. The lovely aroma of mandrakes fills the atmosphere. In the midst of the field and vineyard, love for the Beloved fills the air. In the ancient world the mandrake was a well-known aphrodisiac but also had helpful medicinal properties. (In Genesis 30:1, 14-16, Rachel asked for mandrakes when she could not conceive children.) In the midst of this sweet aroma, all kinds of fruits are laid up for the Beloved. Bearing fruit brings to the bride's life purpose which can be found only in her Beloved. Jesus said, "You did not choose Me but I chose you and appointed you that you should go and bear fruit and that your fruit should remain…" (John 15:16).

As believers we can partake in the enjoyment of pleasant fruits at the gates with our Beloved. There is a harvest; there is revival at our gates. We have the honor of laying up fruits for Him, the old and the new. The truth of the law (old) and grace (new) converge and are perfectly blended for His pleasure. The bride's fruit is full of grace but also true to His Word; it is not rotten, but pleasant and tasty. He promised to climb the towering palm and take hold of the emerging fruit, breasts full of clustering grapes (7:8). The bride now stores them up for her Beloved and takes delight in His pleasure (7:13). Selah!

What happy thoughts and a lovely way to end a chapter! The Bridegroom and bride are working in the vineyards and fields, enjoying the journey together and deeply intimate in the midst of their labor. She gives her love to Him there and opens herself to Him fully. The fragrance of their love fills the atmosphere and will entice others to take this journey into deeper intimacy with Him. So ends Song of Solomon, chapter 7. But the conversation proceeds into chapter 8 as their love story continues.

Before we move on, let's just take a moment to take it in and acknowledge the lover of our souls:

Let's pray:

*Oh, Jesus, how wonderful You are!*

*I love getting to know You as my Bridegroom King.*

*Thank You for eyes to see and ears to hear what the Spirit is saying to the church.*

*I just want to take some time to pause and reflect on this good news.*

*I can maintain intimacy with You in the midst of a busy life.*

*We can be fruitful together in the vineyards and enjoy the work of the harvest.*

*Thank You for drawing me into this intimacy with You.*

*I commit, once again, to run with You.*

*I will give You my love there, in the fields, my Beloved.*

*I will lay up for You fruits for Your good pleasure.*

*Amen.*

## 28

### The Lovesick Bride

*Oh, that you were like my brother…*

*I would kiss you; I would not be despised.*

Song of Solomon 8:1.

The Song is the story of how the bride becomes set on fire from within. We are close to the end of the journey through Song of Solomon in *The Bridegroom Song*. However, the never-ending passion stirred in the little Shulamite maiden will never end. As we come to this final section of the Song, the bride is feeling the electricity of God. She feels so alive because she knows in a deep way who she is and also who the Beloved is. We can be alive like this on the inside only as we walk in the place of radical obedience. This fire makes hearts radiate in this dark world. God has provided this place of absolute surrender as the only route on earth the human heart can fully resonate His glory.

Let us persevere on our path into intimacy with Him.

As the sweet fragrance of passionate love (symbolized by the mandrakes) flows out of our gates, all manner of fruit is waiting for the Beloved. We are about to see how the bride longs to put the Beloved on display and bring Him to mother's house (the church), give Him kisses, and drink the best wine with Him. Yet she is hesitant, distressed that she cannot be more demonstrative in her love without coming under ridicule. "Oh, that you were my brother," she says, and lies back in His arms. She rests in His love as He charges the daughters to back off!

**O That You Were My Brother**

>Oh, that you were like my brother,
>
>Who nursed at my mother's breasts!
>
>If I should find you outside,
>
>I would kiss you;
>
>I would not be despised.
>
>I would lead you and bring you
>
>Into the house of my mother,
>
>She who used to instruct me.

> I would cause you to drink of spiced wine,
>
> Of the juice of my pomegranate.
>
> Song of Solomon 8:1-2

Her love for Him is flowing, but she feels restrained in displaying her affection for the Beloved. She declares the advantage a brother has over a lover in that it is not inappropriate to show public affection for a brother. "Oh, that you were my brother," she says, dreaming of how she would openly express her feelings for her lover. Although it may be hard for us to imagine this in our culture where everything is laid out in full view, at the time Solomon penned these verses, open displays of affection for an intimate lover were less favorably accepted. Relationships between men and women were more discreet. If He were only her brother, she could more freely love and kiss him and publicly acknowledge her love without being despised or ridiculed. To kiss Him speaks of expressing the fullness of all God has allowed her to experience. Her first prayer was for His kisses. She understands this expression of prayer and type of worship is often more appropriate in a small group of believers rather than in a corporate setting. Boldness is combined here with humility and restraint.

She expresses her longing to bring Him into mother's house (SOS 3:11), the church--the place that gave her birth. In that setting she wants to display her love. In the church she was taught and instructed in righteousness, so it seems only fitting to exalt Him in the place God used for her spiritual birth and upbringing. She has no desire to magnify herself but longs to put

Him on display so that He may fellowship among other believers with her, drink the spiced wine and sweet juices of the pomegranate, and be magnified.

God uses members of the body of Christ to produce spiritual birth. She wants to return the blessing to those who nurtured her along the way and give them honor. She is grateful for her spiritual heritage and in essence prays, "I want to bring the fresh presence of God into the house of my mother. I want my Beloved with me in this familiar place and among those who are closest to me. I want to give the best wine to Jesus and share it with those who have been given to me." In the previous chapter we saw the bride wanting to give her love to the Beloved in the fields of ministry, but here she wishes to give back His blessing in her closest relationships in the familiar places of the church. This desire does not come from a place of spiritual superiority but from a place of divine gratitude in her heart. Her yearning is to "...lead You and bring You into the house of my mother and cause You to drink...the best wine!" (SOS 8:2) What a beautiful picture!

**Experiencing God's Embrace**

As these words come from her mouth, she feels His gentle hand under her head. The head represents her understanding. She is familiar with the Beloved's hand reaching to embrace her, and now she feels His support under her head:

> His left hand is under my head
>
> And his right hand embraces me.
>
> Song of Solomon 8:3

The embrace of God is a mysterious thing, but she is beginning to understand the two-fold dimension of being held by her Beloved. His right hand and left hand both surround her, and she acknowledges the importance of each. Let's look a little more closely at the two-armed clasp encircling the bride:

- The left hand--The left hand is strategically placed *under* her head. It is behind her line of vision. He keeps my eyes focused upon his; He holds my mind, will, and understanding. The left hand is the outworking of God's indiscernible activity in her life. It is the unseen work of God and beyond her understanding. He uplifts her even when she cannot recognize Him. The left hand is the intervening grace of God. She does not have a full realization of all the times God has protected her from pain, spared her life, prepared her for something bigger, wooed her heart, or transformed her through His mysterious (and sometimes difficult) ways. Although she may be unaware of all the ways God has worked behind the scenes in her life, she does find comfort in knowing she can trust the invisible actions of God. It is an extravagant expression of His love, and she can rest in knowing He is always working for her benefit.

- The right hand--This touch of God is more easily discernible. These more tangible expressions of God's love are what we crave experiencing daily. The right hand represents the manifest activity of God in her life. These are the obvious and visible blessings God allows her to witness which serve as sweet reminders of His presence, tenderizing her heart toward Him even more. She loves "feeling" loved by Him, and the embrace of His right hand allows her to rest in the assurance of this love. It empowers her and gives her confidence in her position beside Him.

Even though she has some inner reluctance, she feels His hand and steadying embrace in her desire to bring Him to her brothers and sisters in the church. Let us be reminded of the words of Isaiah:

> Don't be afraid, for I am with you.
>
> Don't be discouraged, for I am your God.
>
> I will strengthen you and help you.
>
> I will hold you up with my victorious right hand.
>
> Isaiah 41:10 (NLT)

In SOS 8:3 she enters into another season of experiencing the deep satisfaction of God's embrace. We don't know how long this season lasts, but we do know it is a much-needed time of rest and reassurance in the way the Beloved jealously guards her. She is in a posture of receiving from the Beloved (deeply drinking) without the immediate sacrifice of personal service to others. She is not failing to practice her faith. She is soaking in His love and being filled to the brim. In her first season of intimacy when she felt His hand under her head (SOS 2:6), she was basking in her newly-found passion and acceptance of being the fairest of all. She was in the banqueting house eating raisin cakes and apples. As the journey continued, she was awakened even more, and the process progressed. Now she recognizes the familiar hand and sweet embrace once more as He answers her prayer to be close and holds her gently. She surrenders to the rest. Selah!

**Do Not Disturb**

His sweet voice is heard once more, and He hangs out the "Do Not Disturb" sign:

> I charge you, O daughters of Jerusalem,
>
> Do not stir up or awaken love until it pleases.
>
> Song of Solomon 8:4

Jesus is saying, "I know what she needs!" This is the third time the Beloved has charged the daughters not to disturb her until love pleases. Mike Bickle puts it like this:

> He is solemnly charging other believers not to disrupt

her right now. God has her in a strategic season. There are seasons in God where the Lord [is establishing] people in this sweet revelation and He doesn't want them doing all the activity of the Kingdom. She is fervent, enjoying God but not yet mature. The Lord does not want her judged by religious opinions... "O, daughters of Jerusalem" represents immature believers who lack discernment in the Spirit. These believers do not understand the various operations of the Spirit nor the different seasons in God.[1]

Jesus validated Mary of Bethany by praising her in John 12:3-8 when she poured costly spikenard on His feet while others criticized her. Intimate worship is often ridiculed. Here the Beloved is speaking to the daughters and validating the bride (giving her attestation). These words are His public endorsement of their intimate relationship. He is not ashamed of her and wants everyone to know she is His bride and right where He wants her, in His embrace!

**Coming Up From the Wilderness**

As this season of rest ends, the scene changes; and there again is another question: "Who is this?"

Who is this coming up from the wilderness,

> Leaning upon her beloved?
>
> I awakened you under the apple tree.
>
> There your mother brought you forth;
>
> There she who bore you brought you forth.
>
> Song of Solomon 8:5

"Who is this...leaning upon her beloved?" What a lovely thought! She makes her exit from the wilderness leaning upon her Beloved. "Leaning upon" implies she is relying (or resting) upon Him for support, incapable of standing on her own. A ladder leaning on a wall falls without the supporting structure for stability. She is finding an exodus to this wilderness, and she is leaning hard. Can you see her? Is it you? Are you leaning upon your Beloved so that He bears the weight of your burdens? Just imagine not being able to tell them apart--that they are one, united. She is in Christ.

This wilderness season has brought about such radical change in the bride that her former self is unrecognizable. She is leaning into Him with such intensity that she provokes the question from onlookers, "Who is this?" They are gazing to see who she is. The unseen workings of the Holy Spirit within her have brought about discernible, visual change on the outside.

She has learned to lean on the Beloved's ability instead of trying to do it on her own. She continued to seek without relenting, and the process is producing visible fruit from within. She ceased striving in her own efforts and found herself resting in His arms. His embrace has changed her from the inside out. This surrender of dying to herself caused her to fall back into Him in absolute dependence. She has developed deep humility. This picture is the heavenly life in Christ, who brings us near, as described in Hebrews 12:

> But you have come to Mount Zion and to the city of the living God, the heavenly Jerusalem, to an innumerable company of angels, to the general assembly and church of the firstborn who are registered in heaven, to God the Judge of all, to the spirits of just men made perfect, to Jesus the Mediator of the new covenant, and to the blood of sprinkling that speaks better things than that of Abel.
>
> Hebrews 12:22-24 (ESV)

Did you notice the Scripture says, "you have come" not you *will* come? This tense is the heavenly position of life in Christ. We *have come* to Mount Zion!

**Two Wildernesses**

Two wilderness seasons are found in the Song of Solomon:

1. "Who *is* this coming out of the wilderness?" (3:6)
2. "Who *is* this coming up from the wilderness?" (8:5)

The exit from the first wilderness revealed the provision Jesus made for His bride's redemption, her position, and her protection. This provision is paralleled during the New Testament in Ephesians 2, which speaks of how God, who is rich in mercy, has raised us up together and made us sit together in heavenly places in Christ Jesus. Our position is firmly established in this wonderful place in Christ. The bride has accepted this position, knowing securely where she belongs. From this point onward she makes constant and considerable progress forward.

The exit from the second wilderness passage shows the bride coming up in victory in the midst of temptations, testing, and difficulties. These have purified her life. She did not give up in the wilderness. She has learned that she can do nothing without her Beloved, but with Him she can do all things. She leans upon Him, accepts her seat with Christ in the heavenly places, and sits down with Him in victory!

**Finding Deliverance from the Wildernesses of Life**

Wilderness places are part of living in a fallen world. Israel came through the wilderness. David was often in the wilderness. It is a place where desperation sets in and testing is imminent. We come face to face with our frailty, and our weaknesses become more apparent. The wilderness is a place when we often find ourselves staring into our own inadequacies. The oasis further on is beyond our view. Many times we don't understand the wilderness experience and can't readily see what God is doing in the midst of it. Wilderness experiences are ordained by God so that we can walk out of them empowered in His strength. The Holy Spirit led Jesus into the wilderness immediately after his baptism. Therefore, wilderness is part of the journey. But there is also an exit from the wilderness, and we have to know how to access the off-ramp. The Holy Spirit reveals this to us. Jesus returned from the wilderness in the power of the Spirit and from there began His earthly ministry. In this passage of the Song, we see the bride coming out of the wilderness leaning on her Beloved, His grace leading her out stronger than when she entered. In the wilderness she discovers His sufficiency. Jesus says, "My grace is sufficient for you, for My strength is made perfect in weakness" (2 Corinthians 12:9). She has learned to embrace her own weakness in exchange for His strength. It is the great paradox of grace. She has discovered how to lean, weak-kneed, into Him who lifts her beyond what she could ever ask or imagine. (This is Chapter 8, deep into the journey.)

As the bride ascends and comes up victoriously, she is breathtaking, leaning into her full identity with Jesus as her Beloved. This concept is a deep revelation. She is completely dependent on Him, knowing that without Him she is impotent--a balloon with no air, a sailboat with no wind, a compass without a magnet. Like Jacob, who wrestled for God's blessing and got up with a limp, she is leaning and limping so that He may uphold her completely. He is presenting her with her fully recovered identity. She has learned to lean in both prosperity and adversity. I must lean in hard times as well as when presented with great blessing. It is easy to become presumptuous in times of blessing and become vulnerable to losing dependency.

She has also come to understand who she is without Jesus but knows that with Him she can do all things. In the beginning of the Song her confession was, "I am dark but lovely." She realizes her flesh has a great capacity for sin, but deep down she is beginning to understand that somehow she remains lovely to God. In deep dependence, she *now* knows she is a new creation, and victory is hers! She has learned how to become transparent and vulnerable without fear of her own inadequacy. She trusts in God to be Jehovah Jireh, her Provider, through voluntary weakness. This trust allows His grace to enrich her so that she can become strong. What an awesome Savior! He doesn't just save her--He gives her everything she needs to become His victorious, beautiful bride.

**A Reminder**

As the Beloved Bridegroom and His bride leave the wilderness behind, memories of the beginning of their journey are awakened:

I awakened you under the apple tree.

There your mother brought you forth;

There she who bore you brought you forth.

Song of Solomon 8:5b

Her memory is stirred when the Beloved says, "I awakened you under the apple tree." She remembers the life-changing revelation of His love and how her heart was transformed. God's grace reached, and the mothering of the church covered her with His love. As she sat at the King's table and ate of His provision, He awakened her heart with passion for Jesus. The darkness in her began to fade, and she emerged lovelier still. "Behold, old things passed away and all things become new" (2 Corinthians 5:17).

Perhaps this image stirs memories in you also. Let this be a reminder of when you were awakened and the Beloved began to feed, nourish, and draw you near into His tender and passionate love. Perhaps certain people, songs, or Scripture come to mind. Do you remember the gentle nudges of the lover of your soul over the years? Let us remember and be grateful. The God of the universe has drawn us to Himself in loving-kindness and still whispers gently into our hearts. Would you take this challenge to remember and fall in love with Him all over again?

Let's pray:

# Sarah Ramsey – The Bridegroom's Song

*O Lord! There is so much to take into my heart!*

*Your love has overwhelmed me.*

*You are not only my brother, but You are also my lover.*

*You were not ashamed of me, and I am not ashamed of you.*

*I long to give you my kisses freely.*

*I feel your strong left hand underneath my head, so I can trust you.*

*I recognize your right hand holding me firm.*

*I press my head against your bosom as we exit this wilderness area.*

*Help me lean, Lord--in good times and in challenging circumstances.*

*I want to be anointed and leaning so others may ask, "Who is this?" as I am coming out.*

*Help me remember where I began and how You have gently led me.*

*I am with you, my Beloved! Your grace has delivered me from the wilderness!*

*Thank you!*

*Amen.*

## 29

### The Hot, Fiery Seal

*Set me as a seal upon your heart...*

(Song of Solomon 8:6a).

As she emerges from the wilderness and remembers the beginning of her journey, the bride confidently abandons herself to her Beloved and receives the hot, fiery seal of love upon her heart.

> Set me as a seal upon your heart,
>
> As a seal upon your arm;
>
> For love is as strong as death,
>
> Jealousy as cruel as the grave;
>
> Its flames are flames of fire,
>
> A most vehement flame.
>
> Song of Solomon 8:6

## My Story

Early on this journey of awakening to bridal love and passion for Jesus, the Holy Spirit challenged me to ask for this hot fiery seal. I wasn't familiar with the Song of Solomon and didn't understand it when I read it. As we know, however, God loves to tell us secrets and reveal His treasures. In the early '90s, I aggressively pursued the Bridegroom King and felt called to this message. I was awakened to the message of a heart full of hot, fiery passionate love for Jesus. Mike Bickle was one of my chief teachers. When I heard his testimony about asking for the hot, fiery seal from Song of Solomon Chapter 8, my heart cried out in faith to receive the seal. I began to pray that God would draw me after Himself and committed to run with Him and others. The little Shulamite maiden, who is the bride, showed me the way. I hope you are making this journey, too.

I was able to attend a conference where Mike Bickle was speaking, and I was eager to get to the altar so that he could pray for me. I wanted him to lay hands on me and impart the fiery passion of Jesus. One of the foundational doctrines is the laying on of hands (Hebrews 6:1-3). Paul said, "For I long to see you that I may impart to you some spiritual gift so that you may be established" (Romans 1:11). To *impart* means to give, share, distribute, or grant. The word implies liberality or generosity.[1] So, don't be embarrassed to ask someone who has credibility to lay hands upon you to impart the hot, fiery love of Jesus. Jesus is our bridal seal!

Watchman Nee said the Song of Songs unveils the mystery of passionate intimacy with Christ. I asked for the seal before I knew anything about the journey into intimacy. When I was born again at eight years old, I knew nothing about new birth. This revelation of SOS is the same way. I asked by faith; and Jesus, in His grace and mercy, showed me His love.

During the same time frame in the 1990's, I read Wade Taylor's article in *Pinecrest* magazine about drawing near. It quickened hunger in me to get closer to Jesus. God uses others to help us, and He has a plan to lead us to others who know the way. I was a teaching director at CBS (Community Bible Study) in Cookeville during the time of that personal awakening, and I remember getting my servants' team around me and telling them about what I was seeing. They also became ignited with desire for God's hot fiery seal. We didn't know much, but like Andrew Murray says in the *Holiest of All*, "He will work in our heart more than we can understand with our mind."

During this time, "I fell into a burning ring of fire. And it burns, burns, burns and the flames get higher"[2]--it ignites my heart and burns off the chains. It feels good and hurts at the same time. This journey is the most wonderful of journeys, and I have found great pleasure in it. As the Lord began to help me see Jesus as my Bridegroom King, He led me to Mike Bickle's book, *Passion For Jesus*, in which the author describes the day God revealed Song of Solomon 8:6 to him. As I asked for God's hot, fiery seal to be set on my heart, I trusted the Holy Spirit of Truth, Who leads us and guides us into all truth. My grandson Judah's song says:

> In my head I may not know
>
> What I feel down in my soul
>
> With my eyes I may not see
>
> That fire that burns inside of me![3]

I've learned that "It takes God to love God." I need God to put His own love into my heart so that I can love Him the way He desires (and the way I desire to love Him.) We need to ask for this fiery seal.

> *Lord Jesus, impart that hot, fiery, passionate love for*
>
> *You into my heart and seal it upon my arm!*

I didn't really know what I desired, but I saw the availability in God's word; and He answered the cry of my heart. Let Your fire burn in me, Lord, the most vehement flame.

**The Seal of Love**

The fiery seal has two sides--passion and judgment. The fire releases passion but also burns up all that holds us back from being voluntary lovers. Passion gives us power--not to resist the fire and jump out, but to withstand it. The judgment aspect of God's love comes through the fire as He removes all that hinders bridal love. When we come to God as voluntary lovers, we are consenting to be refined by the flames of His love; but we become ignited in the process!

**The Fiery Seal on My Heart and on My Arm**

Where is this seal? It is on my heart and on my arm—and yours! The heart is the seat of love; in the arm lies strength. This fiery seal on my heart produces wholehearted love for God. Jesus wants to protect my heart, to seal it--from backsliding, sin, bitterness, fear, and slander. His love is stronger than death. He is jealous for me. He is the fire which burns away the impurities of my heart and makes me able to love Him sincerely. He is the All-Sufficient One who keeps my love strong. I am unable to do anything in my own strength. I need to be branded with His fire.

The seal on my arm imparts zeal as I serve others and protects me from burning out. It keeps me from compromise and bitterness which can come from a lack of gratitude as I serve. It gives me power to endure and overcome offense, accusation, defensiveness, and discouragement. It is not me, but Christ in me; a great mystery. The arm represents the public declaration of our love for Him. I am not ashamed of wearing my religion on my sleeve even in the face of persecution. Hitler made the Jews sew a patch on their sleeves. This declaration is mine, but I am asking for the seal of Jesus on my arm. The seal on my heart imparts fiery passionate love for Jesus, while the seal on my arm imparts a fire for ministry that won't get extinguished while doing kingdom work. He has been eternally seared into my bicep, the outworking of my love.

This seal is God's provision. The seal produces a love that will not fail. It enables the bride to love individually and the church to love corporately. Asking for the seal is a welcoming of the branding iron. Though the act is painful, when the seal is set, I am equipped to love with all my heart, soul, strength, and to love my neighbor as myself. It is much more difficult to keep passion alive in the midst of ministry. The seal of fiery love on my arm will protect me from compromise and defilement during the wilderness.

### Some "How-to Ideas"

Here are some ways to practice the command, "set me [as a seal]":

1. **Commune** with Him. Make your desire known--ask.
2. Deliberately **open** your spirit to Him. **Sit** in His presence.
3. **Reach** to Him for fellowship. **Cooperate** with the Holy Spirit in active partnership. **Posture** your soul to

fellowship in faith knowing He wants this more than you do. **Allow** another proven, trustworthy believer to lay hands for impartation through prayer.
4. **Make time** in personal prayer to interact and give yourself to Him.
5. **Believe** that you receive what you ask for in faith.

These disciplines put me in position to receive the Spirit and His power. The disciplines are *not* the fire. The fire is not past victories, but the present Holy Spirit, living today--not tomorrow--but fresh fire today. I don't have to live in failure or defeat, but fire must be fed so that it does not go out. Receive fresh fire today and everyday! The early church of Acts was continually filled with the Holy Spirit, walking in power and purpose; and Christianity spread like wildfire!

**Many Fires Cannot Quench This Love**

In the beginning of her journey, the little shepherdess had prayed for the kisses of His mouth. All she wanted was the power to love God fully. She has made progress over the years and received His kisses. Her heart has become tenderized. Haven't you just loved watching her grow? Her reward is to be enabled to love like Jesus. In John 17:26 Jesus says, "And I have declared to them Your name, and will declare it, that the love with which You loved Me may be in them, and I in them." He answered her prayer, but she has also answered His. Isn't that just the sweetest sight to behold and experience?

This love is planted as a seed at the new birth. It is a gift. It grows as we actively cooperate with God and cultivate it. Nothing can escape or destroy it--no demon, bitterness, or sin. It is His love imparted to me and poured into my heart. "For I am persuaded that neither death nor life, nor angels nor principalities nor powers, nor things present nor things to come, nor height nor depth, nor any other created thing, shall be able to separate us from the love of God which is in Christ Jesus our Lord" (Romans 8:38-39).

> Many waters cannot quench love,
>
> Nor can the floods drown it.
>
> If a man would give for love
>
> All the wealth of his house,
>
> It would be utterly despised.
>
> Song of Solomon 8:7

The seal of His love is supernatural. It does not have a price tag, but it is wealthy love and very costly. Water can't put it out, floods cannot wash it away, and no amount of money can buy it. Nothing in this temporal world could be given in place of it. In this passage, the bride requests of the Lord to give her a permanent place in His heart. She has no intention of ever letting

Him go. She now possesses His empowering love and is well able to overcome difficulties and disappointments, the cares of this world, accusation and condemnation of the enemy, temptation and even prosperity. His desires have become her desires, and she has been eternally changed. How about you?

Let's pray:

*Lord, I wait for your salvation.*

*I reach out to You in fellowship from the secret place.*

*I desire to cooperate with the Holy Spirit.*

*Now I come to Your fire--set my heart on fire for you!*

*Set upon my heart Your seal, O fire of God!*

*Give me eyes to see, O God, so that I may behold your beauty.*

*Lord, Jesus impart Your hot, fiery seal upon my* heart and *upon my arm.*

*Let the flame of Your love burn in my heart, my Beloved.*

*Seal me, Lord, so that I won't grow weary as I wait upon You!*

*Seal me, Lord. Let your hot seal burn in my heart and*

*ignite eternal passion!*

*Brand me, as I yield and wait upon You!*

*No flood can drown Your love, and all the wealth of the world does not compare.*

*Nothing can escape Your love which has been poured out in me!*

*I receive it and proudly wear Your seal. I have been bought by You!*

*Amen.*

Sarah Ramsey – The Bridegroom's Song

## 30

### Little Sister

*We have a little sister…*

(Song of Solomon 8:8).

As the fire seals the bride's heart and the Song ends, her desire is for the little sisters to awaken to the love she has found in the Beloved. She goes to her Beloved and asks what can be done as she labors in prayer and intercedes for little sister. We have learned and watched throughout the journey how the bride surrendered in intercession. She took her seat by the Great High Priest, and now she is warring for her little sister. As fire comes onto her, she can't wait for others to be ignited by the spark!

**The Ever-Interceding Bride**

Now let's take care of the little sister.

We have a little sister,

> And she has no breasts.
>
> What shall we do for our sister
>
> In the day when she is spoken for?
>
> Song of Solomon 8:8

The bride is inquiring of the Eternal Lover, "What shall we do for my little sister?" She wants to know how to make disciples, and He is ready to reveal the plan to her. In the King's chambers, as she beholds His beauty, she begins to inquire of the Lord. Deep commitment to the Lord always extends outward to others.

As she sees the body of Christ, however, she perceives the immaturity and lack of passion for Jesus. She discerns that the immature believers in Jesus have not yet developed passion or the ability to nurture others. The young maidens have not matured to the point of developing spiritual breasts. She knows where to seek the answer and find the solution. She cannot spur them on alone. They need to be wooed by the Beloved, and she wants to cooperate with His plan and show them how to get there. She jealously loves the sisters, as He does, and wants them to find and experience intimacy within the Beloved's chambers as she has done. She is not about keeping Him all to herself. She seeks the Lord and begins to intercede for the maidens in her midst. The bride knows they have a significant place in His kingdom. She desires that they step into that position. Perhaps she remembers when the Good Shepherd told her, "We will make you…"; and she knows the plans He has for the sisters are just as grand.

Isn't it marvelous to know the Beloved has plans for those we love? We want our families, children, and grandchildren to know the Good News and the peace and joy it brings. We long for those who have a special place in our hearts to walk in the fullness of the Lord. Even acknowledging their infancy and immaturity, we can have confidence knowing the Beloved has great plans for our loved ones, even more grand than we can imagine! We don't have to be frustrated or impatient with their apparent lack of progress. We were once there, too, and sometimes even revert back to the more immature stages! He knows how to bring us back and where to position each soul in His kingdom. We need to come alongside Him and pray, "What shall we do?" In other words, what is my part in cooperating with His plan to disciple those around me?

The bride is in partnership with Jesus. She doesn't ask, "What shall I do?" or "what can You do?" but, "what shall *we* do?" She knows she has a part in God's plan for her little sister. She desires to help prepare her to recognize the destiny she is called to fulfill. We can trust God has placed His spiritual DNA in those around us. The seed of the imperishable Word of God is planted deep within each born-again soul. That little seed contains all that is needed to produce the mature spiritual man or woman. Just as in a little baby boy, there is a full man, in that little girl is a grown and mature woman. In the little acorn is the complete oak tree. He will lead them in their calling, but He has called us to run alongside them in partnership with Him. The beauty of the bride's heart is revealed in her willingness to love those He brings into her circle of influence and fold them into her arms.

**My Story**

When I began to see, I wanted those I loved to see, too! I have often gotten too aggressive in my desire to "pass it on," forgetting that prayer is the first step. We must ask, "What shall we do?" and learn to pray for guidance. I feel impotent and ignorant at prayer, but I am learning to pray. I know the Teacher intimately, and He will teach me well and be patient with me. He is my Beloved, and I am His fair one, so when I have a question I know I can inquire. Here the bride is asking, "What about my little sister? We have a little sister, and she has no breasts."

**God Has a Plan**

There is a plan, and it is revealed as she intercedes and begins to ask the Beloved for help. "What shall we do?"

He reveals His plan:

>If she is a wall,

> We will build upon her
>
> A battlement of silver;
>
> And if she is a door,
>
> We will enclose her
>
> With boards of cedar.
>
> Song of Solomon 8:9

If she is a wall...if she is a door, either way He has a plan. Walls speak of defense or protection; doors are entry points to bring others to Christ. We all have different gifts and callings. Some will shepherd the flock (wall), while others will go bring them into the Kingdom of God (door). And God has a plan for each. The "wall" will receive the provision of silver. She will be built upon through the power of redemption. The "door" will be strengthened with cedar boards. The bride will be equipped by Him to equip her little sister to accomplish God's purpose. We can rest assured that each of our destinies has been written in His book since before we were born.

Verse 9 says, "We will," twice. If she is a wall, *we will* build on her a battlement of silver. Silver speaks of redemption and implies that the Lord Himself will call and equip His people through their redemption. None of us are qualified to be agents of the kingdom of God without His redeeming power. He will use the weaknesses and failures of our lives and equip us through redemption (silver) and transformation by His grace. The Lord equips and calls through the five-fold ministry spoken of in

Ephesians chapter 4, which refers to the giftings of pastors, teachers, prophets, evangelists, and apostles. He uses His people to equip His people. If she is a door, she will be equipped to lead others to Jesus, the Door, as God calls and opens hearts to hear His truth. The bride will work by His Spirit to equip her "little sister." Boards of cedar will encircle her. In Scripture, wood often refers to the cross. The sister is a "door" which is bringing others to salvation by way of the cross, and God has made provision by enclosing her with "boards of cedar." She is deeply rooted in her salvation and protected by the blood of Jesus.

**Privilege and Responsibility**

As the bride of Christ prays and intercedes for the harvest, she is aware of the way God has equipped her. In the next passage she confesses with confidence:

> I am a wall,
>
> And my breasts like towers;
>
> Then I became in his eyes
>
> As one who found peace.
>
> Song of Solomon 8:10

Throughout the Song, the importance of developing passion and the ability to nurture has been a priority. These vital attributes are beautifully symbolized by the breasts. In this passage, our attention is drawn to the contrast between the immature little sister who has not yet developed breasts and the mature bride who now has breasts like towers. Remember that in the beginning, her breasts were like fawns; she was immature. Now, she has fully acquired the ability to nurture the body of Christ. She has yielded to the disciplines of the faith that have produced breasts like towers. Now she is equipped to equip her little sister.

The mature bride of Christ values the privilege of who she is in Christ and accepts the responsibility to protect and nurture. She is humble and confident in this role. She is in union with Jesus and is, therefore, dependent and meek, not proud. She is confident in her identity and walks according to His grace, not her own ability, thus producing fruit. She is abiding in the Vine. Jesus is the source of her supply and nourishment. She believes the spoken words the Beloved has poured into to her in previous passages. She is filled with assurance of the Lord's ability in her that free her from fear and doubt. The seal on her heart and arm have released the fire of God to give her sufficiency and the ability not to draw back from the responsibilities set before her. She is able to walk with passion throughout the journey and not burn out. His words are taking root downward and bearing fruit upward, as prophesied in Isaiah:

> And the remnant who have escaped the house of Judah
>
> Shall again take root downward,

> And bear fruit upward.
>
> Isaiah 37:31

She now has the right "equipment," and she is sharing the Good News. 2 Timothy 3:16 says, "All Scripture is given by inspiration of God, and is profitable for doctrine, for reproof, for correction, for instruction in righteousness, that the man of God may be complete, thoroughly equipped for every good work." She declares, "I am a wall, and my breasts are like towers," meaning, "I am a source of protection to many and am able to provide the much-needed nourishment to those around me." She knows her identity yet remains humble and dependent. Then she becomes in His eyes as one who found peace. O, the peace of knowing who I am, and what I am called to do! What confidence we gain when doing the will of God!

**One Who Found Peace**

> Then I became in his eyes
>
> As one who found peace.
>
> Song of Solomon 8:10

The word *then* is significant in Scripture. *Then* always indicates the result of what has just been said. She knows who she is, and this identity brings her peace: "I am a wall." When we know who we are in Christ--when our identity is in Him and we step willingly into that role, *then* we have peace. The peace of God is with her. The Prince of Peace offers her peace, which is not of this world, as He rules in her heart.

Consider how the following verses confirm this:

> The things which you learned and received and heard and saw in me, these do, and the God of peace will be with you. (Philippians 4:9)

> Peace I leave with you, My peace I give to you; not as the world gives do I give to you. Let not your heart be troubled, neither let it be afraid. (John 14:27)

> And let the peace of God rule in your hearts, to which also you were called in one body; and be thankful. (Colossians 3:15)

**Audience of One**

Notice, it is before His eyes that peace has been established in her heart. She has an audience of One! Only in His approving eyes can she be satisfied with peace. She is at peace with who she is only because His eyes are on her, and He is pleased. She knows who she is--and *whose* she is! The Master approves! In His eyes she has found peace. She walks in grace and dignity living before Him, not trying to please others. Deep and lasting peace is found in a life lived before God and for God. Drink in the deep satisfaction of the peace that only He can give as you find the only approval that matters—God's approval. He is her shield and exceedingly great reward (Genesis 15)!

The bride is receiving revelation to recognize and accept her responsibility before God. As God reveals, she believes and gains confidence. This assurance sets her in position to finish strong!

Let's pray:

> *Thank you, Lord, that you have a plan.*
>
> *You have a plan for "little sister" and those around me*
>
> *whom I love.*
>
> *You have a plan for the nurturers.*
>
> *Build walls of redemption, and open doors of salvation*
>
> *so that others may come in!*

### Sarah Ramsey – The Bridegroom's Song

*We seek you; we inquire about Your plan.*

*Spirit of Truth, come lead and guide us into all truth.*

*Teach us all things so that we can develop and become mature.*

*Help us fulfill Jesus' command to go into all the world and make disciples.*

*Help us teach all the things You have commanded.*

*Equip us with Your Word so that we may become equippers for others.*

*Show us where to go and what to do.*

*And thank You, above all else, for Your peace.*

*We long to please You and crave Your acceptance.*

*In Your eyes we rest in peace.*

*Thank You, gracious Lord, for Your peace, which surpasses all understanding.*

*Amen.*

## 31

### The King's Vineyard

*Solomon had a vineyard...*

(Song of Solomon 8:11).

We have come to the end of our journey through the Song of Solomon. The little Shulamite maiden has come so far! And hopefully we have, too. She has been transformed from an insecure maiden darkened by the noonday sun into a vibrant, confident, warring lover of God. She has learned to tend her vineyard fruitfully from the overflow of love in her heart. She has truly become the bride of the King, a voluntary lover and fruitful laborer. She knows where her place is beside Him. In this last portion of chapter 8, the bride acknowledges her accountability to the King. In the following verses we see that the King has a very large vineyard, leased to the keepers; but the bride also has a personal vineyard to tend, and both the bride and the keepers must give an account to the King in silver.

**The Vineyard of the Lord**

Solomon had a vineyard at Baal Hamon;

> He leased the vineyard to keepers;
>
> Everyone was to bring for its fruit a thousand silver coins.
>
> My own vineyard is before me.
>
> You, O Solomon, may have a thousand,
>
> And those who tend its fruit two hundred.
>
> Song of Solomon 8:11-12

The vineyard has been a theme throughout this journey. The vineyard refers to the people of God, or His kingdom. Israel was God's vineyard under the Old Covenant. In the New Covenant, the church is God's vineyard. The vineyard at Baal Hamon, which literally means "father of a multitude," is speaking of the very large vineyard of King Jesus, His kingdom globally throughout the nations. It spans the ends of the earth and will bring forth a vast harvest before the end of the age, as spoken of in Revelation 14. This vast vineyard has many keepers. Here also, at the end of her journey, the bride realizes she has been given a portion of this responsibility through her own individual vineyard. In Chapter 1, the little Shulamite maiden had said, "My own vineyard I have not kept." She remembers, I am sure, the process of coming to know who she is and her place beside her King. She is no longer ashamed of her untended, weedy vineyard. By the end of her journey, she embraces the divine privilege of partaking in His kingdom and savors the responsibility of tending her vineyard so that she may have fruit to bear for her Beloved.

## The King's Vineyard Entrusted to the Church

The King leased His vineyard at large ("Baal Hamon") to keepers, and everyone was expected to do His part by bringing forth a return. Just so, Jesus has entrusted to the Church the awesome responsibility of being the "keepers" of His global kingdom. We have been given stewardship of a very precious commodity. He has sown His very life into His kingdom and likewise desires a full return. But He does not leave us to tend the vineyard alone; He has purposefully equipped us to be fruitful over the specific things entrusted into our care. We can rest assured He will not hold us accountable for things entrusted into someone else's care. "For we are His workmanship, created in Christ Jesus for good works, which God prepared beforehand that we should walk in them" (Ephesians 2:10). But He *will* hold us accountable for the things entrusted into our care. We were created with purpose! The portion of the vineyard entrusted to us usually comes through our neighborhoods, families, workplaces, or other specific tasks He calls us to do. We each have an ordained circle of influence, whether or not we choose to embrace it; and each person will give an account in the coming age.

We know from teachings throughout the Gospels in the form of parables that Jesus expects a return on His investment. Jesus talked about vineyards as He walked His last days on earth: "There was a certain landowner that planted a vineyard...and built a tower. And He leased it to vinedressers and went into a far country" (Matthew 21:33). Here as the Song of Solomon ends, the King who has leased the vineyard comes looking for the fruit. We can count just as assuredly on King Jesus, who is currently in a faraway heavenly country, coming at the end of this age to reap the great harvest at His second coming. We should look forward to that day with great anticipation. Let us not shrink back in fear of meeting Him empty-handed. The bride has learned to step into her position of faithful vinedresser and is excited about sharing in the harvest with Him! She wants to joyfully show Him all that she has done. Let us likewise step into our royal positions and faithfully tend the "vines" in our midst. There is surely no sweeter place on earth or greater eternal reward to come.

In this passage the Beloved is receiving a "full" return, one thousand pieces of silver. One thousand denotes a number of innumerable blessings, with silver being symbolic of redemption. He desired one thousand pieces of silver, and she brings Him in love everything He asks for. She is not afraid of the sacrifice of serving and brings the payment in full. She says, "yes" in spirit and deed in every area required of her. What a powerful life to live on earth! She also acknowledges the rewards that will come to those who have diligently labored with her. She has not done this alone. Others were working alongside and sowing into her life along her journey; and they will receive a just reward in the form of "two hundred" pieces, a portion of her yield. These may be people who encouraged her, prayed over her, and taught her along the way. They will also be rightly honored for the outworking of her fruitfulness.

Diligence and perseverance are two of the main factors in the journey of the bride. The Scripture teaches us that finishing is an important characteristic to develop. As Solomon said, "The end of a thing is better than its beginning," (Ecclesiastes 7:8, NIV). "The latter house will be greater," (Haggai 2:9). Faithfulness in necessary until the end of the journey. At the end of a long day when no progress seems to come, don't give up! "And let us not grow weary while doing good, for in due season we shall reap if we do not lose heart" (Galatians 6:9). Doesn't it give you great hope knowing we can count on God's work for the kingdom being justly rewarded as promised? Rest in the trustworthiness of these promises, dear ones, and finish strong! He will surely see you through to the end.

**The Beloved's Request**

Jesus gives a final commission to the bride. These are His last words to her in the Song:

> You who dwell in the gardens,
>
> The companions listen for your voice--
>
> Let me hear it!
>
> Song of Solomon 8:13

The Beloved calls her "the one who dwells in the gardens," and He instructs His bride not to quit the race. "The companions listen for your voice," He declares. In other words, others still want to hear what you are saying. Her relationship to the body is vibrant and alive; and the ones around her are listening for her voice to guide and encourage them. She is not disqualified just because she has been on this journey for a time, but because she is still standing! So many times we want to run away or quit, but the bride teaches us how to "dwell," or remain. She has maintained her relationships. She has continued in faith. She is at the end of the journey in God's garden. The enemy wants me to believe I am worn out and ineffective, but the Word of God tells me I still have a voice! She has not isolated herself but is still effective and loving the people of God. She didn't stop or shrink back when it got hard. She refused to get offended! Many older believers grow angry, cynical, and bitter after a lifetime's accumulation of trials and offenses. They become less effective rather than more effective as their judgmental attitudes sour their peace and momentum dwindles. It is a powerful testimony when our hearts grow more tender rather than bitter towards the end of our lives. We should be able to walk in even greater humility after a lifetime of hardship, enabling the favor of God to be heaped out in greater portions upon us and others.

Finally, the Beloved says, "Let me hear it!" What a delight! What a responsibility! The Beloved says, "Let me hear your voice!" He had told her in the beginning of the Song that her voice was sweet (2:14). He loves her voice and still wants to hear it. She is not a nag or droning cymbal. He never tires of her. What reassurance! We honor the Lord in many ways with our voices. We can allow Him to hear our voices in worship. Our voices are used to give thanks, to teach others, and to speak words of encouragement. We can let our voices be used to evangelize, speak truth, and tell the good news. He also listens for our voices in prayer when we join Him in the throne room where, "He ever lives to make intercession for the saints" (Hebrews 7:25).

He ends the Song with an affirmation of the two aspects of her initial prayer. When she began her journey into this intimate relationship with the Beloved, her desire was, "Draw me after You and let us run together." Both longings have been fulfilled in her life. She spoke to Him and He responded. She longed for Him and He came. The Creator of our heart always recognizes our cries and will answer a genuine plea and come running after us. Have you ever doubted this truth? Quiet your heart, dear one, and ask Him to come. Patiently wait on the Lord, and ask Him to show Himself to your spirit. "Now we have received, not the spirit of the world, but the Spirit who is from God, that we might know the things that have been freely given to us by God" (1 Corinthians 2:12). Her companions listen for the voice of the bride because she has learned to listen for His.

**The Bride's Request**

The bride's response is immediate when the Beloved yearns to hear her voice. She raises her voice and makes a plea. She intercedes and worships once more with a final cry for Him to come quickly. The shofar (horn calling to battle or to worship) is blowing! Can you hear it?

> Make haste, my beloved,
>
> And be like a gazelle
>
> Or a young stag
>
> On the mountains of spices.
>
> Song of Solomon 8:14

The Song ends with an urgent cry for His return. The Song of Solomon has had so many twists and turns, but listen closely to what she is saying: "Make haste, my beloved...come quickly." Her request is that He be like the young stag who leaps over the mountains as the victorious King who brings triumph over the enemy. This cry echoes the one from the beginning in Chapter 2. She described Him as coming like a gazelle or young stag leaping upon the mountains and skipping upon the hills, running toward His beloved. Christ Himself leads the army of heaven on a white horse (Revelation 19:11-14). He effortlessly spans vast swaths of mountains. No obstacle is too great. His time is drawing nigh. He is swift and virile. He is full of life, and spices abound on His mountain. The mountain of God is His dwelling place, and He reigns as the Eternal King of Kings. The bride is calling Him back to take her home to her eternal dwelling! Could there not be a better ending? Her story is not over--your story is not over; but the Song ends with the bride's anxiously awaiting His return. She eagerly anticipates the consummation of Christ!

Lift your voice, sweet bride of the King, and call your Beloved back to take you home. Let us raise our voices in unison and be confident He will hear our plea to return for us.

## **The Unblemished Bride**

In the Introduction, I made the statement: "The Song of Songs is the story of the bride of Christ developing into maturity. This is an individual process, but it also happens corporately as the Church is made ready for her Bridegroom King." The little Shulamite maiden has become the unblemished bride. You are the bride. Are you prepared for His return? Is your vineyard clean? Do you have fruit to bear? Is your lamp ready? As she has been made fully ready for His return, the Shulamite maiden is calling King Jesus back to the earth. Listen, dear ones, to what the Spirit of God is saying. Assuredly, Jesus Christ is coming back for His bride. Step into your position, and let Him hear your voice. We will corporately arise and call Him, the Maker of heaven and earth, back down from heaven, for the church. Is there any greater calling? The final book and chapter of the Bible affirm her plea. "And the Spirit and the bride say, "Come!" And let him who hears say, "Come!" (Revelation 22:17). The bride is in agreement, and we, too, shall say, "Come, Lord Jesus!"

## **Selah!**

The Shulamite maiden's journey began with a simple request--for His kisses. Although she started as a darkened, unkempt girl, she desired more. "Draw me," she said and asked where to go and be fed. He lovingly claimed her as His "fair one" and showed her where to dwell. She delighted in the shade and sweetness of His provision and learned to feast from His banqueting table. She learned to rest in His embrace. Then He called her to deeper places and, after refusing to go, she experienced the sting of distance. She searched fervently; and He returned, emerging from the wilderness like pillars of smoke. She praised His splendor. The Beloved, in turn, divinely prophesied over her and called her away again, this time to the mountain of myrrh and hill of frankincense; and she reverently responded, "Yes!"

They ascended into a holy position and fought the enemies in the heavenlies. He called her His garden, and she submitted to both the north and south winds. He was so delighted that He brought His friends to enjoy her fruitfulness for a time. As the journey continued, during a night season, He appeared dripping with myrrh and called her away again, this time to a more challenging season of sacrifice. With her hesitancy, He was gone; and once again she experienced His apparent absence.

She became wounded by the watchmen. After being questioned by her friends, she responded with astonishing, detailed descriptions of Him, the Chief among ten thousand. Soon she realized He was in His garden, abiding in Her heart. Once more,

He prophesied her divine features into existence, and she was praised by the daughters.

She journeyed to the garden of nuts, after which time she was affirmed again, emerging with even more mature qualities. She came to fully embrace her position with the Beloved and went with Him to work in His vineyards and fields. Longing to bring Him to the people from her youth, she rested again in His embrace.

She emerged from the wilderness so transformed she was unrecognizable. His fiery seal was set upon her. She became an intercessor for her little sister and also a worthy tenant of His vineyard. She gained a voice in His kingdom. Others listened and responded. He listens, too, for her voice, even now, as she calls Him back.

**The Delightful Journey**

What a delight it has been to take this journey with the little Shulamite maiden. It is an even greater delight knowing I am on this journey of intimacy with Him as my own Beloved. Do you see yourself in her? I do, to the point that it makes me blush to know He sees such intimate details of my life and loves me still. This book was written for you, dear one. It was written for me. Before He even came to the earth and tread the soil of this planet, these words were penned by the Holy Spirit through King

Solomon with you in mind. He knew you would read His Song of Songs and be drawn closer to Him. He wrote this for you. Let Him take you away, over and over again, and stir the deep rivers of your heart as you follow the pattern of the Shulamite maiden. His is the greatest love story ever told. And you, fair one, are a part of it, for now and for eternity.

> He will rejoice over you with gladness,
>
> He will quiet you with His love,
>
> He will rejoice over your with singing.
>
> Zephaniah 3:17

Join me for one final prayer:

> *Jesus, Jesus, Jesus!*
>
> *Dance with me, O Lover of my soul, to the Song of all Songs.*
>
> *You rejoice over me with singing!*
>
> *Help me never stop hearing Your voice, and I will lift mine to You.*
>
> *Let me speak Your words to my little sister, making disciples as I go.*

## Sarah Ramsey – The Bridegroom's Song

*Let my voice never be silent!*

*Let the Word of God spread to the ends of the earth; let it run swiftly!*

*Strengthen me not to draw back and quit, but push forward even harder!*

*Let me join with You in making intercession for Your saints.*

*Let me resist the enemy's strategies and attempts to silence my voice. I cry out!*

*Cry out!*

*I will press in and worship, intercede, teach, tend Your vineyards, and proclaim Your truth.*

*I will not let offense, disappointment, or disapproval stifle*

*My voice, which You long to hear!*

*How lovely is Your dwelling place!*

*Thank You, O Lord, that I am Yours!*

*Amen.*

## _Notes_

Chapter 1

1. Mike Bickle, *Song of Songs: The Ravished Heart of God*, Session 3, p. 2
2. Names of God references: Jeremiah 23:6; Leviticus 20:7-8; Judges 6:24; Ezekiel 48:35; Exodus 15:26; Genesis 22:14; Exodus 17:15; Psalm 23:1

Chapter 2

1. Sarah Ramsey, *Are We There Yet? Journey into the Presence of God* (Book 1 of this series)
2. Judah and the Lion, "Back's Against the Wall" from the album *Sweet Tennessee*

Chapter 3

1. Bickle, Session 6

2. *Random House College Dictionary*
3. Alice Smith, *Intimacy*, p. 79
4. Proverbs 4:23 (NIV) and Psalm 147:13 (NKJV)

Chapter 4

1. Bickle, Session 6, pp. 25-26--The "yes" in your spirit
2. John 6:53-66
3. Derek Prince, "The Divine Exhange," *Atonement*, p. 37
4. Ephesians 2:6
5. Ramsey, pp. 150-175
6. James 1:23

Chapter 5

1. This description of spikenard is taken from the note at John 12:3 in *The Spirit-Filled Life Bible,* Executive Director, Jack Hayford.
2. Mike Bickle, Session 7, p. 3
3. Hebrews 13:15-16
4. Hymn, "A Child of the King," by Harriet E Buell, 1877
5. Mike Bickle, Session 7, p. 4

6. Andrew Murray, *The Blessings of Obedience*, p. 38
7. John Bevere, *Relentless*, pp. 182-183

Chapter 6

1. Bickle, Session 7, p. 10
2. See Psalms 27:4, Luke 10:42, Philippians 3:13
3. "Getting to Know You," *The King and I*, 1951

Chapter 7

1. Dr. Seuss, *Are You My Mother?*
2. Andrew Murray, *The Blessings of Obedience*, p. 55
3. Genesis 3:18, Hebrews 6:8
4. Hebrews 3:1
5. Ephesians 5:18
6. "Love Is a Flag Flown High," author unknown
7. Stuart Hamblin, "It Is No Secret What God Can Do"
8. Proverbs 3:5
9. Madam Guyon, *Britannica.com*

Chapter 8

1. Revelation 12:10
2. John 8:44, Revelation 12:10
3. "my love" is used twenty-two times in Song of Solomon, and "Beloved" is used twenty-two times.

Chapter 9

1. "Bether," *Bible Study Tools*
2. See Hebrews 13:5 and Matthew 28:20.
3. *Spirit-Filled Life Bible,* "Word Wealth," at Hosea 5:15
4. Hymn, "I Will Arise and Go to Jesus"
5. Bickle, "Divine correction is not rejection."
6. Lindell Cooley, "We Will Ride with You"
7. Luke 19:44

Chapter 10

1. Andrew Murray, *The Blessings of Obedience*, p. 39
2. Psalms 40:8
3. Joshua 14:12

(Chapter 10 End Notes, continued)

4. See Matthew 12:46-50, Revelation 12:5
5. See Psalms 27:4, 8 and 14.

Chapter 11

1. Bickle, Session 10, p. 6
2. Hebrews 4:14
3. Matthew 2:11
4. Mark 16:1
5. Exodus 30:1-9 and Leviticus 16:13
6. Revelation 3:8, 8:3-5
7. Hebrews 7:25
8. Luke 22:42
9. See Ephesians 1:19 and 2:4-6.

Chapter 12

1. Mike Bickle with Deborah Hiebert, *The Seven Longings of the Human Heart,* summary of pp. 34, 8, 35, and 37

## Chapter 14

1. Watchman Nee, *Song of Songs*, Part 3, p. 122
2. *Ibid.*

## Chapter 16

1. Throughout Scripture, water is symbolic of the Holy Spirit. In Joel 2:23-29, "as rain that refreshes," and in Acts 2:17 as "the latter rain," which causes the crops to mature. In John 7:37-39, Jesus speaks about the Holy Spirit as a river.
2. John Bevere, *The Holy Spirit*, P. 164
3. Nee, p. 137

## Chapter 17

1. Nee, p. 137
2. See also Genesis 1:26 and Matthew 12:37.

(Chapter 17 End Notes, continued)

3. Bickle, *Song of Songs*, Session 12

Chapter 18

1. Nee, p. 145

Chapter 19

1. Bickle, Session 14

Chapter 22

1. Bickle, Session 16

2. *Ibid.*
3. Alice Smith, *Spiritual Intimacy with God*; Scriptural references for lying spirit and spirit of error, 2 Kings 22:22-23; 2 Chronicles 18:21; 1 John 4:5

Chapter 23

1. Song of Solomon 3:6, 5:9, and 6:1
2. Matthew 5:14
3. Romans 8:17-18 and 5:3-5

Chapter 24

1. Song of Solomon 4:12, 4:15, and 4:16b
2. 4:16c; 5:1; 6:2; 6:11; 7:12; 8:13
3. Andrew Adams, heinspiredme.com
4. Bickle on "the watchmen"

Chapter 25

1. Bickle, Session 17, p. 24

2. Nee, p. 176, and Bickle, Session 16

Chapter 26

1. Bickle, Session 17
2. ---, Session 18, p. 5

Chapter 28

1. Bickle, Session 7, p. 27

Chapter 29

1. impart: to give, "Word Wealth," *Spirit-Filled Life Bible*
2. June Carter Cash and Merle Kilgore, "Ring of Fire"
3. Judah and the Lion

Sarah Ramsey – The Bridegroom's Song

Made in the USA
Columbia, SC
25 July 2020